"This wonderful, important book is ti
just happen; they are made. Based on careful presentation of facts and
development case studies on disaster recovery, *U.S. Emergency Management in the 21st Century* discloses why loss to disasters is growing, even
though research over the past few decades has improved our understanding of the causes of loss. This book thoughtfully proposes how remedies
might be pursued. A must read."

– **Philip Berke**, *Research Professor, UNC Coastal Resilience*
Center, University of North Carolina at Chapel Hill

"Disasters are deeply personal, disrupting and displacing families. This
team drills into the full range of human experiences amid natural disasters, laying out the critical questions our Nation must answer as the
weirdness of climate marches forward."

– **Roy Wright**, *President & CEO, Insurance*
Institute for Business & Home Safety

"*U.S. Emergency Management in the 21st Century*, edited by Rubin
and Cutter (two of the most influential voices in disaster science
and emergency management of our time) and sporting an impressive, multi-disciplinary line up of chapter authors, is an indispensable,
well-chosen collection of studies that manages not only to drill down
deeply in examining some of the major disaster events since the turn
of the millennium, but also to place them in a broader historical, scientific, socio-technical and political context. This volume provides unique
insights into the practical and scientific challenges faced by the United
States government, communities, and academia over the last two decades.
The volume highlights the disruptive and deeply unfortunate impacts of
inequality, mounting political division and political-administrative turbulence and points to the urgency of changing course for a more sustainable and resilient future."

– **Eric Stern**, *Professor of Political Science, College*
of Emergency Preparedness, Homeland Security, &
Cybersecurity, University at Albany

U.S. Emergency Management in the 21st Century

U.S. Emergency Management in the 21st Century: From Disaster to Catastrophe explores a critical issue in American public policy: Are the current public sector emergency management systems sufficient to handle future disasters given the environmental and social changes underway? In this timely book, Claire B. Rubin and Susan L. Cutter focus on disaster recovery efforts, community resilience, and public policy issues related to recent disasters and what they portend for the future.

Beginning with the external societal forces influencing shifts in policy and practice, the next six chapters provide in-depth accounts of recent disasters – the Joplin, Tuscaloosa-Birmingham, and Moore tornadoes, Hurricanes Sandy, Harvey, Irma, Maria, and the California wildfires. The book concludes with a chapter on loss accounting and a summary chapter on what has gone right, what has gone wrong, and why the federal government may no longer be a reliable partner in emergency management.

Accessible and clearly written by authorities in a wide range of related fields with local experiences, this book offers a rich array of case studies and describes their significance in shifting emergency management policy and practice in the United States during the past decade. Through a careful blending of contextual analysis and practical information, this book is essential reading for students, an interested public, and professionals alike.

Claire B. Rubin has more than 40 years of experience in the field of emergency management, having worked as an independent researcher, academic, practitioner, and consultant. As a consultant, she has worked for many organizations – private, nonprofit, and government. Her work includes basic and applied research, the development and presentation of training programs; and the creation and operation of various information dissemination and utilization projects. From 1998–2014 Ms. Rubin was affiliated with the Institute for Crisis, Disaster, and Risk Management at The George Washington University in Washington, DC; she was a research associate and adjunct faculty member there. For the past nine years, she has maintained the blog RecoveryDiva.com. She has published about 100 articles and given many lectures at professional conferences. Rubin is the cofounder and former managing editor of *The Journal of Homeland Security and Emergency Management*, which is now in its 14th year of publication.

Susan L. Cutter is Carolina Distinguished Professor of Geography at the University of South Carolina and director of the Hazards & Vulnerability Research Institute. She is a nationally and internationally recognized scholar, having published more than 14 books and 175 refereed articles and book chapters. Her primary research interests are in the area of vulnerability and resilience science and how they influence place-based differences in disaster recovery. Cutter is an elected fellow of the American Association for the Advancement of Science (AAAS) and a former president of the American Association of Geographers (AAG) and the Consortium of Social Science Associations (COSSA). She served on many national advisory boards and committees, including those of the National Academies of Science, Engineering, and Medicine, National Institute of Standards and Technology, the National Science Foundation, and was a juror for the Rebuild by Design competition for Hurricane Sandy Recovery Projects. She also is an elected foreign member of the Royal Norwegian Society of Science and Letters. She received her master's and doctorate in geography from the University of Chicago.

U.S. Emergency Management in the 21st Century

From Disaster to Catastrophe

Edited by
Claire B. Rubin and Susan L. Cutter

NEW YORK AND LONDON

First published 2020
by Routledge
52 Vanderbilt Avenue, New York, NY 10017

and by Routledge
2 Park Square, Milton Park, Abingdon, Oxon, OX14 4RN

Routledge is an imprint of the Taylor & Francis Group, an informa business

© 2020 Taylor & Francis

Library of Congress Cataloging-in-Publication Data
A catalog record for this book has been requested

ISBN: 978-1-138-35465-4 (hbk)
ISBN: 978-1-138-35466-1 (pbk)
ISBN: 978-0-429-42467-0 (ebk)

Typeset in Adobe Caslon Pro
by Apex CoVantage, LLC

Contents

Detailed Contents

FIGURES

TABLES

Boxes

PREFACE

We chose the title of this book, *U.S. Emergency Management in the 21st Century: From Disaster to Catastrophe*, in order to convey the serious concerns raised in the first two decades of this century stemming from the rapid series of major-to-catastrophic disasters and concerns about the public sector emergency management systems in place to deal with them.[1] This new book follows in the path of *Emergency Management, The American Experience* (3rd edition, 2019), which featured 110 years of emergency management history and policy in the United States, especially the response phase of emergency management. Rather than an updated continuation of the descriptive history of emergency management, we chose a different conceptual framing given that many of the major-to-catastrophic disasters that have occurred since 2000 were different in number, frequency, costs, and impacts from those seen in the last century.

We observed that since 2000, more focused attention is on short-term recovery efforts as well as efforts to foster community resilience at all levels of government and in all sectors of society. These broader concerns and longer-range planning efforts were new and important considerations based on disaster-driven changes that needed changing in public policies, administration, and organizations. What remains worrisome, and appears to be of greater prominence this century, are the observed stresses – and in some cases outright failures – of segments of the current emergency management systems.

Our intended purpose is to explore the shifts in federal emergency management policy and practice as a consequence of the dynamical contexts of environmental change, especially climate, and social and political fragmentation. Using a case study approach based on important focusing events from 2011–2018, the chapters provide context, perspective, and broader meaning to recent major-to-catastrophic disaster events. The authors seek to better understand the short-term impacts, analyze the likely long-term needs and efforts, and provide a base or platform for making changes in emergency management in the years and decades ahead. In fact, the chapter authors themselves are experienced academics, consultants, and practitioners in emergency management, and many of them live and work in the areas affected and have personal experience with the events, adding a richness to the narratives.

The book benefits from the knowledge and experience of many people, including the editors, Claire B. Rubin and Susan L. Cutter. Together, they have more than 75 years of academic, practitioner, and consultant experience in the field of emergency management, helping to put the case studies in larger contexts. They are both strong advocates for translating research into policy and practice, having emergency management practice generate new research needs, and training the next generation of academics and practitioners.

We are grateful for the assistance of many friends and colleagues that we have engaged in discussions of some of the findings and conclusions of the book and for suggestions on earlier drafts of chapters. We especially want to acknowledge the invaluable assistance of Kathryn Abbott, the book development editor. We would also like to thank Erika Pham, University of South Carolina for her cartographic assistance on this project.

Our lingering concern is that the record-setting magnitude, impacts, and costs of disasters in 2017 and 2018 were the result of known hazards – hurricanes and wildfires, for the most part. There are other, lesser-known threats that could post significant challenges to our communities and the nation in the years ahead, such as a massive cyberattack or a global pandemic – all the more reason to attend to repairing and improving our emergency management systems.

Claire B. Rubin and Susan L. Cutter, Coeditors

July 2019

Note

1. Emergency management professionals and disaster scholars define *catastrophe* as a very large event that surpasses local and regional capabilities for response or recovery, and *disaster* as a less severe event, although it, too, might require outside (i.e., federal government) assistance. See Enrico L. Quarantelli, "Emergencies, Disaster and Catastrophes Are Different Phenomena," Preliminary Paper 304 (Newark, DE: Disaster Research Center, University of Delaware, 2000), http://udspace.udel.edu/handle/19716/674.

1

INTRODUCTION

Claire B. Rubin

As the result of an extraordinary series of disasters – major to catastrophic in their impact – in the United States in the 21st century, the field of emergency management is undergoing major changes. These changes are being driven by the word "*more*" – more hazards, more disasters, more people affected, more powerful, more destructive, and more expensive. Essentially more of everything!

From 2000 to 2010 alone, the United States experienced three major-to-catastrophic disasters, which were milestone events for each of the three hazard categories used to characterize disasters in this country:

- **Human-caused/Deliberate**: On September 11, 2001, three terrorist attacks constituted the greatest intentional disaster that has ever occurred on the U.S. mainland. These events are commonly referred to as 9/11.
- **Natural Hazard**: In September 2005, three disasters caused by natural hazards – hurricanes Katrina, Rita, and Wilma – resulted in the most extensive and costly destruction seen to date in the United States in terms of area affected and impacts on people and property on the Gulf Coast. However, the Galveston Hurricane of 1900 still holds the record for the greatest number of deaths.

- **Human-caused/Accidental**: In April 2010, the explosion of the BP Deepwater Horizon oil rig and resultant oil spill caused the largest human-made, accidental event ever to occur in the United States, with the majority of damage affecting Louisiana and the Gulf Coast.

Collectively, these events demonstrated some unusually destructive characteristics, attracted significant international attention, and laid bare many deficiencies in the legislation, plans, systems, and processes used for all phases of emergencies and disasters at all levels of government. Those events were massive and considered "focusing events" or "game changers." Entire books have been written about each one of them.

With all the political, economic, social, technological, and environmental (including climate) changes taking place locally, regionally, and globally in the 21st century, it is important to continue the process of examining some recent disaster events and the adequacy of our emergency management system.

Disasters and Losses, 2010–2019

As we enter the third decade of the 21st century, we struggle in our efforts to deal with disasters and catastrophes, many of which reveal the limitations of emergency management systems in the United States. For disaster researchers, a fundamental question continues to be why is more knowledge about hazards and disasters not reducing the impacts and losses from them?

In the 2010s, we saw dramatic examples of the growing vulnerabilities – frequently affected coastal communities, fire risk in the western states, and vulnerability to hurricanes in the eastern seaboard and gulf coast states as well as U.S. commonwealths and territories in the Caribbean.

The contributors to this book have provided information about recent disaster experiences, offering insights and observations about some of the major events that occurred in the years 2011 through 2019. Indeed, while the authors were writing their chapters, three more major disasters occurred – hurricanes Florence (East Coast: North and South Carolina) and Michael (Gulf Coast and Central America) in 2018 and the Alabama tornadoes in 2019. Although it was not possible to include these events in this book because of the ongoing recovery process, references are made to them as a continuation of the patterns we have observed to date.

The subtitle of the book is "From Disaster to Catastrophe" with good reason. As we enter the third decade of the 21st century, the data about disaster events and losses in recent years are extremely alarming (see Figure 1.1).

With respect to disaster losses, the severity and frequency of extreme events based on U.S. presidential disaster declarations are on the rise. For example, among the top 20 most costly hurricane events to occur in the United States, all but three occurred since 2000. Furthermore, since 2010, the United States has reached new heights in terms of disaster losses, deaths, and inequities in localized impacts. For example, 2017 was the third warmest year in history. It also was the most expensive year ever in U.S. history for weather-related disasters ($306.2 billion). Coastal tidal flooding from rising sea levels produced more than $16 billion in property value losses between 2005 and 2017.[1] Geographically, many areas experienced multiple disaster events – the Gulf Coast, California, and Puerto Rico – but not everyone within those communities was affected equally as some of the case studies illustrate (see Chapter 5 on Hurricane Harvey, and Chapter 8 on Hurricane

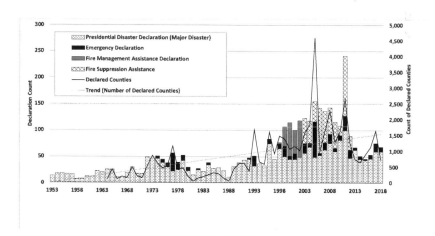

Figure 1.1 Major Disaster and Emergency Declarations 1953–2018

Source: SHELDUS Version 17 (https://sheldus.org). Graphic Courtesy of Dr. Melanie Gall, Arizona State University

Maria). As the average number of decadal billion-dollar weather and climate disasters has inched upwards since 1980, we have reached a tipping point in understanding what is now normal.

Billion-dollar weather disasters are becoming the norm in terms of large, catastrophic events; sadly, they now seem routine, with the expectation of a handful or so every year. Perhaps in the 2020s and beyond, we should adjust our thresholds for these large disasters as multi-billion ($10–50 billion) dollar events, or even mega-billion (>$50 billion) dollar events. A full discussion of the growing burden of uninsured losses from disasters is in Chapter 9.

Additionally, several important new developments have emerged in the past few years:

- In 2017, three major Atlantic hurricanes occurred within a month of one another, affecting major urban areas (Hurricane Harvey, Hurricane Irma, and Hurricane Maria).
- In 2017 and 2018, wildfires in the western states set records for size, cost, and areas of destruction (See Chapter 7 for details.)
- New national legislation – the Sandy Improvement Reform Act (2013) and the National Disaster Recovery Reform Act (2018) – were enacted to remedy the shortcomings uncovered in the federal response to those major disaster events.
- New public-private partnerships (P3s) have been formed to enhance recovery and resilience post-disaster, such as the Rebuild by Design competition and Rockefeller Foundation's 100 Resilient Cities.
- The advent of the Trump administration in 2017 has brought major changes in philosophy of government, as well as major negative changes to emergency management, including significant reductions in programs, staffing, and regulations.

Preview of This Book

Chapter 2: Tipping Points in Policy and Practice provides the context for the detailed case studies in subsequent chapters. Focusing on federal policy changes in emergency management since 2010, this chapter emphasizes shifts in policy and practice in the recovery phase of the emergency management cycle. There are a number of external societal factors influencing these shifts, and they set the stage for creating the tipping points for progressive or regressive changes in emergency management.

Chapter 3: As Tornado Outbreaks Become More Deadly, Major Changes Happen focuses on three of the many tornado events that occurred in the United States from 2011–2013. The tornadoes of 2011 in Tuscaloosa-Birmingham, Alabama, and Joplin, Missouri, and the 2013 Moore, Oklahoma tornados were especially notable for their violent intensity and devastating consequences.

Chapter 4: Hurricane Sandy and the Vulnerability of High-Density Geographic Areas: The New York Experience details the significant impacts on dense urban areas, primarily in New York and New Jersey. It raises many issues, such as vulnerability of high-density areas of national economic importance, special problems finding temporary and permanent housing for thousands of victims, and the fundamental shortcomings of the National Flood Insurance Program.

Chapter 5: Hurricane Harvey: Issues for Urban Development discusses the unprecedented flooding in the metropolitan area of Houston that resulted from Hurricane Harvey in 2018. Houston's experience underscores the relationship between land use and disaster impacts. Among the issues discussed are land use building regulations – or lack thereof – as well as past building practices, issues with the State of Texas' attempts to control both housing and its rainy-day funds, funds designed for these types of events.

Chapter 6: Hurricane Irma and Cascading Impacts focuses on one of the strongest and costliest Atlantic hurricanes in recorded history. Hurricane Irma made landfall in the Florida Keys as a Category 4 hurricane on September 10, 2017, and affected all of the counties in the Florida, causing 42 deaths and an estimated $50 billion in damages. The authors discuss issues of land use and development, especially in the Florida Keys; sea level rise complicating recovery construction; the vulnerability of South Florida, and some of the nation's most expensive real estate, to climate change; and refugees from Puerto Rico who had moved into Florida and other states because of Hurricane Maria.

Chapter 7: California Wildfires details the largest and costliest major wildfire disaster to date. It focuses on the issues of rehousing people within a state that already faced considerable affordable housing problems. It also details the U.S. Congress's refusal to budget adequately for wildfires, even as costs for containing wildfires increases; and the impact of mudslides as a secondary disaster as well as the problems with warning the public of mudslide dangers.

Chapter 8: Hurricane Maria focuses on the extreme destruction in the U.S. commonwealth territory of Puerto Rico, made even worse by the existing internal financial problems. Hurricane Maria caused extensive damage to structures in all sectors, and tens of thousands of people lived on land to which they did not hold legal title. Further, Puerto Rico was unable to temporarily house displaced persons, and many thousands of Puerto Ricans went to mainland cities. It has also faced an elongated response period, perhaps the longest for FEMA to date, leading to a likely record-setting recovery period.

Chapter 9: Loss Reduction and Sustainability highlights the increasing trend in natural hazard losses; explores innovations in loss accounting for disasters and proposed changes; describes increasing difficulty in state matches for disaster relief and recovery expenditures; and explores loss and damage accounts for climate change.

Chapter 10: Summary and Looking Backward and Forward highlights the lessons learned, policy perspectives, and emergency management needs for the future hazards and disaster and not reducing the impacts and losses from them.

While writing the final chapter, the editors noted that in late 2018 and early 2019 the disaster events kept coming. The ongoing occurrence of costly and deadly events continued to affect the U.S., some of the impacts foreshadowed by previous events and preexisting conditions. It is noteworthy that during the study period, 2010–2018, there were two dissimilar political administrations at the national level, each of which demonstrated profoundly different attitudes and actions to address the impacts of disasters on communities and the people who live in them. The authors' ongoing concern is whether the current deficiencies and distortions of the U.S. emergency management system are short-term aberrations or significant lasting changes.

Knowing More but Losing More

In seeking some historical perspective on the fundamental issues regarding the growth of disaster knowledge, major disaster experiences, and the increasing losses, three of the leading scholars in the field have offered their perspectives in this century. In 2001, Gilbert White et al. published an article titled "Knowing Better and Losing Even More: The Use of Knowledge in Hazards Management." The abstract states:

> Although loss of life from natural hazards has been declining, the property losses from those causes have been increasing. At the same time, the volume of research on natural hazards and the books reviewing findings on the subject also have increased. Several major changes have occurred in the topics address. Emphasis has shifted from hazards to disasters. There has been increasing attention to vulnerability. Views of causation have changes. Four possible explanations are examined for the situation in which more is lost while more is known: (1) knowledge continues to be flawed by areas of ignorance; (2) knowledge is available but not used effectively; (3) knowledge is used effectively but takes a long time to have effects; and (4) knowledge is used effectively in some respects but is overwhelmed by increased in vulnerability and in population, wealth and poverty.[2]

Second, in 2014, Susan Cutter gave a slide presentation at the U.S. National Academies for the Gilbert F. White Lecture in the Geographical Sciences, "In Harm's Way: Why More Knowledge is Not Reducing Natural Hazards Losses."[3] In her presentation, Professor Cutter made two key points. First, what accounts for the disaster loss "up-escalator"? Her observations were: 1) smaller magnitude or intensity of events produce greater losses than before; 2) increased exposure and wealth concentrated in high hazard areas; and 3) more frequent events. The second point is, how to reverse the loss escalator? Here Cutter suggests three mechanisms:

improve loss accounting, improve hazard science, and improve the application of hazard science in public policy.

Third, with respect to the continuing challenge to disaster researchers and practitioners, in July 2018 Dr. Lori Peek, the Director of the Natural Hazards Center in Boulder, CO, posed the question: How do we find focus in an era marked by continual catastrophic disruption?[4] She summarized the proceedings of the annual Natural Hazards Conference in July 2018 and then went on to ask

> How do we find and maintain our focus in this time when decades of unsustainable land use planning, lax building code enforcement, rising social and economic inequality, and population growth in risky areas are coming home to roost? How do we find and maintain our focus in an age of weather whiplash and cascading catastrophes that lead us from one affected community to another, one deployment to the next, and yet another study before the previous one was even finished?

Most of the authors of the book's chapters either live or work in the communities affected by the disasters they describe, providing both firsthand experience as well as analytical skills to their chapters. Given the relatively recent occurrence of the disasters described in this book, we expect that new information and developments will become available. Most notable is the delay in federal disaster recovery funds. Since the funding for disaster events that occurred in 2017 was tied up in Congress until June 2019, the full story of recovery for some of our case study communities will have to be completed in the future.

Notes

1. Nicholas Kusnetz, "Coastal Flooding Is Erasing Billions in Property Value as Sea Level Rises. That's Bad News for Cities," *Inside Climate News*, February 28, 2019, https://insideclimatenews.org/news/28022019/coastal-flooding-home-values-sea-level-rise-climate-change-ocean-city-miami-beach.
2. Gilbert F. White, Robert W. Kates, and Ian Burton, "Knowing Better and Losing Even More: The Use of Knowledge in Hazards Management," *Global Environmental Change Part B: Environmental Hazards* 3, no. 3 (2001): 81–92, https://doi.org/10.3763/ehaz.2001.0308. Quote from p. 81.

3. Susan Cutter, "In Harm's Way – Natural Hazards: Why More Knowledge Is Not Reducing Losses," Gilbert F. White Lecture Series, http://dels.nas.edu/global/besr/GW-Lecture.

4. Comments by Director Lori Peek, "Hazards Workshop," July 25, 2018, https://hazards.colorado.edu/news/director/closing-comments-from-the-2018-natural-hazards-workshop.

2

TIPPING POINTS IN POLICY AND PRACTICE

Susan L. Cutter

With each passing decade, emergency management has progressed and regressed with new initiatives undertaken, new leadership, and even new legislation. As explored elsewhere, the American experience in preparing for, responding to, recovering from, and mitigating against hazards and disasters is decidedly a mixed bag of successes and failures. While the philosophical orientation, institutional focus, and administrative location of emergency management changes, there are notable and repeatable patterns from past decades that provide the backdrop for this chapter.

Four key themes emerge from the history of emergency management providing important precursors to the experiences in the 2010s.[1] First, much of the guiding legislation for emergency management in the United States is reactive and in response to a singular focusing event such as Hurricane Katrina, 9/11, or Hurricane Betsy. Second, the administrative positioning of emergency management within the federal bureaucracy guides the uneven focus of activities among natural hazards, terrorism, and nuclear war. During some presidential administrations, emergency management meant civil defense protection against nuclear attack and terrorism, while in others the focus was on natural hazards. Since the mid-2000s, there has been more balance with a clear all-hazards focus. Third, despite the wealth of experience with different events large and small, diverse regions, and changing political administrations, the lessons from past preparedness, response, recovery, and mitigation activities are rarely learned, often forgotten, and then relearned as though they are newly discovered insights. Lastly, losses and impacts continue to increase and often disproportionately affect the most disadvantaged members of communities.

This chapter focuses on federal policy changes in emergency management since 2010. The emphasis is on shifts in policy and practice in the recovery phase of the emergency management cycle. There are a number of external societal factors influencing these shifts in policy and practice and they set the stage for creating the tipping points for progressive or regressive change in emergency management.

What Is the New Normal in the Age of the Anthropocene?

The Anthropocene is the name of the current geologic epoch where humans and human activity are fundamentally altering the earth's basic systems – atmosphere, hydrosphere, biosphere, lithosphere – that provide the basic building blocks and services for human civilization.[2] Compared to geologic time, human impact is rapidly modifying natural systems such as climate, oceans, land masses, and biological communities at spatial scales from local to global. The unprecedented rate and spatial extent of the impact of human activity has not only altered nature, but also societal responses to human-induced changes in the earth's systems governing life as we know it.

In the natural hazards and disasters context, for example, human activity is contributing to climate change, which in turn is increasing the risks of climate-sensitive hazards. The 2014 Intergovernmental Panel on Climate Change (IPCC) Report notes significant increases in human exposure and vulnerability to hazards such as heat waves, droughts, floods, sea level rise and coastal inundation, tropical cyclones, and wildfires.[3] Accordingly, heat waves will become more frequent and last longer. Extreme precipitation events will also become more intense, frequently producing flooding, and warming oceans will cause a rise in sea level producing coastal inundation. Within the United States warming temperatures and changes in precipitation (increases and decreases) will intensify droughts and flooding, produce more extreme heat events, wildfires, and coastal inundation. The U.S. National Climate Assessment concluded the following:

> the evidence of human-caused climate change is overwhelming and continues to strengthen, that the impacts of climate change are intensifying across the country, and that climate-related threats to Americans' physical, social, and economic well-being are rising. These impacts are projected to intensify – but how much they intensify will depend on actions taken to reduce global greenhouse gas emissions and to adapt to the risks from climate change now and in the coming decades.[4]

At the same time that human activity is becoming a more significant geophysical force, society itself is rapidly changing. In the United States, we are becoming a more polarized society. Not only divided politically, which constrains the development of disaster reduction policies especially from elected officials in Congress, which no longer functions in a bipartisan fashion, but we also are divided geographically. More people live along the west and east coasts than in the land mass in between, and there are more people living in urban/suburban communities than in rural areas. More than half of the U.S. population now lives in nine states: California, Texas, Florida, Georgia, Illinois, Michigan, Ohio, Pennsylvania, and New York.[5] According to the National Ocean Service, 39 percent of the nation's population in 2010 lived in counties directly on the shoreline, and this will rise to 47 percent in 2020.[6]

Overall population growth based on natural increases (births minus deaths) has slowed due to an aging population and lower birth rates but that slow growth has been more than offset by immigration.[7] Millennials (born from 1981–1996) are the largest cohort in the labor force, but with an aging population, the old-age dependency ratio ((population aged 65+/population aged 18–64)* 100) will increase from 21 percent in 2010 to 35 percent in 2030.[8] The result of this will be an increasing burden on Social Security with 3.5 working adults needed for every older person on Social Security. In other words, it will take 3.5 working millennials to support one baby boomer. As the population demographically changes, we are becoming a more diverse nation and with that different cultures, mores, attitudes, and life expectancies – all influencers of public policies and emergency response.[9]

But perhaps the most significant demographic change in American society that has a direct impact on emergency management is the increasing income inequality in the nation. The wealth, income, or wage gap between the rich and everyone else has been growing for the last 30 years. The top 10 percent of households have average incomes around $312,000 while the remaining 90 percent average around $34,000.[10] While these figures represent averages, in reality the availability of resources for preparing for, responding to, and recovering from disasters is severely constrained for most Americans. When looking at income inequality by gender or race/ethnicity, the divide is even wider than the averages indicate. Wealth inequality is more extreme than income inequality. Wealth, defined as a household's net worth (sum of assets such as property, savings accounts, etc. minus liabilities such as loans and credit card balances), has increased among the most affluent where the richest 5 percent of Americans own 66 percent of the wealth. The wealth gap is greatest for black and Latino families, many of whom have negative wealth (debts exceed value of assets). Thus, when a disaster occurs, these poorer families are disproportionately affected. The gender wealth gap is more striking, where female-headed households with children have a poverty rate of 35.6 percent, twice that of households led by single men. Poverty is especially acute among women of color who have poverty rates in excess of 21 percent.[11]

The societal shifts in demographics and income affect the capacity of households and the places where they live to prepare for, respond to, and recover from disasters. Such social vulnerability is not geographically uniform across the nation and occurs in urban, suburban, and rural places alike. It is the intersection of social vulnerability with the hazard, which defines where the impacts of disasters are most pronounced, and where differential disaster recovery exists, tipping the balance of who recovers and who does not.[12]

In the Anthropocene, we can expect more human losses and costlier financial impacts. Whether or not emergency management is up to the task is an open question. While there are some hopeful initiatives underway that began in the Obama administration, the Trump administration has reversed course in some areas bringing about major program, staffing, and regulatory changes to the policy and practices of emergency management.

Crowdsourcing Situational Awareness

While emergency management maintains a command and control structure through the National Incident Management System (NIMS), the communication of risk, warning, and response information has become democratized through advancements in mobile technologies and devices, increased internet access, and social media.[13] However, a digital divide continues to exist among American households. According to a Pew Research Center analysis, nearly 35 percent of households with annual incomes less than $30,000 do not have a high-speed internet connection in their home, and this is highest among African American and Hispanic households.[14] Many school-aged children, especially those in high school who live in such households now face a "homework gap" because they are unable to complete assignments that require internet access at home. The homework gap can decrease academic performance, making students even more disadvantaged.

Social media is the primary mechanism for distributing information about disaster preparedness, response, and recovery by FEMA (www.fema.gov/social-media) and state emergency management officials.[15] Using official accounts on different platforms, such as Instagram, LinkedIn, YouTube, Facebook, and Twitter, there is an instantaneous and two-way exchange of information – text, maps, graphics, videos – between the public and emergency managers, especially pre-event warning information. Twitter's cofounder sent the first tweet on the platform on March 21, 2006, and five months later, after a mild earthquake in northern California, the development team realized the potential of the platform for real-time hazard event reporting. FEMA Director Fugate began using

Twitter regularly in August 2009 in his official capacity.[16] The multi-lingual FEMA App (www.fema.gov/mobile-app) for mobile devices, launched in 2010, provides real-time alerts, but also emergency safety tips, locations of open emergency shelters and disaster recovery centers, and emergency kit checklists.[17] The app also facilitates online registration for disaster assistance and uploading and sharing crowdsourced disaster photos via its *Disaster Reporter*.

There is now such a demand for instantaneous information that emergency management entities at both state and federal levels have social media specialists maintaining social media accounts, coordinating the messaging and creating content, and responding to social media queries from the public. As technology and social media platforms change, the demand for such specialists is bound to increase. As FEMA Director Craig Fugate stated in his testimony to Congress,

> Communication in and around a disaster is a critical, life-saving part of FEMA's mission. Social media provides the tools needed to minimize the communication gap . . . because it helps to facilitate the vital two-way communication between emergency management agencies and the public. . . . Most importantly, social media is imperative to emergency management because the public uses these communication tools regularly. Rather than trying to convince the public to adjust to the way we at FEMA communicate, we must adapt to the way the public communicates.[18]

Finally, during the 2017 and 2018 hurricane seasons, FEMA established a Crowdsourcing Exchange to coordinate data from digital humanitarian volunteers. The exchange provided for the collection, cleaning, and validation of crowdsourced data along with its analysis and mapping to assist in real-time situational awareness. Efforts to formalize rules governing the validation of crowdsourced geographic information helps build trust in the quality and accuracy of the data.[19] The use of crowdsourced, social media, and big data analytics – derived from advanced technological systems such as unmanned aerial vehicles or drones and other mobile sensors – is revolutionizing how emergency managers prepare for and respond to disasters.[20]

Time and Space Compression of Events

The rapid succession of events in a single season, or the cumulative impacts of discrete events on a particular place, inevitably put stresses on emergency response and recovery. Described as social cascades, disasters that happen in quick succession have a "perverse multiplier effect (tipping point)" in compounding response and recovery and in some instances exacerbate the conditions of vulnerability.[21] There are examples of cascading impacts prior to 2010, most notably in 2004 when hurricanes Charley, Frances, Ivan, and Jeanne struck Florida within six weeks of each other, creating massive power outages. Similarly, in 2005, hurricanes Katrina, Rita, and Wilma arrived in close succession to the Gulf Coast states including Florida, the latter already reeling from the impacts of the four storms the year before.

The 2017 Atlantic hurricane season accelerated cascading impacts even further, not only because of the short time between landfalls but also as a consequence of the hurricanes' strength, impacts affecting major urban areas – Houston, San Juan, and Miami – and overall losses, placing them in the top five most damaging hurricanes in U.S. history. The temporal and spatial connection between these events (see Chapters 5, 6, and 8) produced differential impacts on residents. They also influenced the ability of the federal response system, already stressed by deployments in Texas, Louisiana, and Florida, to adequately respond and provide disaster relief to Puerto Rico.

Much like the failure of response to Hurricane Katrina, the failed response in Puerto Rico to Hurricane Maria was the result of administrative shortcomings in senior-level staffing within FEMA due to slowness in appointments by the Trump administration. It was also a function of the lack of understanding of the fragility of the island's infrastructure, especially the electrical grid and residential dependency on it, and the failure to anticipate what cascading hurricanes would do to the island and its residents.[22] One of the real lessons learned in Puerto Rico was how ill-prepared the agency was to manage an emergency including logistical problems outside the continental United States. There were issues in finding temporary housing given the level of damage, thus many of the survivors relocated to Florida, stressing the resources of many local host communities (see Chapter 6).

In addition to the hurricanes, the 2017 wildfires in California (Chapter 7) also highlighted emerging response and recovery challenges of cascading events. FEMA did not have a sufficient workforce (known as surge capacity) to meet the response needs, and many of the workers were serving in capacities they were not qualified to hold. There were also shortages in the availability of contractors, delaying both debris removal and the distribution of food and other essential supplies. According to the GAO report:

> The 2017 hurricanes and wildfires reaffirmed the existence of some longstanding response and recovery challenges, but also highlighted several new challenges related to (1) the near-sequential timing of the disasters, (2) housing assistance, (3) workforce management, and (4) public assistance.[23]

Conflicting Demands for Fast Recovery

Local residents and elected officials want to recover quickly, and normally define recovery as reconstruction of buildings and infrastructure – tangible elements of recovery – not other elements of recovery such as restoration of livelihoods, social networks, or cultural and environmental assets. The desire to rebuild quickly – but not always better, safer, or for the long-term sustainability of the community – underscores the need for pre-event planning for post-disaster recovery.[24] This tension between rebuilding quickly and rebuilding slower with considerations for more equitable, resilient, and safer structures strikes at the core of many federal policies.

More broadly, the time compression associated with post-disaster urban development fundamentally alters the nature of recovery at the local level where physical construction, financing, social capital formation, and community buy-in occur at different times and often involve different sets of actors, and proceeds without a predetermined recovery plan.[25] Added to this is the bifurcation of recovery responsibilities between multiple federal agencies – FEMA (for short-term), and HUD (for longer-term recovery).

The *National Disaster Recovery Framework* (NDRF) is one of five documents governing federal emergency management.[26] The initial NDRF, published in 2011, underwent a revision in 2016. It defines the capabilities needed to help restore communities affected by an event and provides the mechanism for engagement of the whole community in the process.

Recovery activities begin at the pre-event stage and continue long-term, spanning months to years depending on the event's severity and impact. The recovery continuum has four timeframes (see Figure 2.1) and necessitates cooperation between federal agencies and state, tribal, and local partners, as well as nongovernmental entities such as voluntary organizations in disasters, faith-based groups, and local community groups. Short-term recovery led by FEMA with support from other agencies includes debris removal and restoration of critical infrastructure and lifelines, as well as the provision of emergency shelters. These short-term activities range from one to 180 days and are guided by resources provided under the Stafford Act via the Disaster Relief Fund obligations (individual assistance, public assistance), federally backed insurance programs (e.g. FEMA's National Flood Insurance Program (NFIP), U.S. Department of Agriculture (USDA) crop insurance), federally backed loans from the Small Business Administration (SBA), FEMA hazard mitigation grant programs (pre-and post-disaster), among others.

During the short to intermediate term (within the 180 day window), the state engages in the planning for recovery process and the submission of the state's recovery action plan to the Department of Housing and Urban Development (HUD), for additional funding for unmet needs in the community after the disaster (e.g., disaster relief, long-term recovery, housing, infrastructure restoration, and economic revitalization).[27] Once a congressional appropriation for Community Development Block Grant Disaster Recovery (CDBG-DR) is given, the grantee (generally a state, county, or city) receives the allocation from HUD and expends funds based on the action plan.

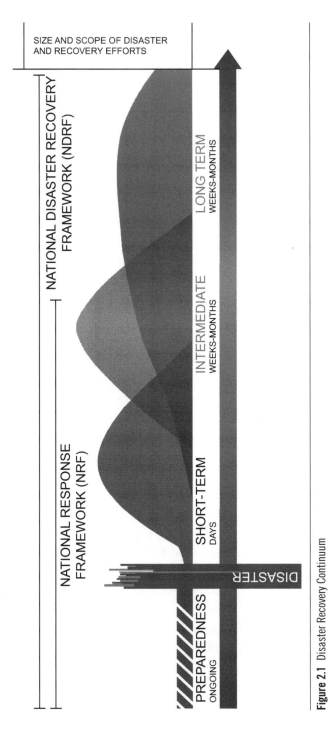

Figure 2.1 Disaster Recovery Continuum

Source: Department of Homeland Security (DHS), National Disaster Recovery Framework, 2nd edition (Washington DC: DHS, 2016). Graphic redrafted by Erika Pham, University of South Carolina

The federal process for distributing disaster relief can be relatively fast for immediate individual assistance and public assistance. However, as recovery proceeds from meeting the immediate needs of the whole community to longer-term issues of permanent housing, permanent infrastructure, and opportunities to build back stronger, the recovery timeline stretches from months into years. Because of the lag time (months after the event) in submitting CDBG-DR recovery plans, some communities wait years for CDBG-DR funds, frustrating residents and public officials alike. While there are many obstacles that slow or halt the recovery process, a list of the most significant follows.[28]

- First, recovery is not easy, and there is not enough time, nor enough money, to meet all the demands. The recovery will be uneven, and the competing interests of stakeholders will defy what is often the right and just thing to do, such as buying out high-risk properties and moving people out of harm's way versus rebuilding.
- Second, recovery takes years and moves from easier solutions involving emergency actions and community services restoration to more complex and perhaps contentious issues of rebuilding, replacing, and improving.
- Third, disaster programs, policies, and procedures are moving targets with assistance policies frequently changing as political administrations come and go; oftentimes different agencies have conflicting rules, regulations, and/or accountability measures that complicate the process.
- Fourth, there are many possible options for recovery, but the community may not be able to recover to where they were before the disaster because of regulatory, institutional, and/or financial constraints.
- Fifth, there is considerable help available to assist communities in the recovery process and no need to reinvent the wheel, especially when neighboring communities or states, federal officials, and disaster professionals have the experience and can help.
- And sixth, if the community has experienced a disaster once, it can and does happen again. Lessons learned in the recovery provide

useful information for inclusion in future pre-impact recovery
plans so the next time the community can recover faster and better
than before.

Policy Action, Inaction, and Reaction

Each successive presidential administration comes into governmental service with the expectation of either continuing the policies of the previous
administration, modifying existing policy, or even, in extreme circumstances, radically reversing the policy. During the Obama administration,
emergency management implemented a whole community approach,
with emergency management recognized as a shared responsibility
among governments at all levels, the private sector, faith-based organizations, voluntary organizations, and citizens. There was also an emphasis
on catastrophic planning, efforts to prepare for climate change through
adaptation planning, the recognition of disaster resilience as a key part
of the whole community approach, and the increased use of technology
and social media in emergencies. Given experienced leadership at local
and state levels of emergency management and at FEMA, response and
recovery efforts, while not perfect, were much improved.

With the Republican Party controlling Congress after the 2012 election, there were relatively few legislative disaster policies enacted in the
2010s (Table 2.1). Among the most notable was the response to Superstorm Sandy in 2012, which led to the Sandy Recovery Improvement
Act of 2013 (SRIA), notable for streamlining the administrative burden and providing greater flexibility in the use of disaster relief funds for
Public Assistance applicants. The other was the 2018 Disaster Recovery
Reform Act (DRRA), which provided a major change in the Stafford
Act concerning recovery management and reimbursable costs. With over
50 different provisions – ranging from simplifying management costs for
HMGP to streamlining the Public Assistance program to provide more
flexibility, to broadening eligibility for mitigation funding for wildfires –
the reforms are far-reaching. Despite these two bipartisan laws, perhaps
the most telling characteristic of disaster policy initiatives during the
2010s was the extensive use of presidential policy directives (PPD) and
executive orders (EO).

Table 2.1 Major Disaster Policy Initiatives 2010–2018

Title (Date)	Signal or Focusing Event[1]	Significance
Sandy Recovery Improvement Act (SRIA), 2013	Superstorm Sandy	Added tribal governments as equivalencies to states in securing and administering public assistance funds; capped fixed estimates for timely repair work; provided for less administrative burden in requesting and expending funding, and provided greater flexibility in the use of funds by Public Assistance applicants (www.congress.gov/113/plaws/publ2/PLAW-113publ2.pdf); www.fema.gov/sandy-recovery-improvement-act-2013)
Biggert-Waters Flood Insurance Reform Act (2012)	Superstorm Sandy	Moved insurance rates to an actuarial basis, subsidized rates for non-primary residences phased out; authorized and funded the risk mapping program, re-authorized and extended the National Flood Insurance Program (NFIP) for five years (www.naic.org/documents/cipr_events_2012_cipr_summit_overview.pdf; www.fema.gov/media-library/resources-documents/collections/341)
Homeowners Flood Insurance Affordability Act (2014)	None	Delayed certain provisions of Biggert-Waters including restoration of grandfathering, limits to rate increases, includes annual surcharge; conducted an affordability study (www.fema.gov/media-library/assets/documents/93074; www.fema.gov/media-library-data/1396551935597-4048b68f6d695a6eb6e6e7118d3ce464/HFIAA_Overview_FINAL_03282014.pdf)
Weather Research and Forecasting Innovation Act (2017)	None	Improved NOAA assets to deliver weather data, expanded weather research including hurricane warnings, becomes a companion to the National Earthquake Hazards Research Program (NEHRP) in advancing weather-related hazards science and application (www.congress.gov/115/plaws/publ25/PLAW-115publ25.pdf)
Disaster Recovery Reform Act (2018)	2017 Hurricane season and wildfires	Major reforms to the Stafford Act in terms of flexibility in rebuilding under the Public Assistance program, increased funding for mitigation and resilience, improved state capacity to manage disaster recovery with increased allowable management costs, enhanced mitigation programs and funding for wildfires and windstorms. (www.fema.gov/news-release/2018/10/05/disaster-recovery-reform-act-2018-transforms-field-emergency-management; www.fema.gov/disaster-recovery-reform-act-2018)

[1] A signal or focusing event draws attention to harms or impacts that are concentrated geographically or within special communities of interest that garner the interest of the public and policy makers leading to mobilizations for enacting changes in public policy.

Source: T.A. Birkland, "Focusing Events, Mobilization, and Agenda Setting," *Journal of Public Policy* 18 (1), 2018: 53–74

Among the many executive orders, the presidential policy directive –
PPD-8 – signed by President Obama in 2011 is significant for its long-
term impacts on emergency management. The PPD-8 had as its stated
goal:

> A secure and resilient nation with the capabilities required
> across the whole community to prevent, protect against, miti-
> gate, respond to, and recover from the threats and hazards that
> pose the greatest risk.[29]

The national preparedness goal organized national capabilities into five
mission areas, and national frameworks developed to support each one.
PPD8 also established systems of training and exercises, including processes for the identification and assessment of risks and capabilities,
known as THIRA (Threat and Hazard Identification and Risk Assessment). THIRA provides a standardized guide to help communities identify hazards and threats of concern, how they will affect the community,
the core capabilities needed to meet the overall national preparedness
goal, and then apply the results.[30]

The other mechanism routinely used to implement disaster policy after
2010 were presidential executive orders. On November 1, 2013, President
Obama signed Executive Order 13653 in order to improve the preparedness and resilience of federal agencies and their programs to the impacts
of climate change. Agencies modernized and reformed programs, policies,
rules, and operations to support climate-resilient investments, developed
data and tools to support risk-informed decision making, and developed
climate change adaptation plans.

Two months into his administration President Trump revoked
(EO13783) the Obama executive order, solidifying his view that climate
change is a hoax and fulfilling a campaign promise to pull out of the 2015
Paris Agreement on climate change. A second important executive order,
EO13690, signed in January 2015 by President Obama, established a
flood risk standard that held new federal infrastructure to a higher flood
standard. It required federal agency-sponsored projects to use methods
informed by climate science to build two feet higher than the base-flood

elevation and build to the 500-year flood elevation. President Trump also revoked this order (EO13708) on August 15, 2017, a few weeks before Hurricane Harvey.[31]

Near the end of his administration, President Obama signed two additional executive orders focused on risk reduction and enhanced resilience for wildfires and earthquakes, both of which remain in place. The first, Executive Order 13717, established a federal earthquake risk management standard that applied to all federal buildings. Specifically, any new designs, construction, and retrofits of federal buildings would now have to meet modern seismic building codes. The second, Executive Order 13728, focused on mitigating wildfire risks to federal buildings on public lands and new buildings and retrofitted buildings comply with the International Wildland-Urban Interface Code.

The Reality of Unsustainable Losses and the Push Towards Disaster Resilience

In 2005, the National Science and Technology Council's (NSTC) Subcommittee on Disaster Reduction (SDR) issued their *Grand Challenges* report, fundamentally altering the approach to disaster management. As they state at the onset,

> We have reduced the number of lives lost each year to natural disasters, but the costs of major disasters continue to rise. A primary focus on response and recovery is an impractical and inefficient strategy for dealing with these ongoing threats. Instead, communities must break the cycle of destruction and recovery but enhancing their disaster resilience.[32]

This executive branch report was a tipping point for federal interest in and engagement with disaster resilience as a loss reduction strategy. In 2008, federal agencies approached the U.S. National Academies to undertake a consensus study of disaster resilience. By 2009, eight federal agencies and one National Laboratory signed on to support the effort (see Box 2.1: *Disaster Resilience: A National Imperative*).

Box 2.1 Disaster Resilience: A National Imperative

The consensus report commissioned by multiple federal agencies stands as a landmark in the national effort to increase resilience at all levels from communities to the federal government. The committee tasks as defined by sponsors were:

Tasks

1) "Define *national resilience* and frame the primary issues related to increasing national resilience (resilience at federal, state, and local community levels) to hazards and disasters in the United States;

2) Provide goals, baseline conditions, or performance metrics for resilience at the U.S. national level;

3) Describe the state of knowledge about resilience to hazards and disasters in the United States;

4) Outline additional information or data and gaps and obstacles to action that need to be addressed in order to increase resilience to hazards and disasters in the United States; and

5) Present conclusions and recommendations about what approaches are needed to elevate national resilience to hazards and disasters in the United States."

(National Research Council, 2012: 20).

Recommendations

Among the actionable recommendations were to create a culture of resilience for the nation and to develop mechanisms for measuring resilience. The full recommendations were:

1) "Federal government agencies should incorporate national resilience as a guiding principle to inform the mission and actions of the federal government and the programs it supports at all levels.

2) The public and private sectors in a community should work cooperatively to encourage commitment to and investment

in a risk management strategy that includes comple-
mentary structural and nonstructural risk-reduction and
risk-spreading measures or tools.

3) A national resource of disaster-related data should be
established that documents injuries, loss of life, property
loss, and impacts on economic activity.

4) The Department of Homeland Security – in conjunction
with other federal agencies, state and local partners, and
professional groups – should develop a National Resilience
Scorecard.

5) Federal, state, and local governments should support the
creation and maintenance of broad-based community resilience coalitions at local and regional levels.

6) All federal agencies should ensure they are promoting and
coordinating national resilience in their programs and policies. A resilience policy review and self-assessment within
agencies and strong communication among agencies are
key to achieving this kind of coordination." (National
Research Council, 2012:8–9).

The National Research Council (NRC) report released in 2012 highlighted the need for fostering a culture of resilience for the nation, engaging not only local, state, and federal governments but also the private
sector, community members, and everything in between in the process –
in other words, the whole community.[33] Coming on the heels of PPD-8
and other efforts at the federal level, agencies took the recommendations
to heart and began to refocus some agency policies and practices.

In the Obama administration, all-hazards resilience was a focal point
for the National Security Council (NSC) with a Senior Director for
Preparedness Policy leading in the development and implementation
of PPD-8. Climate resilience also included a wide portfolio of activities
within the Office of Science and Technology Policy (OSTP), including an interagency White House Council on Climate Preparedness and
Resilience, co-chaired by the Council on Environmental Quality, OSTP,

and the National Security Council. The focus on all-hazards preparedness and community resilience was clear from the agency (FEMA) level
to the West Wing itself during the Obama years.

Once in office in early 2017, President Trump appointed another
career emergency management professional, Brock Long, as director. To
mute the anti–climate-change stance in the Trump administration, federal agency career officials substituted the word *resilience* for the words
climate change and *adaptation*.[34] In downplaying the science on the causal
association between weather-related disasters and climate change, the
Trump administration developed a broader focus beyond response, moving to preparedness and resilience. Reorganization at FEMA under
Long, who served for only two turbulent years, included the elevation of
the Resilience Portfolio, created in September 2018 as a separate entity,
with direct oversight by the number-two person at FEMA, the deputy
administrator. The Trump administration reduced but did not eliminate
disaster resilience, with OSTP maintaining a small focus on the impacts
of natural hazards and extreme weather and critical infrastructure security and resilience through the Committee on Homeland and National
Security.

While federal governmental interest began to wane, disaster resilience
came of age during this period in philanthropy engagements, private/
public partnerships, and through science outreach to communities. Following are brief descriptions of these efforts.

Disaster Resilience Philanthropy

In the aftermath of 2012's Superstorm Sandy, Governor Cuomo appointed
the president of the Rockefeller Foundation, Judith Rodin, to co-chair
the NYS 2100 Commission. The commission's charge was to provide recommendations on preparing New York to respond more effectively to
and bounce back from future storms – in other words become resilient.
Combined with Sandy's impacts and experiences and the foundation's
long-standing interests in global challenges and promoting well-being,
especially in cities, the Rockefeller Foundation launched the 100 Resilient Cities (100RC) program to help other cities become more resilient

to present and future physical, social, and economic challenges.[35] The goal of the 100RC was to build a network of global resilience practices in cities that integrated governments, NGOs, the private sector, and citizens. Resources provided for a Chief Resilience Officer (CRO) in each city to lead the efforts, coordinating the development and implementation of the resilience strategy, and working cooperatively with the 100RC network to build the community of practice. In the summer of 2019, Rockefeller formally ended its financial support of the 100RC program, midway through its initial timeline.[36]

Public/Private Partnerships

In the immediate aftermath of Superstorm Sandy and its unprecedented impact on the New York metropolitan region, President Obama launched the Hurricane Sandy Rebuilding Task Force. The task force, chaired by the secretary of the Department of Housing and Urban Development (HUD), had two main tasks: align local needs and priorities with available federal policies and resources and provide recommendations for rebuilding to move toward long-term resilience. The HUD secretary, Shaun Donovan, had prior experience in New York as housing authority commissioner and a background in planning and design. Keeping in mind the need for local input and cooperation, the task force recommended a competition to develop innovative resilience designs for rebuilding that combined the politics and local engagement, planning, and design, called Rebuild by Design (RBD). The task force also recommended an upfront funding commitment for the competition and the funding for the first-phase implementation of the winning designs.[37] There was $15.2 billion allocated for Hazard Mitigation Grant Program-Disaster Recovery (HMGP-DR) funding to support the implementation of the program among others. RBD also had partnerships with philanthropic organizations, including the Rockefeller Foundation. The foundation provided financial resources for the research and design phase, community organizing, collaboration with the design teams a central project manager, and staffs for each team. At the same time, four partner organizations within the New York metropolitan region – New York University Institute for

Public Knowledge, the Municipal Art Society, Regional Plan Association, and Van Allen Institute – also provided scientific and local knowledge support to the teams.

Following the global call for interdisciplinary teams, 148 teams representing 15 countries applied. Ten teams had successful pre-proposals and began the planning and design process and the development of full proposals.[38] In 2014, HUD announced six winning proposals with an allocation of $930 million in funding granted to New York City, New York state, New Jersey, and Connecticut with the stipulations that the grantees incorporate the design into their broader disaster recovery plan submitted to HUD with the funds completely expended by 2022.

The success of the RBD Hurricane Sandy Design competition paved the way for other resilience projects nationwide. In 2014, HUD announced a $1 billion CDBG-National Disaster Resilience program.[39] The competition was open to states, counties, and local governments who had a major disaster declaration in any year between 2011 and 2013, with potential applicants invited to Phase I workshops. The Rockefeller Foundation hosted workshops in multiple locations throughout the country. The workshops provided technical expertise to potential applicants on hazard identification, resilience concepts, and tools and data to support applicants. The initial review of applications resulted in invitations to 40 states and communities to move forward and submit full proposals, including the identification of how the proposal related to the recovery from the specific disaster affecting the state or community. In early 2016, HUD announced 13 CDBG-NDR finalists. Eight states – California, Connecticut, Iowa, Louisiana, New Jersey, New York, Tennessee, and Virginia – received awards between $15 million and $120 million for their proposed projects. An additional $17 million to $176 million went to five cities or counties: New York City, New Orleans, Minot, North Dakota, Shelby County, Tennessee, and Springfield, Massachusetts for resilience actions.[40]

Full Circle: Science Outreach to Communities[41]

The 2012 National Academies report launched a national conversation on resilience and mechanisms and building blocks for action based on its recommendations. There were multiple briefings to the White House, the House Committee on Homeland Security, senatorial and house members, as well as federal agencies and other interested parties in the year following the report's release. In January 2014, the National Academies (NASEM) established their Roundtable on Risk and Resilience of Extreme Events to implement four of the recommendations through a pilot community program starting with two communities – Linn County, Iowa and Charleston, South Carolina.[42] In February 2015, a third pilot community, Seattle, Washington, joined and by September, the fourth community, Tulsa, Oklahoma, was on board. Outreach to local communities continued throughout 2016–2018. The ResilientAmerica Roundtable rebranded with four pillars: 1) understand and communicate risk; 2) identify measures of community resilience; 3) share information and data to enhance decision making for building more resilient communities; and 4) build/strengthen partnerships/coalitions within and among communities for resilience.[43] In addition to the community pilot program and the consensus studies it facilitates, the ResilientAmerica Roundtable continues its role as a convener and incubator of workshops, expert meetings, and public events to foster national resilience to disasters and extreme events. Their most recent reports examined measuring community resilience and urban flooding.[44]

The Trump Era and the Regression of Federal Capabilities

The tipping point in practice occurred in the latter half of the 2010s with the incoming Trump administration, which embarked on a policy of dismantling federal agencies. Brock Long, the Trump-appointed FEMA administrator, left after two years amid ongoing recovery from a dozen or more major catastrophes (the case studies in this book). The inability or unwillingness to fill and retain senior-level positions in the agencies, especially in DHS where FEMA is located, led to a decline in the trained workforce and administrative capacity, as well as the loss of institutional memory. What this means is that the federal government is no longer a reliable partner with state and local entities in emergency management. This recalcitrance, coupled with an antagonistic Republican-led congress that repeatedly held up disaster relief appropriations, left state and local emergency managers to fend for themselves, especially in Puerto Rico (2017 Hurricane Maria) and the Midwest (2019 flooding).

Congress has also not solved the flood problem, simply granting extensions on extensions for the National Flood Insurance reauthorization multiple times. As listed by the Association of State Floodplain Managers (ASFPM), priorities for reform should include funding and enhancing the national flood mapping program; ensuring that the expansion of private-sector insurance does not erode the existing comprehensive flood risk management system in place already; addressing the affordability issue; and supporting increased cost of compliance and pre-disaster mitigation of repetitive loss properties.[45]

Finally, while placing an emphasis on enhancing resilience to natural hazards and disasters in the early 2010s, there is currently no federal structure for such programs. In particular, there are no legislative mandates or administrative authority, such as the Stafford Act, for a focus on resilience nor is there a funding stream for it. The case studies in subsequent chapters of this book highlight these overarching issues and much more.

Notes

1. William L. Waugh and Kathleen Tierney, ed., *Emergency Management: Principles and Practice for Local Government*, 2nd edition (Washington, DC: International City/County Management Association (ICMA), 2007); Richart T. Sylves, *Disaster Policy and Politics: Emergency Management and Homeland Security* (Los Angeles: Sage, 2015); George J. Haddow, Jane A. Bullock, and Damon P. Coppola, *Introduction to Emergency Management*, 6th edition (Cambridge, UK: Butterwork-Heinenmann, 2017); Claire B. Rubin, ed., *Emergency Management: The American Experience*, 3rd edition (Milton Park, UK: Routledge, 2019).
2. Will Steffen, Paul J. Crutzen, and John R. McNeill, "The Anthropocene: Are Humans now Overwhelming the Great Forces of Nature?" *Ambio* 36, no. 8 (2007): 614–621; Simon L. Lewis and Mark A. Maslin, "Defining the Anthropocene," *Nature* 519 (March 12, 2015): 171–180.
3. IPCC, *Climate Change 2014: Synthesis Report. Contribution of Working Groups I, II and III to the Fifth Assessment Report of the Intergovernmental Panel on Climate Change*, edited by Core Writing Team, R.K. Pachauri and L.A. Meyer (Geneva, Switzerland: IPCC, 2014).
4. Alexa Jay, D.R. Reidmiller, C.W. Avery, D. Barrie, B.J. DeAngelo, A. Dave, M. Dzaugis, M. Kolian, K.L.M. Lewis, K. Reeves, and D. Winner, "Overview," in *Impacts, Risks, and Adaptation in the United States: Fourth National Climate Assessment, Volume II*, edited by D.R. Reidmiller, C.W. Avery, D.R. Easterling, K.E. Kunkel, K.L.M.

Lewis, T.K. Maycock, and B.C. Stewart (Washington, DC: U.S. Global Change Research Program, 2018), 26. https://doi.org/10.7930/NCA4.2018.CH1.

5. Florence Fu and Chris Weller, "Half of the US Population Lives in These 9 States," *Business Insider*, June 22, 2016, www.businessinsider.com/half-of-the-us-population-lives-in-just-9-states-2016-6.

6. NOAA, National Ocean Service, "What Percentage of the American Population Lives Near the Coast?" 2018, https://oceanservice.noaa.gov/facts/population.html.

7. William H. Frey, *US Population Growth Hits 80-year Low, Capping off a Year of Demographic Stagnation* (Washington, DC: Brookings Institution Press, December 21, 2018), www.brookings.edu/blog/the-avenue/2018/12/21/us-population-growth-hits-80-year-low-capping-off-a-year-of-demographic-stagnation/.

8. Jonathan Vespa, David M. Armstrong, and Lauren Medina, "Demographic Turning Points for the United States: Population Projections for 2020 to 2060," *Current Population Reports*, P25-1144, March 2018, www.census.gov/content/dam/Census/library/publications/2018/demo/P25_1144.pdf.

9. William H. Frey, *Diversity Explosion: How New Racial Demographics Are Remaking America* (Washington, DC: Brookings Institution Press, 2018).

10. Institute for Policy Studies, "Income Inequality in the United States," https://inequality.org/facts/income-inequality/.

11. Ibid.

12. Susan L. Cutter, Ronald L. Schumann III, and Christopher T. Emrich, "Exposure, Social Vulnerability and Recovery Disparities in New Jersey after Hurricane Sandy," *Journal of Extreme Events* 1, no. 1 (2014), 23 pp.; Susan L. Cutter, Christopher T. Emrich, Jerry T. Mitchell, Walter W. Piegorsch, Mark M. Smith, and Lynn Weber. *Hurricane Katrina and the Forgotten Coast of Mississippi* (New York, NY and Cambridge, UK: Cambridge University Press, 2014).

13. Adam Crowe, "6 Ways to Utilize Social Media Before a Disaster Strikes," *Emergency Management*, August 8, 2012, www.govtech.com/em/disaster/6-Ways-Utilize-Social-Media-Disaster.html.

14. Monica Anderson and Andrew Perrin, "Nearly One in-Five Teens Can't Always Finish Their Homework Because of the Digital Divide," *FactTank: News in the Numbers*, Pew Research Center, October 26, 2018, www.pewresearch.org/fact-tank/2018/10/26/nearly-one-in-five-teens-cant-always-finish-their-homework-because-of-the-digital-divide/.

15. See "Social Media," FEMA, last updated August 23, 2018, www.fema.gov/social-media.

16. "@CraigatFEMA," FEMA, www.fema.gov/twitter-archive/CraigatFEMA/.

17. "Mobile App," FEMA, last updated May 2, 2019, www.fema.gov/mobile-app.

18. Craig Fugate, "Understanding the Power of Social Media as a Communication Tool in the Aftermath of Disasters," written statement of Craig Fugate, administrator, Federal Emergency Management Agency, before the U.S. Senate Committee on Homeland Security and Governmental Affairs, Subcommittee on Disaster Recovery and Intergovernmental Affairs (Washington, DC, May 4, 2011), www.dhs.gov/news/2011/05/04/written-statement-craig-fugate-administrator-federal-emergency-management-agency.

19. Michael F. Goodchild and J. Alan Glennon, "Crowdsourcing Geographic Information for Disaster Response: A Research Frontier," *International Journal of Digital Earth* 3, no. 3 (2010): 231–241.

20. Amir Elichai, "How Big Data Can Help in Disaster Response," *Scientific American*, December 13, 2018, https://blogs.scientificamerican.com/observations/how-big-data-can-help-in-disaster-response/.

21. Susan L. Cutter, "Compound, Cascading, or Complex Disasters: What's in a Name?" *Environment: Science and Policy for Sustainable Development* 60, no. 6 (2018): 16–25; quote from p. 24.

22. FEMA, "2017 Hurricane Season: FEMA After-Action Report," July 12, 2018, www.fema.gov/media-library-data/1531743865541-d16794d43d3082544435e147 1da07880/2017FEMAHurricaneAAR.pdf; Arelis R. Hernandez and Joel Achenbach, "Failure of Imagination Hindered Federal Puerto Rico Response Amid Rough Hurricane Season," *The Washington Post*, July 13, 2018, www.washingtonpost.com/national/failure-of-imagination-hindered-federal-puerto-rico-response-amid-rough-hurricane-season/2018/07/13/8ab2b1ea-86b0-11e8-8553-a3ce89036c78_story.html?noredirect=on&utm_term=.b9e464a5080b.

23. Government Accounting Office, *Hurricanes and Wildfires: Initial Observations on the Federal Response and Key Recovery Challenges* (Washington, DC: GAO-18-472, 2018), 23. www.gao.gov/assets/700/694231.pdf.

24. Gavin Smith, *Planning for Post-disaster Recovery: A Review of the United States Disaster Assistance Framework* (Washington, DC: Island Press, 2012).

25. Ibid.; Robert B. Olshansky, Lewis D. Hopkins, and Laurie A. Johnson, "Disaster and Recovery: Processes Compressed in Time," *Natural Hazards Review* 13, no. 3 (2012): 173–178.

26. Department of Homeland Security (DHS), *National Disaster Recovery Framework*, 2nd edition (Washington, DC: DHS, 2016), www.fema.gov/media-library-data/1466014998123-4bec8550930f774269e0c5968b120ba2/National_Disaster_Recovery_Framework2nd.pdf.

27. Department of Housing and Urban Development (HUD), "Fact Sheet," n.d., www.hudexchange.info/resources/documents/CDBG-DR-Fact-Sheet.pdf.

28. Natural Hazards Center, *Holistic Disaster Recovery: Ideas for Building Local Sustainability After a Natural Disaster* (Boulder, CO: Natural Hazards Center, 2001), www.preventionweb.net/files/1746_2206589.pdf; Cutter, *Hurricane Katrina*, 169–173; A.R. Siders, "Government-Funded Buyouts after Disasters are Slow and Inequitable – Here's How That Could Change," *The Conversation*, October 19, 2018, https://theconversation.com/government-funded-buyouts-after-disasters-are-slow-and-inequitable-heres-how-that-could-change-103817.

29. FEMA, "National Preparedness Goal," 2018, www.fema.gov/national-preparedness-goal.

30. FEMA, "Comprehensive Preparedness Guide (CPG) 201: Threat and Hazard Identification and Risk Assessment (THIRA) and Stakeholder Preparedness Review (SPR) Guide," last updated May 31, 2018, www.fema.gov/media-library/assets/documents/165308.

31. Kriston Capps, "Trump Rolled Back the Government's Best Flood Protection Standard," *City Lab*, August 28, 2017, www.citylab.com/environment/2017/08/trump-flooding/538203/.

32. Subcommittee on Disaster Reduction (SDR), *Grand Challenges for Disaster Reduction* (Washington, DC: National Science and Technology Council, 2005), 1.

33. National Research Council (NRC), *Disaster Resilience: A National Imperative* (Washington, DC: National Academies Press, 2012).

34. Miranda Green, "Trump Administration Swaps 'Climate Change' for 'Resilience'", *CNN*, September 30, 2017, www.cnn.com/2017/09/30/politics/resilience-climate-change/index.html.

35. Judith Rodin, *The Resilience Dividend: Being Strong in a World Where Things go Wrong* (New York: Public Affairs, 2014).

36. Laura Bliss, "'100 Resilient Cities' Is No More. Now What?" *CityLab*, April 11, 2019, www.citylab.com/environment/2019/04/rockefeller-100-resilient-cities-climate-philanthropy-end/586522/.
37. Josh Bisker, Amy Chester, and Tara Eisenberg, eds., *Rebuild by Design* (New York: Rebuild By Design, 2015).
38. Ibid.
39. Department of Housing and Urban Development (HUD), "National Disaster Resilience," last updated 2019, www.hudexchange.info/programs/cdbg-dr/resilient-recovery/.
40. Ibid.
41. I want to thank Lauren Alexander Augustine, Elisabeth Eide, Danielle Goldsmith, and the ResilientAmerica program team at the National Academies of Sciences, Engineering, and Medicine (NASEM) for their assistance in compiling the chronology of National Academies' resilience outreach.
42. NRC, *Developing a Framework for Measuring Community Resilience: Summary of a Workshop* (Washington, DC: The National Academies Press, 2015), https://doi.org/10.17226/20672.
43. National Academies of Sciences, Engineering, and Medicine (NASEM), "ResilientAmerica," http://sites.nationalacademies.org/PGA/ResilientAmerica/PGA_086235.
44. NASEM, *Building and Measuring Community Resilience: Actions for Communities and the Gulf Research Program* (Washington, DC: The National Academies Press, 2019), https://doi.org/10.17226/25383; NASEM, *Framing the Challenge of Urban Flooding in the United States* (Washington, DC: The National Academies Press, 2019), https://doi.org/10.17226/25381.
45. Association of State Floodplain Managers, "ASFPM Detailed Priorities for 2019 NFIP Reauthorization and Reform," last updated April 1, 2019, www.floods.org/ace-images/ASFPMPriorities4NFIP2019ReauthorizationApr1_2019.pdf.

3

AS TORNADO OUTBREAKS BECOME MORE DEADLY, MAJOR CHANGES HAPPEN

Lucy A. Arendt, Jane Cage, and Renee White

Tornadoes are not unusual in a country known for its "Tornado Alley" and "Dixie Alley" – the 13 states in the United States known for their frequent tornadoes. On average, there are at least 1,000 recorded tornadoes in the United States annually; more EF4 and EF5 tornadoes occur in the United States each year than they do anywhere else.[1] Despite their relative frequency, three tornadoes in particular have contributed to important changes in federal policy and practice in the last decade: 1) the 2011 Tuscaloosa-Birmingham, Alabama, tornado; 2) the 2011 Joplin, Missouri, tornado; and 3) the 2013 Moore, Oklahoma, tornado.

What are the broad lessons for policy makers and those charged with proposing changes in practice? First, events sufficiently shocking in their intensity and consequences may make the need for change more salient and urgent to those having decision-making power, such as leaders at all levels of government.[2] Second, data collected from such events may affirm existing beliefs, generate new insights, and suggest more changes. The 2011 tornadoes in Tuscaloosa-Birmingham and Joplin, along with the 2013 tornado in Moore, have affirmed the veracity of these broad lessons. With respect to specific lessons learned, this chapter describes three categories of changes made at the federal level. The changes were selected for their potential to influence decision making prior to and in the aftermath of tornado events and for their likely impact on community recovery and resilience. They include: 1) community empowerment in the aftermath of disaster; 2) disaster recovery procedures; and 3) broad-based safety improvements.

Three Extraordinary Tornado Events

Although the United States had thousands of tornado events between 2011 and 2013, the tornadoes of 2011 in Tuscaloosa-Birmingham and Joplin and the 2013 Moore tornado were especially notable for their violent intensity and devastating consequences. Damages to property were extensive. Loss of life and injuries were significant. The psychological and emotional toll on residents, first responders, and others is ongoing and incalculable. No other tornadoes in recent memory have produced the same degree of scientific and general interest as these three. Before diving into the changes made to federal policy and practice resulting from these tornadoes, we briefly describe each tornado event and its immediate consequences. Of course, the consequences of each event continue to accumulate many years later.

The Tuscaloosa-Birmingham, Alabama Tornado (April 2011)

During the late afternoon and early evening of Wednesday, April 27, 2011, an EF4 multiple-vortex tornado struck the communities of Tuscaloosa and Birmingham in Alabama, along with smaller communities lying between the two cities. The maximum path width was approximately 1.5 miles, and highest winds recorded at 190 miles per hour (mph) (see Figure 3.1). The tornado was on the ground for approximately 91 minutes, with damages estimated at $2.4 billion (in 2011 dollars). The tornado damaged and destroyed homes, apartment complexes, cell towers, warehouses, vehicles, shopping centers, railroad trestles, boats, restaurants, churches, commercial buildings, office buildings, and more. Sixty-five people were killed, and another 1,500 injured by the tornado that left a path of destruction 80.68 miles long.[3]

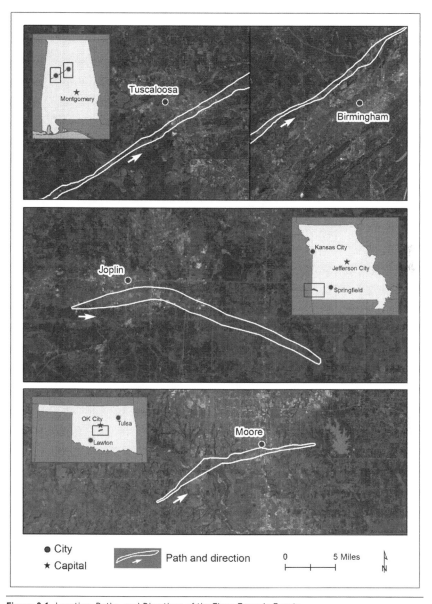

Figure 3.1 Location, Paths, and Directions of the Three Tornado Events

Source: Data compiled from National Weather Service events archives. Graphic Courtesy of Erika Pham, University of South Carolina

The Joplin, Missouri Tornado (May 2011)

Late in the afternoon and early evening of Sunday, May 22, 2011, an EF5 multiple-vortex tornado tracked eastward across the city of Joplin, continuing its eastward trajectory into rural Jasper and Newton counties. The third tornado to strike Joplin since 1971, the 2011 tornado reached a maximum width of nearly one mile during its journey through the southern one-third of the city (see Figure 3.1). The highest winds had speeds greater than 200 mph. The tornado was on the ground for approximately 38 minutes, and damages estimated to be $2.8 billion (in 2011 dollars). The tornado damaged and destroyed homes, apartment complexes, several big box commercial buildings, shopping centers, restaurants, churches, schools, medical buildings (including one hospital), nursing homes, convenience and grocery stores, warehouses, a bank, vehicles, power poles, cell towers, and more. The tornado killed 161 people and injured 1,150 more, making it the deadliest tornado since modern records began in 1950. The path of destruction was 22.1 miles long.[4]

The Moore, Oklahoma Tornado (May 2013)

Midway through the afternoon on Monday, May 20, 2013, a violent EF5 tornado moved eastward through the communities of Newcastle, Moore, and south Oklahoma City. Moore had experienced four major tornadoes in fewer than 14 years, beginning in May 1999. The tornado reached a maximum width of 1.1 miles and highest winds recorded at 210 mph. The tornado was on the ground for approximately 39 minutes, with damage estimated at $2 billion (in 2013 dollars). The tornado damaged and destroyed a bridge, homes, an oil production site, farms, vehicles, a bowling alley, convenience store, a cemetery, industrial buildings, power poles, and two schools – Briarwood Elementary and Plaza Towers Elementary. Seven children died at the latter site. The tornado was responsible for 24 deaths and 212 injuries. Its path of destruction was approximately 14 miles (see Figure 3.1).[5]

When Tornadoes Change Federal Policy and Practice

These three tornadoes led to several major shifts and changes in federal emergency management policy and practice. In some cases, the shifts were underway prior to the tornadoes and the tornadoes lent urgency and saliency to the need for change. In other cases, evidence gathered in the wake of the tornadoes led to review, refreshing, and overhaul of existing policies and practices. Whether the three tornadoes indirectly or directly contributed to the changes, what is clear is that the changes have been intended to guide actions taken to mitigate, prepare, respond, and recover from tornadoes going forward.

Community Empowerment in the Aftermath of Disaster

In December 2011, the Federal Emergency Management Agency (FEMA) published *A Whole Community Approach to Emergency Management*.[6] Developed under the leadership of Craig Fugate, the document offers three guiding principles and describes six strategic themes. The three principles – understand and meet the actual needs of the whole community, engage and empower all parts of the community, and strengthen what works well in communities on a daily basis – recognize that communities must discover and implement their own recovery paths in the aftermath of disaster.[7] Approaches to emergency management that fail to take into account the specific character, culture, and leadership of a given community are unlikely to yield optimal results. Instead, the "Whole Community," defined as "residents, emergency managers, organizational and community leaders, and government officials," must come together and evaluate how best to organize and capitalize on its "assets, capacities, and interests."[8]

While describing each of the principles in detail is outside the scope of this chapter, we have decided to highlight one of them, "Engage and Empower All Parts of the Community." The principle states that,

> Engaging the whole community and empowering local action will better position stakeholders to plan for and meet the actual needs of a community and strengthen the local capacity to deal with the consequences of all threats and hazards.[9]

Illustratively, FEMA's Office of Disability Integration and Coordination emphasizes the need to engage the WHOLE Whole Community (repetition intended). They offer community stakeholder forums for members of disability groups, nonprofit organizations, and state and local government to discuss disaster planning and assistance for people with disabilities and those with access and functional needs. They deploy Regional Disability Integration Specialists to assist with inclusive, community-wide emergency management and they have assigned Disability Integration Advisors to FEMA Incident Management Assistance Teams to ensure that the needs of people with disabilities are met in the immediate and near-term aftermath of disasters.[10] The Office asserts "emergency managers at all levels share responsibility for meeting the needs of the whole community – including people with disabilities."[11] Together, the Office's activities intend to mitigate the negative consequences often disproportionately suffered by underrepresented populations in disasters.

The *Whole Community* document further delineates this philosophy by describing six strategic themes:

- Understand community complexity;
- Recognize community capabilities and needs;
- Foster relationships with community leaders;
- Build and maintain partnerships;
- Empower local action;
- Leverage and strengthen social infrastructure, networks, and assets.

The document further specifies who plays what role in a community's emergency management. Fundamentally, affected communities lead while federal agencies follow and support. For example, FEMA staff members tasked with facilitating community recovery might first observe and listen during meetings with community leaders and the public and then make recommendations founded in best practices that complement the community's character. In the end, they acknowledge that ultimate decision making lies with the community's leaders.

The *Whole Community* publication cites both Tuscaloosa-Birmingham and Joplin as examples of strategic themes in practice. One theme – "Recognize Community Capabilities and Needs" – asks community members to recognize their "private and civic capabilities, identify how they can contribute to improve pre- and post-event outcomes, and actively engage in all aspects of the emergency management process."[12] In the aftermath of the spring 2011 tornadoes, members of the Tuscaloosa and Birmingham communities created the Alabama Interagency Emergency Response Coordinating Committee, led by individuals from Independent Living Resources of Greater Birmingham, United Cerebral Palsy of Greater Birmingham, and the Alabama Governor's Office along with representatives from FEMA and the American Red Cross. Daily conference calls brought together up to 60 individuals from agencies serving individuals with disabilities and chronic illnesses and led to the creation of the Disaster Recovery Resource Database. It included information on shelters, health care services, food assistance, dependent care, animal shelters and services, and more.[13] This collaboration reflected the belief that acting in unison was essential to the community's recovery.

Joplin's Citizens Advisory Recovery Team (CART) illustrates the strategic theme of "Empower Local Action."[14] For this theme, those involved in emergency management are encouraged to "enable the public to lead, not follow, in identifying priorities, organizing support, implementing programs, and evaluating outcomes."[15] Led by community leader and one of this chapter's authors, Jane Cage, the CART's purpose was to engage Joplin's residents in dialogue about the community's recovery goals. While Cage and others were supported by federal agencies – e.g., FEMA's Long-Term Community Recovery Task Force – it was the CART that brought together community residents in several public listening sessions during the summer of 2011 to brainstorm around housing and neighborhoods, schools and community facilities, infrastructure and environment, and economic development (Figure 3.2). The CART compiled the results of these sessions into a report shared with the City Council on November 7, 2011. The report, *Listening to Joplin*, led to the creation of the CART Implementation Task Force that met to devise specific action steps that the community might undertake for its recovery. Three months later, the Implementation Task Force presented its report, *Listening to Joplin – Next Steps*, to a joint meeting of the Joplin City Council, the Duquesne Board of Aldermen, the Joplin School Board, the Joplin Area Chamber of Commerce, and the CART Board. The report was unanimously ratified. The work of the CART has continued to influence the community's recovery efforts, providing support for the belief that, "community ownership of projects provides a powerful incentive for sustaining action and involvement."[16]

Figure 3.2 Community Meeting, Joplin, Missouri, July 12, 2011
Source: FEMA photo/Steve Castaner

The Whole Community philosophy and its attendant practices have served as the foundation of FEMA's efforts since 2011. While perhaps not always successful in practice, the approach does appear fundamental to facilitating effective emergency management and resilience within communities.

Disaster Recovery Procedures

The Sandy Recovery Improvement Act of 2013 (SRIA),[17] amended Title IV of the Robert T. Stafford Disaster Relief and Emergency Assistance Act (42 U.S.C. 5121 et seq.) that addresses the federal assistance that FEMA may deliver to survivors of a disaster. While named for Hurricane Sandy, much of the legislation's content was conceived in the aftermath of the 2011 tornadoes in Tuscaloosa-Birmingham and Joplin.[18] The procedures described in SRIA provide greater flexibility in the use of federal funds and acknowledgement that disaster recovery depends on meeting immediate needs and mitigating against future risk.[19] A key element of SRIA is the identification of five alternative procedures for debris removal. Repairing infrastructure and rebuilding housing, both essential activities in the aftermath of a disaster, depend on efficient and swift debris removal.

Debris Removal: Pre-testing for SRIA in the Aftermath
of the 2011 Tornadoes

On April 28, 2011, one day after the Tuscaloosa-Birmingham tornado, President Barack Obama declared a major disaster for the state of Alabama. The declaration included provisions for individual assistance, debris removal, and emergency protective measures. "Operation Clean Sweep" was responsible for removing an estimated 10 million cubic yards of debris from streets, curbsides, and private property (see Figure 3.3). The federal program paid for 75 percent of cleanup costs; state and local governments shared the remaining 25 percent of costs. By September 2, 2011 – less than six months after the tornado – around 95 percent of the estimated debris had been cleared, and "Operation Clean Sweep" deemed a success.[20]

Approximately one week after the Joplin tornado, on May 31, 2011, FEMA authorized Expedited Debris Removal (EDR), a pilot program that increased the Federal cost share of all debris removal from 75 percent to 90 percent for areas with extensive or catastrophic damage. EDR

Figure 3.3 Tuscaloosa Debris Removal
Source: FEMA photo/Steve Castaner

applied to the first 75 days of operations, backdated to the day of the tornado, May 22, 2011 through August 7, 2011.[21] EDR allowed the increased cost share for removing debris from qualifying parcels of private property and rights-of-way. While it had much in common with Alabama's "Operation Clean Sweep," Joplin's debris removal program was designed specifically to assess the efficacy of tying increased federal funding to a shortened time period, one of the alternative procedures that would later appear in SRIA. Joplin met the August 7, 2011, deadline for 90 percent federal cost sharing. The state agreed to fund the 10 percent match. Mark Rohr, Joplin's city manager from 2004–2014, affirmed that EDR was the key to Joplin's rapid recovery.[22]

The outcomes of both EDR in Joplin and "Operation Clean Sweep" in Tuscaloosa helped inform the alternative procedures for debris removal listed in SRIA and articulated in the *Public Assistance Alternative Procedures (PAAP) Pilot Program Guide for Debris Removal* (Version 6.1).[23] SRIA requires FEMA to regularly revisit and consider extending the timing for the pilot program. Accordingly, while the original legislation addressed five alternatives for debris removal, the current *PAAP Pilot Program for Debris Removal*, renewed through June 2019, includes just two of the five procedures listed in SRIA:

- Reimbursing base and overtime wages for the employees of state, tribal or local governments, or owners or operators of private non-profit facilities performing or administering debris and wreckage removal; and
- Providing cost-share incentives to a state or tribal or local government to have a debris management plan accepted by the FEMA and have pre-qualified one or more debris and wreckage removal contractors before the start of the declaration's incident period.[24]

The remaining three alternative procedures are not included in the current version of the pilot program. The first of these, which addresses the potential for grants made by FEMA based on fixed estimates, has been set aside while FEMA works to improve its debris estimating methodologies.[25] FEMA has also discontinued the final two alternative procedures described in SRIA,[26] after determining that neither of the two procedures met intended goals. According to the *PAPP Guide*, "the Sliding Scale [for determining the federal share] has not resulted in more timely or cost effective completion of debris removal operations and less than one percent of applicants have participated in the Recycling Revenue procedure."[27] While the first part of this statement appears at odds with the debris removal experience in Joplin that Mark Rohr and others praised,[28] no additional detail has been made public as to the specific issues with the sliding scale approach that caused FEMA to set it aside. While the overall pilot program continues, much has changed since the passage of the SRIA with respect to the alternative procedures intended to incentivize swift and cost-efficient debris removal.

Donated Resources and Community Recovery

While not addressed specifically in SRIA, another of FEMA's policies related to debris removal underwent significant review after the Joplin tornado. After Joplin's tornado, people donated time, money, goods, and services to its response and recovery. Tens of thousands of volunteers helped with a wide range of activities, including hauling debris to curbs and picking through debris for salvageable items, organized primarily by the AmeriCorps St. Louis Emergency Response Team. According to Younker,

> Through January 30, 2014, the city of Joplin in partnership with AmeriCorps tracked 182,044 volunteers.... More than 1.5 million hours of service were recorded from all organizations and agencies reporting to either the city or AmeriCorps, equating to more than 176 years' worth of service.[29]

Leslie Haase, Joplin's finance director, states, "The $17.7 million of donated resources is the largest amount recorded in the history of Missouri and in FEMA Region VII. . . . Not only did the volunteers help clean up Joplin, but they also helped us financially recover a significant amount of expense."[30] It is this last comment that bears highlighting. In addition to the direct advantages associated with volunteer labor and efforts, the City of Joplin also reaped an important indirect advantage – the ability to claim its scrupulously recorded volunteer hours as part of the contribution needed to match the federal funds needed for its recovery.

FEMA Recovery Policy RP9525.2 established the criteria by which applicants received credit for volunteer labor, donated equipment, and donated materials used in the performance of eligible emergency work. In the case of Joplin, the Federal share for debris removal was for 90% inside the EDR zone. Debris removal outside the EDR was covered by the normal FEMA reimbursement of 75 percent. RP9525.2 was later archived and its information incorporated into the *Public Assistance Program and Policy Guide* (*PAPPG*) published on January 1, 2016. FEMA's updated Public Assistance Donated Resources Recovery Policy[31] provides for the application of the value of donated resources (third-party in-kind contributions) toward the nonfederal cost share of eligible emergency work projects and direct federal assistance (DFA).

One cannot overstate the value of public assistance from FEMA with respect to its potential impact on a community's recovery. Donated labor, equipment, and materials ease a community's financial burden at a time when revenues may be severely affected.[32] In the case of Joplin, the AmeriCorps St. Louis Emergency Response Team was on the ground within hours of the tornado. They coordinated the efforts of individuals as well as those of more than 2,200 different groups.[33] They had a volunteer reception center in place to help with documenting volunteer hours along with a donations coordination center, a multi-agency donated goods warehouse, and points of distribution throughout the community. Managing donations as meticulously as was done in Joplin yields clear positive benefits that complement those associated with expedited debris removal.

Broad-based Safety Improvements

The National Institute of Standards and Technology (NIST) sent a four-person reconnaissance team to Joplin from May 25–28, 2011. This initial team determined that the tornado represented a "significant opportunity to learn from what happened and to improve safety in the future.'[34]

Two months later, a National Construction Safety Team (NCST) of four researchers was established. Its 494-page final report, published in March 2014, includes 47 findings and 16 recommendations "for improvements to building and emergency communications codes, standards and practices that lead to more tornado-resilient communities."[35]

The final report has three categories of recommendations: 1) improving the characteristics of tornado hazards and their associated wind fields; 2) improving how buildings and shelters are designed, constructed, and maintained in tornado-prone regions; and 3) improving emergency communications systems and public response.[36] Several report findings also align with observations made after the May 20, 2013, Moore, Oklahoma, tornado. Table 3.1 lists the recommendations and the agencies expected to facilitate their implementation.

The safety improvements recommended in the NCST's report intend to yield positive and sustainable changes for communities that enhance their resilience. Significant progress has been made in the five years since the final report's publication. Routine reports to the NCST Advisory Committee[37] suggest a structured process with consistent leadership that understands the complex interdependencies among the recommendations and the need to engage various stakeholders in careful study and extensive dialogue.

Improving Tornado Hazard Characteristics

A key discovery NCST made while conducting its investigation was that "operational weather radar technology [was] incapable of determining tornado occurrence and intensity for heights at which most structures are built."[38] The result? Inadequate warning lead time and all-too-frequent false alarm rates, both believed to have contributed to the significant number of casualties associated with the Joplin tornado. The team also found that point-based estimates of the tornado hazard were insufficient, as

> demonstrated by the larger spatial extent and longer duration of the wind field in Joplin compared to tornado hazard models . . . and by the amount and effects of wind–borne debris in Joplin.

Table 3.1 NIST NCST Team Recommendations

	R#	Recommendation Summary	Lead
Hazard Characteristics	R1	Develop and deploy instrumentation systems that can measure and characterize actual tornadic near-surface wind fields	NOAA
	R2	Improve publicly available tornado event databases	NWS
	R3	Develop tornado hazard maps for use in the engineering design of buildings and infrastructure	NIST
	R4	Standardize and improve the Enhanced Fujita Scale through addition of scientific/quantifiable damage indicators	NWS
Buildings, Shelters, Designated Safe Areas, and Lifelines	R5	Develop performance-based standards for tornado-resistant design	ASCE
	R6	Develop performance-based tornado design methodologies	NIST, FEMA
	R7	Develop tornado shelter standard for existing buildings; install tornado shelters in more buildings in tornado-prone regions	ICC
	R8	Develop and implement uniform national guidelines that enable communities to create safe, effective public sheltering strategies	FEMA
	R9	Develop guidelines for selection of best available refuge areas	FEMA
	R10	Prohibit aggregate used as surfacing for roof coverings and aggregate, gravel, or stone used as ballast in tornado-prone regions	ICC
	R11	Develop requirements for enclosures of egress systems in critical facilities	ICC, NFPA
	R12	a) Develop tornado vulnerability assessment guidelines for critical facilities b) Performance of vulnerability assessments by critical facilities in tornado-prone regions	FEMA
Emergency Communication	R13	a) Develop codes, standards, and guidance for emergency communications b) Develop joint plan by emergency managers/media/NWS for consistent alerts	NFPA
	R14	Deploy "push" technologies for transmission of emergency information	FEMA
	R15	Research to identify factors to enhance public perception of personal risk	NSF, NIST
	R16	Develop technology for real-time, spatially resolved tornado threat information	NOAA

Source: National Institute of Standards and Technology (NIST), *NIST NCSTAR 3 – Final Report, NIST: Technical Investigation of the May 22, 2011 Tornado in Joplin, Missouri* (Washington DC: NIST, March 2014)

Debris from structures was shown to have significantly contributed to the overall damage state . . . and to the potential for
injuries and fatalities in Joplin.[39]

Essentially, point-based methods underestimate actual damage. Finally,
the team observed that the existing Enhanced Fujita intensity scale did
not adequately distinguish tornado intensity due to the lack of adequate
damage indicators (DIs) and corresponding degrees of damage (DoDs).
This made it difficult to describe tornadoes and their associated risk
accurately.

Approximately eight years after Joplin's tornado, enhanced tornado
hazard maps are under development[40] and key stakeholders have participated in workshops intended to review the utility of the work completed
thus far.[41] A new ASCE/SEI/AMS "Standard on Wind Speed Estimation in Tornadoes and Other Windstorms" is also under development
along with a new approach to assigning wind speeds for each DoD for
all DIs. New DIs are being developed, including several specific to rural
areas.[42] Finally, NIST has been working with NOAA on tornado database structure and data collection procedures improvements as well as
data archival and access improvements.[43]

Performance of Buildings, Shelters, and Designated Safe Areas

Of the 16 recommendations in the NCST's final report, fully half are in this
category. Two recommendations address the need for performance-based
design as it relates to tornado and wind hazards. Specifically, the team recommended that buildings and their components and systems in tornado-
prone areas of the country be built to withstand tornado hazards to the
extent made possible by performance-based design. The team noted "there
are no standards for the tornado-resistant design of ordinary buildings
and infrastructure, except for *safety–related structures in nuclear power
plants and storm shelters or safe rooms*" (italics original).[44] Remedying this
oversight is expected to yield "more tornado-resilient communities (in
terms of enhanced occupants' life safety and reduced property damage
and economic loss)."[45] The team also observed that building codes at the

time did not consider the "inconsistent performance of different building components (e.g., walls versus roof) . . . when subjected to tornado hazards."[46] The outcome? Even when building structures withstood collapse, the damage to building components and systems often led to extensive damage, loss of functionality, and casualties. The same observations were made in the wake of the 2013 Moore tornado. In response, NIST is leading a new ASCE Tornado Task Committee charged with developing tornado load provisions.[47]

Three recommendations address shelters and refuge areas. The NCST found unexpectedly high casualties in several high-occupancy commercial box-type structures (BST) (e.g., Home Depot) and in multifamily housing units and nursing homes. The best available refuge rooms in the BSTs did not adequately protect occupants. The lack of community shelters or shelters/safe rooms in several multifamily housing units and nursing homes left their residents with no safe place to shelter. Emergency plans often directed building occupants to interior corridors or restrooms, areas that provided little or no protection.[48]

In response to the need for community shelters, requirements for installation of storm shelters on school campuses expanded and changes adopted in the 2018 editions of the International Building Code (IBC) and the International Existing Building Code (IEBC).[49] The International Code Council (ICC) changed the IBC to require that new buildings on existing school campuses in tornado-prone regions include ICC 500 compliant tornado shelters. The ICC also changed the IEBC to require that additions to existing school campuses include tornado shelters. They further required retrofits of tornado shelters in existing buildings. Both codes added provisions for minimum shelter capacity and maximum travel distance to the shelters.

Nearly everyone killed in the Joplin tornado was inside a building. Most of the buildings where the fatalities were found were either heavily damaged or destroyed by the tornado. Often, these individuals had sheltered above ground in these heavily damaged buildings. Few had access to below-grade or tornado-resistant shelters (see Figure 3.4).[50] At the time, there were no community tornado shelters or public safe rooms in Joplin. The NCST final report recommended the development and

Figure 3.4 Storm Shelter, Moore, Oklahoma, May 22, 2013

Source: FEMA photo/Andrea Booher

implementation of uniform national guidelines for public sheltering strategies. In response, FEMA significantly expanded its tornado safe room guidance[51] to include more information on siting, designing, installing, and operating public tornado shelters and safe rooms. The ICC also published a commentary to their ICC/NSSA Standard for Design and Construction of Storm Shelters[52] with guidance on design and installation of both residential and community tornado shelters.[53]

The NCST team also observed that best available refuge areas within buildings were often selected for reasons other than structural safety. To address this issue, the National Fire Protection Association (NFPA) included additional guidance for selection of facilities to use as shelters and best available refuge areas for tornadoes into its updated NFPA 1616, Standard for Mass Evacuation, Sheltering, and Re-entry Programs,[54] first published in 2017.

The practical implications of these building performance recommendations and actions are readily observable. In Oklahoma, for example, the number of safe rooms has increased dramatically since 2013.[55] While the Tuscaloosa-Birmingham tornado occurred on a Wednesday after the school day had ended, and the Joplin tornado occurred on a

Sunday, the Moore tornado occurred as the school day was ending. Seven children at Plaza Towers Elementary School in Moore were killed.[56]

Funding for safe room construction in Oklahoma is primarily through a mix of bond issues and FEMA Hazard Mitigation Grant Program grants, which pay for up to 75 percent of building projects. Still, many districts have been unable to generate the funds needed to build safe rooms. While the cost of building a safe room is approximately the same throughout the state, rural communities may not be able to generate the additional funds needed to fund these spaces.[57] As a result, students in poorer districts may continue to huddle in hallways, in closets, and in rooms without windows – places that cannot ensure reasonable levels of safety.

Risk Communication

One challenge faced by people living in tornado-prone areas is whether to respond to a weather-related warning and how quickly they need to act. In the case of Joplin, NOAA observed "the majority of Joplin residents did not take protective action until processing additional credible confirmation of the threat and its magnitude from a non-routine, extraordinary risk trigger."[58] At least some people hesitated to seek shelter, and many lost their lives or were injured as a result.

One outcome of their uncertainty was that many people found themselves outside or in vehicles as the tornado bore down on them. Why might this uncertainty have occurred, especially in an area where tornadoes were common? Several possibilities have been proffered, including a belief that the "*perceived* frequency of siren activation in Joplin led the majority of survey participants to become desensitized or complacent to this method of warning."[59] In its final report, the NCST also observed that the different means used by communities to disseminate emergency communications for tornadoes may confuse people.[60] In the case of Joplin, for example, the protocol required that sirens cease after three minutes. On May 22, 2011, the first siren sounded for three minutes at 5:11 p.m. Not realizing that the three-minute sounding was the standard, at least some people interpreted the siren's cessation to mean that the danger had passed. When a second siren sounded for three minutes at 5:38 p.m., many were further confused. Was there or wasn't there a tornado? By that time, the tornado was bearing down on Joplin, and people's uncertainty meant that many were not sheltered properly when it struck.

With these observations in mind, the NCST final report[61] recommended standardization of emergency communications, enhanced distribution of emergency communications protocols, and adoption of current and next-generation emergency communication "push" technologies (e.g., GPS-based mobile alerts). In response, NIST published a technical note providing alerting guidance and the NFPA incorporated guidance on public alerts and warnings, and application of social media to support emergency communications into its NFPA 1616 Standard for Mass Evacuation, Sheltering, and Re-entry Programs.[62]

The report also recommended the development of technology that provides tornado threat information on a spatially resolved real-time basis so that people might have better information when they need it. The objective of the Forecasting a Continuum of Environmental Threats (FACET) program at NOAA's National Severe Storms Laboratory is to enhance tornado warnings such that they are more precise, offer more lead time, and generate fewer false alarms.[63] The current polygon used to illustrate where a tornado is likely to strike is problematic in that communities may not have consistent lead time and not all communities affected. The FACET program introduces technology that more narrowly confines the range of the warning map while updating it more frequently, giving enhanced lead time. These changes are expected to be implemented by 2021.[64]

Learning From Tornadoes

The lessons learned from the 2011 Tuscaloosa-Birmingham and Joplin tornadoes and the 2013 Moore tornado are increasing safety throughout the U.S.'s tornado-prone areas. The changes highlighted in this chapter are not the only ones; others have happened at both state and local levels. Community recovery and resilience depend on correctly applying lessons learned from many communities while also understanding the unique constellation of factors that characterize a community.[65]

Challenges to learning remain. For example, people's preferences can stall or stop the implementation of lessons. In 2013, not long after its tornado, a story on Moore noted that it had no local ordinance or building code requiring below-ground shelters.[66] Such ordinances are often considered cost prohibitive and anathema to those who believe that such ordinances conflict with individuals' property rights. At the time, the Moore website explained the lack of a community shelter by noting that people wouldn't have time to get to it and would be less at risk in a "reasonably well-constructed residence," though "well-constructed" may not have included a safe room or below-ground shelter.[67] In addition to cost concerns, people accustomed to living in "tornado alley" may see tornadoes as a fact of life that no cost outlay can protect them from.[68]

Another potential obstacle to learning is a lack of consensus around the solution. Experts may disagree. Available evidence may not point to a solution where the benefits clearly outweigh the costs. Various contingency factors, such as building type, may further affect a proposed solution's generalizability. One example is the decision to shelter in place versus evacuate. If the experts cannot agree on what people should do, how can the average person decide?

In addition, experience can change expert opinions. One example of this is the advice on whether sheltering in hallways is appropriate. In the case of Joplin, for example, school hallway cameras in two schools revealed that the hallways acted as wind tunnels.[69] Had students been in those hallways, crouched in typical duck-and-cover position, there may have been more injuries and fatalities as large debris flew through the air. Fortunately, school was not in session.

Eight years after the 2011 Joplin tornado, individuals at NIST and other federal agencies continue to work on recommendations resulting from expert technical analysis of that event and its aftermath. As Hobbes writes, "Every discovery . . . no matter how significant, must compete with the traditions, assumptions and financial incentives of the society implementing it."[70] Change in the way we view and deal with tornado events will take substantial effort, significant time, and sizeable amounts of money. The work is ongoing.

Notes

1. NOAA, "Severe Weather 101: Tornado Basics," accessed March 1, 2019, www.nssl. noaa.gov/education/svrwx101/tornadoes/.
2. Lucy A. Arendt and Daniel J. Alesch, *Long-Term Community Recovery from Natural Disasters* (Boca Raton, FL: CRC Press, Taylor & Francis Group, 2014).
3. "Tuscaloosa-Birmingham Tornado – April 27, 2011," National Weather Service (NWS), accessed March 1, 2019, www.weather.gov/bmx/event_04272011tuscbirm.
4. "7th Anniversary of the Joplin Tornado – May 22nd, 2011," National Weather Service (NWS), accessed March 1, 2019, www.weather.gov/sgf/ne`ws_events_2011may22.
5. "The Tornado Outbreak of May 20, 2013," National Weather Service (NWS), accessed March 1, 2019, www.weather.gov/oun/events-20130520.
6. FEMA, *A Whole Community Approach to Emergency Management: Principles, Themes, and Pathways for Action* (Washington, DC: FEMA, December 1, 2011), accessed November 1, 2018, www.fema.gov/media-library/assets/documents/23781.
7. Arendt and Alesch, *Long-Term Recovery*.
8. FEMA, *Whole Community*, 3.
9. Ibid., 4.
10. "Office of Disability Integration and Coordination 2013 Fact Sheet," FEMA, accessed March 28, 2019, www.fema.gov/office-disability-integration-and-coordination-2013-fact-sheet.
11. Ibid.
12. FEMA, *Whole Community*, 8.
13. FEMA, *Whole Community*.
14. See for example, www.joplinareacart.com.
15. FEMA, *Whole Community*, 15.
16. Ibid., 14.
17. "Public Law 113-2-Jan. 29, 2013, Disaster Relief Appropriations, Division B – Sandy Recovery Improvement Act of 2013," FEMA, accessed December 11, 2018, www. fema.gov/sandy-recovery-improvement-act-2013.
18. R. Serino, personal correspondence, 2018.
19. Arendt and Alesch, *Long-Term Recovery*.
20. Jason Morton, "Debris Removal Nearly Complete," *Tuscaloosa News*, September 2, 2011, www.tuscaloosanews.com/news/20110902/debris-removal-nearly-complete.
21. FEMA, *The Response to the 2011 Joplin, Missouri, Tornado: Lessons Learned Study* (Washington, DC: FEMA, December 20, 2011), https://kyem.ky.gov/Who%20 We%20Are/Documents/Joplin%20Tornado%20Response,%20Lessons%20 Learned%20Report,%20FEMA,%20December%2020,%202011.pdf.
22. Mark Rohr, *Joplin: The Miracle of the Human Spirit* (Mustang, OK: Tate Publishing & Enterprises, 2012).
23. FEMA, *Public Assistance: Alternative Procedures Pilot Program Guide for Debris Removal (Version 6.1)* (Washington, DC: FEMA, June 28, 2018). www.fema.gov/ media-library-data/1531832460665-eefa838f818a3215e9480d71954a5ec9/PAAP_ Debris_Guide_V6.1_6-28-2018_508.pdf.
24. Ibid.
25. Ibid.
26. FEMA, "Public Law."
27. FEMA, *Public Assistance*, 2.
28. Rohr, *Joplin*.
29. Emily Younker, "Five Years after 2011 Tornado, Joplin Continues to Attract Volunteers." *The Joplin Globe*, July 16, 2016, www.joplinglobe.com/news/local_news/

five-years-after-tornado-joplin-continues-to-attract-volunteers/article_6a876a57-e7b8-5663-a956-78c08af30fc0.html.

30. Jono Anzalone, "FEMA Releases Updated Donated Resources Policy," *National Mass Care Strategy*, March 20, 2014, https://nationalmasscarestrategy.org/fema-releases-updated-donated-resources-policy-2/.

31. FEMA, "Recovery Policy: Public Assistance Donated Resources," June 25, 2018, www.fema.gov/media-library-data/1530129122565-bbfdac5b88ffc3d7c59bef ce5593c993/Donated_Resources_Policy_2018_508.pdf.

32. Arendt and Alesch, *Long-Term Recovery*.

33. Todd C. Frankel, "How 80,000 Volunteers Showed Joplin, Mo., that 'the World Cared'," *St. Louis Post-Dispatch*, December 25, 2011, www.stltoday.com/news/local/metro/how-volunteers-showed-joplin-mo-that-the-world-cared/article_ceede6f5-7025-56d9-b0c3-00444234db5e.html.

34. National Institute of Standards and Technology (NIST), *NIST NCSTAR 3 – Final Report, NIST: Technical Investigation of the May 22, 2011 Tornado in Joplin, Missouri* (Washington, DC: NIST, March 2014), xliv, https://doi.org/10.6028/NIST.NCSTAR.3.

35. NIST, *Final Report*, ix.

36. Ibid., 357.

37. NCST Advisory Committee agendas, minutes, and presentations are available at: www.nist.gov/topics/disaster-failure-studies/national-construction-safety-team-ncst/advisory-committee-meetings.

38. NIST, *Final Report*, 358.

39. Ibid., 360.

40. Judy Mitrani-Reiser, Long Phan, Marc Levitan, and Erica Kuligowski, "Summary of Progress on Implementation of the Joplin Tornado Investigation Recommendations," *NCST Advisory Committee Meeting*, September 28, 2017, www.nist.gov/sites/default/files/documents/2017/09/28/02_mitrani_joplin_introduction.pdf.

41. Marc Levitan and Erica Kuligowski, "Tornado Hazard Characteristics, and Emergency Messaging and Communication," *NCST Advisory Committee Meeting*, August 30, 2018, www.nist.gov/sites/default/files/documents/2019/01/28/02_phan_levi tan_kuligowski_ncstac_aug2018_joplin_recommendations_update_final.pdf.; Long Phan, "Summary of Progress on Implementation of Recommendations from the Joplin Tornado Investigation," *NCST Advisory Committee Meeting*, August 30, 2018, www.nist.gov/sites/default/files/documents/2019/01/28/summary_of_progress_on_implementation_of_recommendations_from_the_joplin_tornado_investigation.pdf.

42. Ibid.

43. Ibid.

44. NIST, *Final Report*, 362.

45. Ibid.

46. Ibid., 363.

47. Marc Levitan, Long Phan, and Erica Kuligowski, "Update on Implementation of Recommendations from the Joplin Tornado Investigation," *NCST Advisory Committee Meeting*, February 2018, www.nist.gov/sites/default/files/documents/2018/02/20/04_update_on_implementation_of_recommendations_from_the_joplin_investigation.pdf.

48. NIST, *Final Report*.

49. Levitan et al., "Update on Implementation."

50. NIST, *Final Report*.

51. FEMA, *FEMA P-361, Safe Rooms for Tornadoes and Hurricanes: Guidance for Community and Residential Safe Rooms, 3e.* (Washington, DC: FEMA, March 31, 2015), www.fema.gov/media-library/assets/documents/3140.
52. ICC, "ICC 500-2014: ICC/NSSA Standard for the Design and Construction of Storm Shelters, 2e.," 2014, www.fema.gov/media-library-data/1444388800229-090 2a12ce6670c6f96d8419c7464ca67/Highlights_of_ICC_500.pdf.
53. Levitan et al., "Update on Implementation."
54. Available at www.nfpa.org/codes-and-standards/all-codes-and-standards/list-of-codes-and-standards/detail?code=1616.
55. Darla Slipke and Ben Felder, "Dozens of Schools Built Safe Rooms Following Moore Tornado," *NewsOK*, May 20, 2018, https://newsok.com/article/5595052/dozens-of-schools-built-safe-rooms-following-moore-tornado.
56. Kiel Ortega et al., "Damage Survey and Analysis of the 20 May 2013 Newcastle-Moore EF-5 Tornado," *Special Symposium on Severe Local Storms*, American Meteorological Society. Atlanta, GA, February 2014.
57. Slipke and Felder, "Dozens of Schools."
58. U.S. Department of Commerce, National Oceanic and Atmospheric Administration, National Weather Service, Central Region Headquarters, *NWS Central Region Service Assessment: Joplin, Missouri Tornado – May 22, 2011* (Kansas City, MO: NOAA, July 2011), iii–iv, www.weather.gov/media/publications/assessments/Joplin_tornado.pdf.
59. Ibid.
60. NIST, *Final Report*, 368.
61. Ibid., 367–370.
62. Levitan and Kuligowski, "Tornado Hazard"; Phan, "Summary of Progress."
63. Jon Erdman, "The Future of Tornado Warnings: More Precise, More Lead Time, Fewer False Alarms," *Tornado Central, The Weather Channel*, March 24, 2017, https://weather.com/storms/tornado/news/tornado-warnings-future-facets-nssl.
64. Ibid.
65. Arendt and Alesch, *Long-Term Recovery*.
66. John Schwartz, "Why No Safe Room to Run To? Cost and Plains Culture," *The New York Times*, May 21, 2013, www.nytimes.com/2013/05/22/us/shelter-requirements-resisted-in-tornado-alley.html.
67. Ibid.
68. Ibid.
69. Stephanie Pappas, "Schools Need Better Tornado Protection, Scientists Say," *Live Science*, June 24, 2014, www.livescience.com/46497-schools-need-tornado-protection.html.
70. Michael Hobbes, "Everything You Know About Obesity is Wrong," *Huffpost: Highline*, September 19, 2018, https://highline.huffingtonpost.com/articles/en/everything-you-know-about-obesity-is-wrong/.

4

HURRICANE SANDY
THE NEW YORK CITY EXPERIENCE

Donovan Finn

Superstorm Sandy struck the New York metropolitan region on October 29, 2012. The storm, which became a tropical cyclone, or hurricane, on October 24 near the island of Jamaica, had lost its hurricane-strength winds by the time it made landfall in southern New Jersey, hence the "superstorm" moniker. The storm was massive, with a peak diameter of 870 nautical miles and a storm surge that caused devastating flooding across the region.[1] Because it struck such a heavily populated and economically important part of the country, Sandy forever changed disaster recovery in the United States. However, as Rubin has argued,[2] this is true for almost every major disaster. Each new "focusing event" that we experience can help public officials and disaster managers refine and improve responses for future events.

Two aspects of the Sandy experience, however, are unique among previous large disasters. First, the Sandy region is densely urbanized with highly vulnerable coastal areas. This created unique recovery challenges – such as finding temporary and permanent housing for affected residents – and highlighted the deficiencies in federal disaster recovery programs when applied to dense urban areas.[3] Yet the storm also struck one of the world's premiere metropolitan areas, which possesses perhaps unparalleled access to financial resources, professional expertise, and political capital. These two intertwined aspects of the Sandy experience – the region's unique vulnerabilities as well as its unique recovery capacity – provide the basis for drawing out some important lessons about disaster response and recovery, especially in dense urban areas. Although the storm struck a huge region, this chapter examines the post-Sandy recovery process in New York City specifically, focusing on housing recovery, business recovery and workforce development, and community recovery. A few important questions guide this discussion. What were the key recovery challenges in New York City after Sandy? What programs were created to address these unique local conditions? How did these efforts affect recovery outcomes? And what national recovery policies were altered as a result of the Sandy experience in New York?

Sandy's Impacts on New York City

Sandy was a large and powerful storm that also caused damage in Jamaica, Cuba, the Bahamas, and 24 U.S. states; it killed at least 117 people in the U.S. alone.[4] When the storm struck the New York metropolitan region on October 29, 2012, it was the largest Atlantic hurricane ever recorded.[5] In all, 12 states and the District of Columbia received disaster declarations, with Sandy causing $71.5 billion in damage. Most of this money went to heavily damaged New York and New Jersey. Of the hundreds of hurricanes to strike the United States since 1851,[6] only 2005's Hurricane Katrina (with damages of $163.8 billion) and 2017's hurricanes Harvey ($126.3 billion) and Maria ($90.9 billion) caused more damage than Sandy.[7]

This damage was widespread across New Jersey, New York City, and New York State's suburban Long Island region (e.g., Nassau and Suffolk counties). The storm's unusual trajectory funneled a large storm surge into the region causing extensive flooding along coasts, bays, and rivers (see Figure 4.1).[8] Peak storm tides – surge plus high tide – measured more than fourteen feet above the average height of the lowest daily tide at the Battery on Manhattan Island's southern tip near the Financial District.[9] Entire neighborhoods were flooded, infrastructure was destroyed, beach-front homes were moved off their foundations or washed out to sea, and large parts of the region were without power for days (Figure 4.2). The

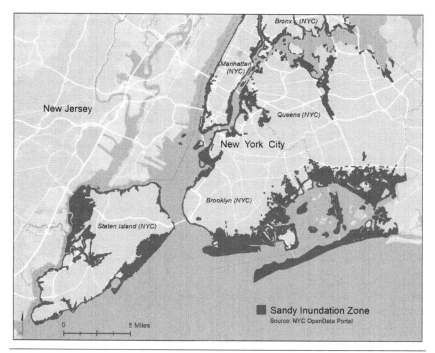

Figure 4.1 Hurricane Sandy Inundated Areas in New York City

Source: Data from New York City Department of Small Business Services (SBS) via the city's NYC OpenData portal. Graphic provided by Erika Pham, University of South Carolina

Figure 4.2 Rockaway Peninsula Boardwalk

Source: Photo by author

storm caused shutdowns of the New York Stock Exchange for two days, the New York City transit system for three days, and the city's school system for a week. There were approximately 69,000 housing units in New York City directly damaged by Sandy, and many thousands more affected by utility outages or damage to surrounding neighborhoods.[10] Seventeen percent of New York City's land area – or almost 51 of its 303 square miles – flooded.[11] Heavily damaged infrastructure systems included the flooding of eight of New York City's subway tunnels and both of LaGuardia Airport's runways.

Sandy in Context

Recovery from a major disaster is an incredibly challenging undertaking because communities are complex places.[12] Recovery efforts must somehow repair various urban systems including housing, business, infrastructure, social services, and others by not only rebuilding their damaged components but also stitching back together the interconnected economic and social networks that underpin these systems. Recovery also requires that actions happen not only across these many interrelated sectors but at multiple scales – from the individual household and firm to the block, neighborhood, municipal, and state levels – all within a framework dictated by federal laws and policies. Federal programs, however, are sometimes too blunt and inflexible to address specific local and individual contexts. At the same time, the federal government is a critically important stakeholder in the recovery process, even in a resource-rich region like the New York metropolitan area (see Federal and State Housing Recovery Programs, following).

While every recovery process is inherently complicated, for a host of reasons, the New York City context amplifies this dynamic. The largest city in the nation, New York had, in 2012, a population of 8.4 million with a population density of over 27,000 people per square mile. New York City's population is more than twice as large as the next largest U.S. city, Los Angeles, and larger than all but 11 U.S. states. Spread across 303 square miles, the city's diverse geography, urban form, and socio-demographics present daunting challenges to one-size-fits-all recovery strategies. The city's sheer size complicates even basic recovery tasks such as face-to-face meetings between affected residents and recovery officials. For many residents, especially for the many New Yorkers who don't own a car, even the seemingly simple task of visiting a citywide recovery office is a time-consuming activity.

The city's housing also presented complications. According to the U.S. Census, New York City residential rents are 1.4 times the national average, and housing prices are almost 2.8 times the national average. Recovery costs like construction labor, materials, and temporary housing are higher in the region than other parts of the country. Even the form of homeownership for many New Yorkers is atypical. Of the city's 1,038,200 owner-occupied housing units, 43 percent are either cooperatives or condominiums, ownership types poorly served by federal disaster recovery programs because they are relatively rare outside of a few major cities.[13] The typical American single-family home – the model for which most federal recovery programs are designed[14] – is the exception rather than the rule in New York.[15] Some Sandy-flooded areas, such as Staten Island and the Rockaways, have more single-family-home residences than other parts of the city. Still, some 70 percent of the housing units affected by the surge were in buildings larger than four units.[16]

New York City's social dynamics also created recovery challenges.[17] While the poverty rate in the United States was 15 percent when Sandy struck, New York City's poverty rate adjusted for housing costs was 45.2 percent.[18] Over a quarter of the households in Sandy's flood zone included senior citizens and 12.1 percent contained senior citizens living alone.[19] There are more than 200 languages spoken in the city, with more than half of New Yorkers speaking a language other than English at home, a factor that can hamper even simple recovery tasks such as filling out paperwork and speaking with case workers. Additionally, where people live, the degree of damage they experience, and the degree and type of social capital present in the community all affect recovery outcomes.[20] In a city as large and diverse as New York, that meant that recovery capacity varied widely from neighborhood to neighborhood,[21] further complicating efforts to address the myriad of differing recovery contexts.

Finally, an effective recovery process is more than merely a series of individual rebuilding projects. It also demands that communities create and rework local policies and programs for the post-disaster context. New York City has invested millions of dollars in site-specific recovery and resilience measures since Sandy, such as $28 million in resiliency upgrades for Staten Island University Hospital, $15 million to revitalize and protect commercial corridors in the Rockaways, and $12 million to restore 68 acres of the Saw Mill Creek marsh on Staten Island.[22] Yet, while these large place-based capital investments are valuable, it is also important to create and revamp citywide policies and programs so that individual residents and business can rebuild and contribute to community-wide recovery. Since Sandy, the city has begun to infuse lessons learned across policy and operations at all levels of local government, as illustrated in the following.

While this chapter focuses on the recovery process in New York City after Sandy, the city's own municipal government was only one of many actors involved in this process. The federal government and New York State also expended significant effort to facilitate the city's recovery. Through the federal government's Disaster Relief Appropriations Act of 2013 (DRA), also known as the Sandy Supplemental, approximately $50 billion was allocated for storm recovery. New York City ultimately received $4.2 billion in Community Development Block Grant–Disaster Recovery (CDBG-DR) allocations from the U.S. Department of Housing and Urban Development (HUD) and the state received a comparable allocation. Because of their flexible nature, CDBG-DR funds are particularly useful for recovery because they allow local and state governments to develop programs that address locally specific needs.

Housing Recovery in New York City

In the aftermath of a major disaster, one of the most urgent objectives is typically to assure that affected residents have adequate shelter.[23] So important is housing to a community's ability to recover from a disaster that housing is one of the Federal Emergency Management Agency's (FEMA) six key Recovery Support Functions (RSFs) around which the agency's recovery framework is designed. Due to the unique nature of New York City's land use patterns and building and zoning codes, as well as Sandy's widespread damage, housing-related issues presented enormous challenges for recovery officials and required the development of many new strategies.

Federal and State Housing Recovery Programs

One of the first challenges encountered after Sandy was the realization that federal recovery programs designed for predominantly suburban contexts did not always address the needs of affected New Yorkers.[24] The week after Sandy's landfall FEMA created the Hurricane Sandy Catastrophic Disaster Housing Task Force in New York and New Jersey to help consolidate housing-related issues and focus on some of the region's unique challenges. There were many federal programs created or modified to account for local conditions, such as FEMA's new Sheltering and Temporary Essential Power (STEP) program.[25] Designed to address the dual challenges of high housing costs and inadequate supply of temporary shelter options in the Sandy region, plus the imminent onset of winter weather, STEP focused on funding emergency home repairs that allowed residents to shelter in place during long-term rebuilding[26] instead of relying on hotels and rental housing (which were in short supply) or FEMA trailers (for which no vacant land was available).

A second FEMA shelter-in-place program known as the "5/25/5" initiative is an expedited claims process for the National Flood Insurance Program (NFIP) providing recoupable rapid grants of $5,000 to replace household contents, $25,000 for heat and electricity restoration, and $5,000 to repair damaged doors and windows. FEMA also increased rental assistance payouts to 125 percent of HUD's 2013 fair market rates instead of the standard 100 percent, providing displaced residents more purchasing power.[27] Finally, FEMA revived its Disaster Housing Assistance Program (DHAP) originally created in response to hurricanes Katrina and Rita and used again after hurricanes Ike and Gustav. Given the Sandy region's low supply of and high costs for housing, DHAP-Sandy paired residents seeking emergency housing with case managers who assisted residents with finding available housing. DHAP also made rental payments directly to landlords for twelve months and assisted with upfront costs that often act as a barrier for disaster-affected residents, such as security and utility deposits. While the Sandy recovery context was unique from many previous disasters, these examples show how the federal response exhibited significant flexibility in developing or modifying housing recovery programs to fit local needs. Although the focus of this chapter is on New York City, it is worth noting that most of these programs were applied throughout the Sandy-affected region with calibration for varied local contexts.

State efforts also played a significant part in the city's recovery. New York Governor Andrew Cuomo established a Governor's Office of Storm Recovery (GOSR) using the state's own $4.4 billion CDBG-DR allocation and developed statewide programs that also made valuable contributions to the unique needs of New York City residents such as a set of voluntary Buyout and Acquisition Programs that operated in a few particularly hard-hit and vulnerable neighborhoods. The Buyout Program purchased damaged homes at pre-storm value, converting the parcels into permanent open space. The Acquisition Program purchased homes and then auctioned them off to new owners with stringent requirements for resilient redevelopment. A smaller set of the most at-risk homeowners in designated Enhanced Buyout Areas in Staten Island and in neighboring suburban Suffolk County were eligible for additional incentives of up to 15 percent above their homes' pre-storm value.[28]

Rapid Repairs and Build It Back Programs

State and federal efforts were critical to housing recovery efforts in New York City, but using its significant CDBG-DR allocation, the city also developed its own housing recovery programs to deal with uniquely local issues shaped by the city's physical landscape, its sheer size, and the amount of damage sustained. Within days of landfall, then-mayor Michael Bloomberg had created the Office of Housing Recovery Operations (HRO) inside city hall. Taking over housing-related recovery tasks from the city's Office of Emergency Management (OEM), the HRO was initially an ad hoc unit staffed by personnel from city agencies, later becoming a standing unit known as The NYC Mayor's Office of Housing Recovery Operations. Rapid Repairs, the city's initial emergency housing recovery program, launched in late November of 2012 as the city's actualization of FEMA's STEP program,[29] financing short-term emergency repairs in order to make homes habitable, even if not fully repaired, while the long-term rebuilding process played out. Rapid Repairs applicants were eligible for up to $10,000 worth of emergency repairs to electrical, heat, and hot water systems as well as emergency exterior repairs such as plywood coverings for damaged doors and windows. Consistent with STEP funding regulations and in order to assist households in a time of need, the city placed repair crews on retainer and assigned them to damaged neighborhoods rather than having homeowners find, hire, and pay their own contractors In four months, the ambitious program made repairs to over 20,000 units serving more than 54,000 people at a cost of $640 million fronted by the city in anticipation of recouping the expenditures from expected federal aid packages.[30]

Build It Back (BIB), the successor to Rapid Repairs, launched in May of 2013. Moving beyond Rapid Repairs' focus on short-term emergency accommodation, BIB was a larger program using HUD CDBG-DR funds and designed to facilitate permanent rebuilding of damaged housing units as well as mitigate future flood risks (Figure 4.3). Created by the Bloomberg administration, BIB was a concerted attempt to avoid some of the problems seen in previous large-scale housing recovery programs such as waste, contractor fraud, noncompliant repair work, and homeowner overburden. The city also developed a system to prioritize low-and moderate-income households for the first 1,000 BIB funding cases based on research showing that higher income households were generally better able to qualify for disaster aid because of more complete record-keeping and documentation.[31] The program, however, faced significant delays and extensive criticism, and in early 2014 new mayor Bill de Blasio modified the program to speed up aid distribution, including removing the income prioritization levels.

Like Rapid Repairs, BIB was both a grant program and a construction management program. For the BIB Single Family Program (from one- to four-unit properties), the city managed rebuilding projects in an attempt to increase efficiency and reduce complications for homeowners. Single Family Program applicants were tracked into one of five pathways based on type and severity of damage and homeowner preference: Repair, Repair with Elevation; Rebuild, Reimbursement; or Acquisition

Figure 4.3 NYC/Build It Back

Source: Photo by author

for Redevelopment. Residential buildings with more than five units – including rental buildings, condominiums, and cooperatives – were eligible for the BIB Multi family Program that included forgivable loans and grants for repairs and resiliency upgrades but no construction management assistance. A Temporary Relocation Assistance program was added to BIB in April 2015 to assist homeowners that were required to temporarily vacate their primary residence or place their possessions in offsite storage to facilitate reconstruction work.

Originally launched with a $2.2 billion budget and a two-year timeline, BIB had more than 20,000 applicants in its first few months. Despite a much-criticized slow start, the program eventually helped repair, rebuild, or purchase more than 8,300 rental and owner-occupied buildings containing more than 12,500 units. In total 1,375 buildings were elevated (see Figure 4.4), 6,675 received partial reconstruction assistance, and

Figure 4.4 Housing Reconstruction

Many storm-damaged homes such as these on New York City's Rockaway peninsula were elevated during rebuilding.

Source: Photo by author

approximately 250 were acquired by the city; almost 20,000 more units in larger buildings also received BIB assistance through the Multi family Program.[32]

Public Housing Recovery

While Rapid Repairs and BIB focused on private market housing recovery, the New York City Housing Authority (NYCHA) (the city's public housing agency) faced a completely different set of challenges. NYCHA manages 175,636 city-owned public housing units for some 392,259 low-income New Yorkers, almost 5 percent of the city's total population.[33] Some of NYCHA's largest complexes are located in vulnerable waterfront neighborhoods like Red Hook and the Rockaways where Sandy caused extensive damage, affecting hundreds of buildings in 33 different NYCHA developments. Additionally, 402 buildings were without power and 386 lacked heat or hot water, some for extended periods.[34] Emergency repairs were made in the immediate aftermath of Sandy, but the majority of recovery work did not begin until December of 2015 when NYCHA received $3 billion in FEMA recovery funds. NYCHA ultimately plans to spend more than $1.7 billion on Sandy repairs and an additional $1.4 billion on risk mitigation, such as flood-proofed heat and hot water equipment in 20 complexes and whole-building emergency generators in 210 buildings.[35]

Business Recovery and Workforce Development

Like its housing recovery efforts, the city's business recovery programs by design, filling gaps not fully addressed by programs like the federal Small Business Administration's (SBA) Disaster Loan Assistance program and the state's NY Rising Small Business Program. A month after Sandy, the NYC Department of Small Business Services (SBS) and the Economic Development Corporation (EDC) created the Business Recovery Zone Initiative (BRZ), assigning SBS and EDC staff to business recovery assistance programs in five heavily storm-damaged areas of the city. SBS Restoration Business Acceleration Teams (RBATs) also assisted damaged businesses in navigating city permit and inspection processes and facilitating fee waivers in order to get businesses back open as soon as possible. SBS also added recovery expertise to their seven existing Business Solutions Centers around the city and held a series of Business Recovery Plan workshops. EDC, meanwhile, created the Resiliency Innovations for a Stronger Economy (RISE: NYC) competition to generate high-tech ideas specifically focused on helping small businesses recover and become more resilient. In April 2014 the mayor announced 11 winning RISE: NYC entries that would receive a combined $30 million in CDBG-DR funds for implementation of renewable-based backup power systems, deployable flood protections, and free community Wi-Fi systems. Other city agencies also took on recovery and resilience efforts such as the Industrial Development Agency, which provided more than $2.8 million in tax exemptions to assist in business recovery.

To further support its recovery efforts, the city also solicited philanthropic assistance from some of the city's major employers. A $15 million Emergency Loan Fund created by the EDC, Goldman Sachs, and the New York Bankers Association offered $25,000 loans to small businesses at 1 percent interest. Borrowers were also eligible for a $10,000 grant if they sustained flood damage or power outages that displaced their business. SBS operated a separate Small Business Assistance Grant program for small repairs supported by Barclays, Citibank, and investment bank UBS. MasterCard sponsored a Capacity Building and Strategic Planning process for commercial districts, Citi Community Development funded an ad campaign to support small businesses affected by Sandy, and the Mayor's Fund to Advance New York City supported a citywide Storefront Improvement Program, allocating $1 million to renovate commercial facades damaged by Sandy. As of April 2014, the city had provided $23.4 million in loans and grants to over 650 businesses.[36]

Particularly after Mayor de Blasio took office in 2014, the city also moved more aggressively to harness the potential for workforce development as part of the recovery process, owing in part to advocacy from a coalition of influential community and labor groups, including the Alliance for a Just Rebuilding. The city's strategy had multiple components, but the largest was the Sandy Recovery Hiring Plan, created as part of the mayor's larger HireNYC initiative, which established apprenticeship and local hiring requirements for BIB contracts. BIB also developed Sandy Recovery Workforce1, an extension of SBS's preexisting Workforce1 program. Funded by $3 million of the city's CDBG-DR allocation, Sandy Recovery Workforce1 established a career center in Coney Island, providing job counseling and employment referrals for affected residents to jobs in recovery-related fields like construction, architecture, and recovery case management, as well as vouchers for union constructions skills training programs. As a result of this effort, 22 percent of BIB's workforce came from neighborhoods impacted by Sandy, including 982 workers hired directly by BIB and an additional 62 hired through Workforce1. The latter program also placed 467 affected residents with other employers and 137 residents into construction apprentice programs.[37]

Community Recovery

Alongside recovery programs specific to housing and businesses, whole-community recovery is the third major aspect of recovery planning. Admittedly a broad term, community recovery overlaps with housing recovery and business recovery but also focuses on restoration and resilience of infrastructure systems, community-scale risk mitigation, and community-wide issues like social equity, livability, and sustainability. A wide variety of community recovery efforts commenced including programs spearheaded by the federal government, the state, and the city.

In addition to federal and state efforts, New York City moved quickly to develop its own long-range rebuilding and resiliency plan, launching the Special Initiative for Rebuilding and Resiliency (SIRR) only weeks after the storm. Housed in the NYC EDC and building on the city's ongoing sustainability planning efforts, the SIRR released a detailed citywide resilience plan, "A Stronger, More Resilient New York,"[38] eight months after Sandy containing 257 action items totaling $20 billion in investments. The Mayor's Office of Long-Term Planning and Sustainability was initially charged with implementing SIRR, but in 2014 that task moved to a new Office of Recovery and Resiliency (ORR) created by incoming mayor Bill de Blasio.

Other city agencies also integrated resiliency into their ongoing work. The New York City Department of Housing Preservation and

Development (HPD), as part of its larger suite of neighborhood planning efforts, began a Resilient Edgemere Community Planning Initiative in 2015 to address the neighborhood's Sandy-related damage, preexisting issues such as an abundance of vacant land and widespread disinvestment as well as risks associated with its low-lying waterfront location. The 18-month planning process included public workshops and other efforts leading, in early 2017, to the release of the Resilient Edgemere Community Plan, a 60-point, 10-year plan addressing hazard mitigation as well as economic development, infrastructure, social equity, and livability issues.[39]

The Department of City Planning (DCP) also created a new resilience-focused neighborhood planning process after Sandy, while simultaneously beginning to address resilience-oriented deficiencies in the city's zoning code. The Resilient Neighborhoods Initiative, funded by $8.4 million from the city's CDBG-DR allocation, used extensive public engagement to develop post-storm rebuilding and resilience plans in ten economically and physically vulnerable areas of the city. DCP has also continued to methodically refine the city's zoning code to ensure that it reflects newly urgent resilience goals and federal guidelines. The DCP has also worked to make certain that the city's building and zoning regulations do not contradict one another. Three months after Sandy, the mayor issued an executive order to suspend some existing zoning rules to facilitate resilient reconstruction in affected neighborhoods. In October 2013, the City Council approved the Flood Resilience Zoning Text Amendment and later the Special Regulations for Neighborhood Recovery zoning text amendment. However, both were temporary, and from 2016 to 2018 DCP conducted 110 public meetings to inform the Zoning for Flood Resiliency permanent zoning code update that will be presented to the city council for adoption in 2020.

Lessons From a Recovery

This chapter has so far outlined some of the basic ways that New York City addressed recovery and attempted to facilitate resilient rebuilding after one of the most devastating storms in U.S. history. This brief account can only begin to portray the complexity of this task and highlight the successes and challenges of the city's many efforts. Moreover, focusing mostly on the efforts of New York City necessarily sidelines the work done by the federal government and New York State to help the city and the broader region recover.[40] It does not even begin to catalog the equally instructive efforts undertaken in neighboring Nassau County and Suffolk County, nearby municipalities like Long Beach, New York and Hoboken, New Jersey, or neighboring states. This discussion also omits the incredibly important response and recovery work done by hundreds, likely thousands, of nonprofit organizations and philanthropies across the city and region. The efforts of these groups, many of which did not exist before Sandy, were of incalculable importance to the region's recovery. Nonetheless, the focus on one municipal government's response to a major disaster allows consideration of a few key lessons that can be instructive for management of future recovery programs in densely populated urban centers. To unpack some of these lessons, it is useful to return to the questions posed at the beginning of this chapter. First, given New York City's unique vulnerabilities and physical and social characteristics, what were some of the city's key recovery challenges? With the city's significant resources, what innovative programs did it develop to address these unique local conditions and how did these efforts affect recovery outcomes? And finally, what national recovery policies were altered as a result of the Sandy experience in New York?

New Approaches and Uncertain Outcomes

Clearly, New York City has vulnerabilities that are unique, or at least heightened, as compared to most other American municipalities. It quickly became clear after Sandy that business as usual recovery strategies, particularly federal ones, were often untenable in the New York City context. Many of the challenges were unique to and exacerbated by the city's density and geographic and social diversity. The sheer scale of the disaster made it difficult to focus resources. The areas most affected by Sandy, with a few exceptions, included many low-income, working-class, and middle-class New Yorkers, who often lacked the kinds of safety nets that are so critical for recovery.[41] The city is incredibly diverse by every measure, and everything is expensive, from housing to labor to materials.

The city's density often created logistical challenges for rebuilding damaged homes and businesses. Moreover, the recovery was also complicated by the way a large city, by necessity, is organized, with dozens of city agencies and newly created recovery entities having overlapping and sometimes conflicting agendas and responsibilities. And federal programs were often ill-suited to the city's context because household reimbursement limits were insufficient given the city's high cost of living or because rebuilding programs were better suited to single family detached housing units, among many other disconnects. Because recovery programs need to be tailored to address local conditions, it also means that local governments must have their own preexisting recovery capacity and resources, and outside expertise can only provide limited assistance.

Even for a high-capacity city like New York, it is also enormously difficult to scale up major recovery programs quickly from the ground up.[42] As Brad Gair, the original director of New York City's HRO and a creator of BIB explained in public testimony at a U.S. House of Representatives Committee on Homeland Security Field Hearing on Staten Island in July of 2016,

> the current recovery system requires affected communities to essentially create and setup [sic] in a few months what amounts to a multibillion dollar corporation with hundreds of employees and contractors, numerous storefront locations, a broad-based marketing campaign, and integrated customer service operations while tens of thousands of desperate customers must wait anxiously for help as hope dwindles.[43]

These efforts are often new and untested, unlike existing federal programs that have been refined over multiple applications. While this presents an opportunity for creativity and innovation, it also creates risk that programs will not work as well as anticipated. Though New York City's recovery process has been largely effective in a broad sense, it has not been flawless, and many individual households, businesses, and even neighborhoods have not approached anything resembling full recovery though many years from the storm most have settled into some kind of "new normal."

Especially in their early stages, many of the city's recovery programs faced major challenges. Rapid Repairs, for instance, came in for sharp criticism including complaints from homeowners about delays, missed appointments, and poor work quality.[44] Build It Back was even more problematic (Figure 4.5). Though developed quickly by an overstretched local government during a challenging time, the program was anything but a hasty afterthought. The Boston Consulting Group under a $6.1 million city contract, with subcontractors Public Financial Management, URS Group, Inc., and Solix Inc., designed the program and had responsibility for technical support and case management at an anticipated cost of $50 million.[45] But the program languished in its first few months, which were also the waning days of the Bloomberg mayoral administration. By the time Bloomberg left office on December 31, 2013 – fourteen months after Sandy – not a single BIB reimbursement check had gone out.[46] BIB subsequently went through multiple directors with an additional $500 million eventually added to its budget.[47]

But the slow pace of reconstruction was not BIB's only problem. A total of 11,691 applicants eventually withdrew from the program, and

Figure 4.5 Make Us All a Priority

Source: Photo by author

scores of others complained about confusing and contradictory information.[48] The city-managed program also struggled at times to acquire construction permits due to the complexity of the city's construction and zoning codes.[49] Elected officials decried costs that sometimes exceeded the pre-storm value of the repaired homes[50] and called for the firing of BIB's director.[51] The program even received public criticism from its creator[52] and a scathing audit from the city's comptroller.[53] Later a group of six homeowners on Staten Island filed a class action lawsuit in July of 2018 over shoddy workmanship on their elevated homes.[54] While Build It Back was pointedly designed to avoid some of the pitfalls experienced by other large-scale housing recovery programs, the complexity of the challenge nonetheless overwhelmed even a bureaucracy as large and generally capable as New York City's, highlighting in stark terms just how difficult and durable the challenges of recovery are for local governments.

NYCHA's recovery efforts were another blemish on the city's record. In early 2017 New City Council members admonished NYCHA officials for having finished work at only one of 33 damaged complexes.[55] By the following year, the agency had 3,375 active contracts totaling $1.8 billion[56] and estimated completion of all work by 2021.[57] Post-Sandy repairs are all the more urgent given NYCHA's overall deferred maintenance backlog, estimated as high as $45.2 billion.[58] Additionally, the overall recovery-related experience of NYCHA residents has often been markedly different from the experiences of the rest of the city. Graham, for instance, reports that while owners and renters in the private market were prioritized for household-level recovery programs and selected to actively participate in deliberations about community-wide recovery and resiliency-building programs, NYCHA residents often felt marginalized and excluded from the recovery process.[59]

While many of New York City's challenges were unique, this is also true of every other disaster because every community is unique in its own way and one-size-fits-all approaches will never work perfectly anywhere. The challenge is to strike a balance so that the design of federal programs is useful across a variety of contexts yet also nimble and flexible enough to apply in each of the specific and unique contexts in which disasters occur. Local governments possess a nuanced understanding of local conditions but may not have the expertise, experience, or resources to create and implement contextually appropriate programs even when federal funding is flexible.

As the New York example illustrates, when local governments possess significant recovery capacity, they will design programs that are responsive to local needs and in many cases move the needle significantly about what we know about designing effective recovery programs. At the same time, these programs are inherently complex and by their very nature are experimental and unproven. Mistakes will be made. But lessons learned from New York City's post-Sandy efforts can nonetheless help us see new approaches that other communities might use in their own local contexts.

Sandy's Effect on National Recovery Policies

Sandy also significantly influenced national recovery policy. While many factors, perhaps most importantly presidential leadership, are central to how the federal government responds to a major disaster, the context of the disaster also shapes the federal response. Sandy struck the most densely populated region in the United States and one of the world's most important economic centers. It is thus unsurprising that the federal response was robust, but the region's own capacity, in addition to its intense need in a moment of crisis, contributed to the kind of federal response that occurred. President Obama created the cabinet-level Hurricane Sandy Rebuilding Task Force (HSRTF) on December 7, 2012, and appointed HUD Secretary Shaun Donovan as the Task Force Chair. The HSRTF released its *Hurricane Sandy Rebuilding Strategy* (HSRS) in August of 2013 as a framework for spending Sandy Supplemental funds.[60]

As illustrated by the 69 recommendations in the HSRS, the federal government's post-Sandy approach "shows an unprecedented commitment to coordination across federal agencies and collaboration between the federal, state, and local governments and key local constituencies," according to Puentes and Katz of the Brookings Institution.[61] The HSRS also prioritized local decision making and regional coordination and emphasized future resilience in addition to rebuilding. Part of the reason for this was clearly the scale of Sandy's devastation and the region's density and jurisdictional complexity. However, another component was the region's capacity to participate actively in its own recovery.

One example of this more ambitious and creative federal approach to recovery was HUD's Rebuild by Design (RBD)[62] program, a recovery and resiliency planning and design competition created in response to HSRS recommendation #3: "Create a design competition to develop innovative resilient design solutions that address the Sandy-affected region's most pressing vulnerabilities."[63] RBD's philanthropically funded design competition (led by the Rockefeller Foundation) helped HUD determine how to spend $920 million in CDBG-DR recovery funds on resiliency projects in the Sandy region. Nearly 150 interdisciplinary design teams applied to the first RBD solicitation. In August 2013 ten of these teams were chosen for a year-long participatory planning and design process that ultimately included hundreds of community meetings and design workshops. The ten final proposals included a 10-mile levee around lower Manhattan and a multi-faceted resilience plan for the New Jersey. In June of 2014, six of the ten projects received $20 million to $335 million for initial implementation.[64] The RBD process was also the model for HUD's 2014–2016 National Disaster Resilience Competition (NDRC), which allocated an additional $1 billion to 13 jurisdictions affected by disasters between 2011–2013 (see Chapter 2).

Implementation of RBD projects has been slow, however, particularly in New York City. The proposals were essentially conceptual designs developed without much local government input and lacking detailed engineering analysis or implementation plans. For instance, one winning proposal was The Big U, a 10-mile-long waterfront levee doubling as publicly accessible open space stretching around lower Manhattan. The city initially received $335 million to implement the design proposal, which was split into smaller implementation components with the first phase – known as the East Side Coastal Resiliency Project (ESCR) – extending 2.4 miles along the city's east side from 25th Street to Montgomery Street. The city then spent two years conducting a significant public engagement process that further reshaped the project. After the city and local residents came to consensus on a final plan, the city unexpectedly scrapped the first design in early 2018 just as it was set to break ground, citing an internal review that exposed insurmountable logistical hurdles.

A new plan announced in October of 2018 instead proposed to raze and elevate all of East River Park at a new cost of $1.45 billion. But in throwing out the original plan completely, the city generated vocal community backlash over the new design, the delays, the three-year closure of East River Park, and the absence of community input in the new plan.[65] However, city officials have thus far remained steadfast, arguing that the new design will be a more effective flood barrier, create more usable public space, and be completed faster and with fewer construction-related impacts on nearby neighborhoods. Adjacent sections of the former Big U are now part of the city's Lower Manhattan Coastal Resiliency project which includes $500 million worth of shoreline protection projects for an additional 2.3 miles of coastline and a $10 billion plan to extend the city's shoreline 500 feet into the East River adjacent to the Financial District

Figure 4.6 East Side Coastal Resiliency Project Meeting

Source: Photo by author

and South Street Seaport even though funding for this plan has not yet been identified.[66]

The administration of President Donald Trump has taken a much different approach to post-disaster recovery than the Obama administration, as more recent hurricane disasters such as hurricanes Harvey, Irma, and Maria illustrate (see Chapters 5,6, and 8).[67] Part of that difference was attributable to the uniqueness of the Sandy context. It also points to the outsize role that federal leadership plays in local recovery, from working with Congress to pass disaster funding bills, to appointing effective and empowered agency leadership to using their bully pulpit, presidents will always have a significant impact on recovery on the ground in local communities. Sandy illustrated a federal government that was empowered and emboldened to innovate and find effective ways to work within the strictures established by Congress. After Sandy, FEMA, HUD, and other agencies sought out new approaches that emphasized speed and effectiveness, focused on deliberation and social equity, and attempted to move beyond in-place rebuilding to future resilience. While that mind-set does not appear to have been permanently ingrained into the federal recovery approach, it was nonetheless an important beginning. Recovery officials at the federal, state, and local levels have now seen what is possible with prioritized goals, and it is clear from talking to officials on the ground that many of the lessons facilitated by the federal approach to Sandy have opened new pathways for approaching recovery.

Conclusion

According to the metrics used by the city, the recovery and rebuilding process from Sandy was largely complete by 2019, with programs like Build It Back wrapping up all of their planned work and federal recovery money fully allocated to ongoing projects. The city then began to shift its efforts toward creating more broad-based resilience against future extreme events as well as slow-onset climate change and risks like extreme heat, regular tidal flooding, vulnerable housing stock, aging infrastructure and social inequities. In acknowledgement of that redirection, in January of 2019 the Mayor's Office of Recovery and Resiliency dropped "Recovery" from its name and was renamed the Mayor's Office of Resiliency with primary responsibility for the city's climate change adaptation efforts as part of the larger NYC Mayor's Office of Climate Policy and Programs. Much like the city's recovery efforts, New York's resiliency efforts provide a valuable lens for other communities to better understand both the challenges and opportunities that can arise in the post-disaster period.

Resilience has become an orienting theme for city efforts and was one of the four key pillars of Mayor de Blasio's 2015 strategic plan *One New York: The Plan for a Strong and Just City*,[68] more commonly known as OneNYC. Enhancing the resilience of the city's housing stock, including in neighborhoods unaffected by Sandy, is now a multi-agency priority. The Office of Resilience recently partnered with the state's GOSR and the nonprofit Center for NYC Neighborhoods to operate the FloodHelpNY Home Resiliency Audit Program, which provides an online flood risk mapping tool, free home resilience audits, and assistance acquiring affordable flood insurance in vulnerable New York City neighborhoods. In June 2017 the New York City Council added a Special Coastal Risk District to the city's suite of special zoning districts and mapped those districts in neighborhoods like Broad Channel and Hamilton Beach in Queens and the state's Enhanced Buyout Areas on Staten Island including Graham Beach, Ocean Breeze, and Oakwood Beach, seeking to limit new development in vulnerable areas.

The city's overall resilience efforts have also increasingly begun to dovetail with other goals, such as the mayor's 2017 *Housing New York 2.0* plan[69] aimed at creating or preserving 300,000 units of affordable housing by the year 2026. Near the end of 2018, the city's Department of Housing Preservation and Development (HPD) announced a new Resilient Homes program designed to increase the supply of affordable housing for first time buyers and continue to address Sandy-related damage. The program invited qualified developers to propose new housing units on 30 sites (38 total housing lots) within FEMA's Special Flood Hazard Areas ("100-year" floodplain) in parts of Staten Island, Brooklyn, and Queens that the city acquired through Build It Back's Acquisition for Redevelopment Program. Eligible projects must meet the NYC Building Code Appendix G: Flood-Resistant Construction standards which include flood-resistant materials and elevation of living areas and mechanical systems. Construction financing will be secured under the city's preexisting Open Door program, which provides low-interest construction loans and $1 sales of city-owned land for developers who build affordable housing units.

As all of the preceding examples help to illustrate, New York City is undoubtedly more prepared, overall, for another major disaster because of its experience with Sandy and the efforts it has taken to enhance its resilience as part of the recovery process. New policies and regulations have been put in place, coastal protection projects have been implemented, and numerous site-scale improvements have been made to homes and businesses. Residents and city officials also have a new appreciation for the risks the city faces. Yet some of the challenges faced during the long-term recovery from Sandy will continue to complicate efforts to address resilience, such as the city's sheer size and diversity, social issues like income inequality and lack of affordable housing, the costs of protecting more than 8 million residents from a wide variety of potential future hazards, and the political and economic pressures to develop despite known risks. At the same time, the city is also at an advantage because it is fortunate to have the capacity to sustain and even grow its efforts to address the intertwined challenges of sustainability and resilience.[70]

Notes

The author would like to thank the editors, Claire B. Rubin and Susan L. Cutter, as well as Rob Olshansky, Laurie Johnson, Divya Chandrasekhar, Yu Xiao, and John Travis Marshall for helping in their own ways to make this chapter possible. This research was funded, in part, by the National Science Foundation under award #1335109.

Notes

1. Eric S. Blake, Todd B. Kimberlain, Robert J. Berg, John P. Cangialosi, and John L. Beven II, *Tropical Cyclone Report, Hurricane Sandy (AL182012), 22–29, October 2012* (Miami, FL: National Hurricane Center, 2013), www.nhc.noaa.gov/data/tcr/AL182012_Sandy.pdf.
2. Claire B. Rubin, ed., *Emergency Management: The American Experience*, 3rd edition (Milton Park, UK: Routledge, 2019).

3. Donovan Finn and John Travis Marshall, "Superstorm Sandy at Five: Lessons on Law as Catalyst and Obstacle to Long-Term Recovery Following Catastrophic Disasters," *Environmental Law Reporter News and Analysis* 48 (2018): 10494–10519.

4. Centers for Disease Control and Prevention, "Deaths Associated with Hurricane Sandy, October–November 2012," *Morbidity and Mortality Weekly Report*, May 24, 2013, www.cdc.gov/mmwr/preview/mmwrhtml/mm6220a1.htm.

5. Blake et al., *Tropical Cyclone Report*.

6. Eric S. Blake, Edward N. Rappaport, and Christopher W. Landsea, *The Deadliest, Costliest, and Most Intense United States Tropical Cyclones from 1851 to 2006 (And Other Frequently Requested Hurricane Facts)*, NOAA Technical Memorandum NWS TPC-5 (Miami, FL: National Weather Service, National Hurricane Center, 2007), www.nhc.noaa.gov/pdf/NWS-TPC-5.pdf.

7. National Oceanic and Atmospheric Administration, "U.S. Billion-Dollar Weather & Climate Disasters 1980–2018," www.ncdc.noaa.gov/billions/events.pdf.

8. Christopher E. Schubert, Ronald J. Busciolano, Paul P. Hearn Jr., Ami N. Rahav, Riley Behrens, Jason S. Finkelstein, Jack Monti Jr., and Amy E. Simonson, *Analysis of Storm-tide Impacts from Hurricane Sandy in New York* (Reston, VA: U.S. Geological Survey Scientific Investigations Report 2015–5036, 2015), https://pubs.usgs.gov/sir/2015/5036/sir20155036.pdf.

9. Blake et al., *Tropical Cyclone Report*.

10. City of New York, "NYC Recovery: Community Development Block Grant Disaster Recovery, The City of New York Action Plan Incorporating Amendments 1-8A," February 13, 2015, www1.nyc.gov/assets/cdbgdr/documents/amendments/CDBG-DR%20Action%20Plan%20Amendment%208%20[English].pdf.

11. Special Initiative for Rebuilding and Resiliency, *PlaNYC: A Stronger, More Resilient New York* (City of New York, 2013), www1.nyc.gov/site/sirr/report/report.page.

12. Daniel J. Alesch, James N. Holly, and Lucy A. Arendt, *Managing for Long-Term Community Recovery in the Aftermath of Disaster* (Alexandria, VA: Public Entity Risk Institute, 2009); Daniel J. Alesch and William Siembieda, "The Role of the Built Environment in the Recovery of Cities and Communities from Extreme Events," *International Journal of Mass Emergencies and Disasters* 32, no. 2 (2012): 197–211; Laurie A. Johnson and Robert B. Olshansky, *After Great Disasters: An In-Depth Analysis of How Six Countries Managed Community Recovery* (Cambridge: Lincoln Institute of Land Policy, 2017).

13. Finn and Marshall, "Superstorm Sandy."

14. Max Weselcouch, *Sandy's Effects on Housing in New York City* (New York: Furman Center for Real Estate and Urban Policy, 2013), http://furmancenter.org/files/publications/SandysEffectsOnHousingInNYC.pdf.

15. New York City Rent Guidelines Board, "2018 Housing Supply Report," www1.nyc.gov/assets/rentguidelinesboard/pdf/18HSR.pdf.

16. Weselcouch, *Sandy's Effects*.

17. Louise Comfort, Ben Wisner, Susan L Cutter, Roger Pulwarty, Ken Hewitt, Anthony Oliver-Smith, John Wiener, Maureen Fordham, Walter Peacock, and Fred Krimgold, "Reframing Disaster Policy: The Global Evolution of Vulnerable Communities," *Environmental Hazards* 1, no. 1 (1999): 39–44. https://doi.org/10.3763/ehaz.1999.0105; Sharona Hoffman, "Preparing for Disaster: Protecting the Most Vulnerable in Emergencies," *UC Davis Law Review* 42 (2009): 1491–1547; Brenda D. Phillips, William C. Metz, and Leslie A. Nieves, "Disaster Threat: Preparedness and Potential Response of the Lowest Income Quartile," *Global Environmental Change Part B: Environmental Hazards* 6, no. 3 (2005): 123–133, https://doi.org/10.1016/j.hazards.2006.05.001.

18. City of New York, *New York City Government Poverty Measure 2005–2016: An Annual Report from the Office of the Mayor* (New York: Mayor's Office of Operations, 2018), www1.nyc.gov/assets/opportunity/pdf/18_poverty_measure_report.pdf.
19. Weselcouch, *Sandy's Effects.*
20. Phil Berke, Jack Kartez, and Dennis Wenger, "Recovery after Disaster: Achieving Sustainable Development, Mitigation and Equity," *Disasters* 17, no. 2 (1993): 93–109, https://doi.org/10.1111/j.1467-7717.1993.tb01137.x; Gavin Smith, *Planning for Post-Disaster Recovery: A Review of the United States Disaster Assistance Framework* (New York: Island Press, 2012); Andrew Rumbach, Carrie Makarewicz, and Jeremy Németh, "The Importance of Place in Early Disaster Recovery: A Case Study of the 2013 Colorado Floods," *Journal of Environmental Planning and Management* 59, no. 11 (2016): 2045–2063, https://doi.org/10.1080/09640568.2015.1116981.
21. Leigh Graham, Wim Debucquoy, and Isabelle Anguelovski, "The Influence of Urban Development Dynamics on Community Resilience Practice in New York City after Superstorm Sandy: Experiences from the Lower East Side and the Rockaways," *Global Environmental Change* 40 (2016): 112–124.
22. City of New York, "Mayor de Blasio Announces Key Resiliency Investments to Support Small Businesses and Jobs, Including New Business Resiliency Program and Major Upgrades Across Sandy-Impacted Neighborhoods," Press release, December 19, 2014, www1.nyc.gov/office-of-the-mayor/news/568-14/mayor-de-blasio-key-resiliency-investments-support-small-businesses-jobs-#.
23. Mary C. Comerio, "Housing Issues After Disasters," *Journal of Contingencies and Crisis Management* 5, no. 3 (1997): 166–178.
24. Finn and Marshall, "Superstorm Sandy."
25. Jared T. Brown, and Daniel J. Richardson, *FEMA's Public Assistance Grant Program: Background and Considerations for Congress* (Washington, DC: Congressional Research Service Report 43990, 2015), https://digitalcommons.ilr.cornell.edu/key_workplace/1414/.
26. Federal Emergency Management Agency, "Sheltering and Temporary Essential Power (STEP) Pilot Program" (FEMA Recovery Program Guidance, November 16, 2012), www.fema.gov/media-library-data/20130726-1858-25045-8258/step_pilot_program_final_111612.pdf.
27. Craig Fugate, Written testimony of FEMA Administrator Craig Fugate for a Senate Committee on Homeland Security and Governmental Affairs, Subcommittee on Emergency Management, Intergovernmental Relations, and the District of Columbia hearing titled "One Year Later: Examining the Ongoing Recovery from Hurricane Sandy" (Washington, DC, 2013), www.dhs.gov/news/2013/03/20/written-testimony-fema-administrator-craig-fugate-senate-committee-homeland-security.
28. Governor's Office of Storm Recovery, "NY Rising Buyout and Acquisition Program Policy Manual Version 3.0," 2015, https://stormrecovery.ny.gov/sites/default/files/uploads/po_20150415_buyout_and_acquisition_policy_manual_final_v3.pdf.
29. City of New York, "Mayor Bloomberg Announces NYC Rapid Repairs Program Has Completed Work on More Than 10,000 Residences Damaged by Sandy," Press release, January 20, 2013, www1.nyc.gov/office-of-the-mayor/news/031-13/mayor-bloomberg-nyc-rapid-repairs-program-has-completed-work-more-10-000; Diane P. Horn, *Federal Disaster Assistance: The National Flood Insurance Program and Other Federal Disaster Assistance Programs Available to Individuals and Households After a Flood* (Washington, DC: Congressional Research Service Report 44808, 2018), https://fas.org/sgp/crs/homesec/R44808.pdf.

30. William Goldstein, Amy Peterson, and Daniel A. Zarrilli, *One City, Rebuilding Together: A Report on the City of New York's Response to Hurricane Sandy and the Path Forward* (New York, 2014), www1.nyc.gov/assets/home/downloads/pdf/reports/2014/sandy_041714.pdf.

31. Russ Buettner and David W. Chen, "Hurricane Sandy Recovery Program in New York City Was Mired by Its Design: Broken Pledges and Bottlenecks Hurt Mayor Bloomberg's Build It Back Effort," *New York Times*, September 5, 2014, www.nytimes.com/2014/09/05/nyregion/after-hurricane-sandy-a-rebuilding-program-is-hindered-by-its-own-construction.html.

32. Amy Peterson, "Testimony of Mayor's Office of Housing Recovery Operations Before the New York City Council Committee on Environmental Protection, April 12, 2018," www1.nyc.gov/assets/housingrecovery/downloads/pdf/2018/04-12-18_build_it_back_city_council_testimony_submitted_final.pdf.

33. New York City Housing Authority, "NYCHA 2018 Fact Sheet," www1.nyc.gov/assets/nycha/downloads/pdf/NYCHA-Fact-Sheet_2018_Final.pdf.

34. Goldstein et al., *One City*.

35. New York City Housing Authority, *Recovery to Resiliency: NYCHA's Hurricane Sandy Recovery Program* (New York, 2016), https://issuu.com/nycha/docs/recovery_to_resiliency_04.11.16.

36. Goldstein et al., *One City*.

37. City of New York, *Mayor's Management Report: September 2017* (New York, 2017), www1.nyc.gov/assets/operations/downloads/pdf/mmr2017/2017_mmr.pdf.

38. Special Initiative for Rebuilding and Resiliency, *PlaNYC*.

39. New York City Department of Housing Preservation and Development, "Resilient Edgemere Community Plan," 2017, www1.nyc.gov/assets/hpd/downloads/pdf/community/resilient-edgemere-report.pdf.

40. Donovan Finn, Divya Chandrasekhar, and Yu Xiao, "Planning for Resilience in the New York Metro Region after Superstorm Sandy," in *Spatial Planning and Resilience Following Disasters: International and Comparative Perspectives*, edited by Stefan Greiving, Michio Ubaura and Jaroslav Tesliar (Bristol, UK: Policy Press at the University of Bristol, 2016), 117–135.

41. Susan L. Cutter, Bryan J. Boruff, and W. Lynn Shirley, "Social Vulnerability to Environmental Hazards," *Social Science Quarterly* 84, no. 1 (2003): 242–261.

42. Finn and Marshall, "Superstorm Sandy"; Holly M. Leicht, *Rebuild the Plane Now: Recommendations for Improving Government's Approach to Disaster Recovery and Preparedness* (New York: Community Preservation Corporation, 2017).

43. Brad Gair, "A Prepared Community Is a Resilient Community," Statement to U.S. House of Representatives Committee on Homeland Security's Subcommittee on Emergency Preparedness, Response, and Communications, Staten Island Field Hearing, July 11, 2016, https://docs.house.gov/meetings/HM/HM12/20160711/105146/HHRG-114-HM12-Wstate-GairB-20160711.pdf.

44. Emily Nonko, "Inside the Failures of Post-Hurricane Sandy Build It Back Program," *Curbed NY*, October 27, 2017, https://ny.curbed.com/2017/10/27/16554180/hurricane-sandy-relief-build-it-back-housing; Tom Wrobleski, "Some Scathing Reviews of Rapid Repairs' Debut on Staten Island," *SILive.com*, December 23, 2012, www.silive.com/news/2012/12/some_scathing_reviews_of_rapid.html.

45. Scott Stringer, "Audit Report on the Administration of the New York City Build It Back Single Family Program by the Mayor's Office of Housing Recovery Operations," FM14-115A, March 31, 2015, https://comptroller.nyc.gov/wp-content/uploads/documents/FM14_115A.pdf.

46. Nonko, "Inside the Failures."

47. Katie Honan, "'Build It Back' Helping Fewer Homeowners, but Needs $500M More, City Says," *DNAinfo.com*, September 23, 2016, www.dnainfo.com/new-york/20160923/broad-channel/build-it-back-hurricane-sandy-rebuilding-problems-funding/.

48. Katie Honan, "'Build It Back' Head Should Quit or Be Fired, Councilman Says," *DNAinfo.com*, July 18, 2016, www.dnainfo.com/new-york/20160718/rockaway-park/head-of-citys-failed-build-it-back-should-resign-or-be-fired-official/; Katie Honan and James Fanelli, "City Forced Us from Our Homes for Sandy Fixes Months Ago, Residents Say," *DNAinfo.com*, May 10, 2016, www.dnainfo.com/new-york/20160510/rockaway-beach/city-forced-us-from-our-homes-for-sandy-fixes-months-ago-residents-say/.

49. Honan and Fanelli, "City Forced Us."

50. Honan, "Helping Fewer Homeowners."

51. Honan, "Head Should Quit."

52. Nicholas Rizzi, "Build it Back Was a 'Categorical Failure,' Its Creator Says," *DNAinfo.com*, July 12, 2016, www.dnainfo.com/new-york/20160712/ocean-breeze/build-it-back-was-categorical-failure-its-creator-says/.

53. Stringer, *Audit Report*.

54. Amanda Farinacci, "Homeowners to File Class Action Lawsuit Against Build it Back Program," *NY1.com*, July 30, 2018, www.ny1.com/nyc/all-boroughs/news/2018/07/31/homeowners-to-file-class-action-lawsuit-against-build-it-back-program.

55. Ben Kochman, "City Pols Slam NYCHA for Delays in Hurricane Sandy Building Repairs," *New York Daily News*, February 28, 2017, www.nydailynews.com/news/politics/city-pols-blast-nycha-delays-sandy-repairs-article-1.2985097.

56. New York City Housing Authority, Recovery and Resilience Department, "List of All Contracts Encumbered Related to Sandy Recovery," last updated February 13, 2018, www1.nyc.gov/assets/nycha/downloads/pdf/List%20of%20all%20Sandy%20contracts%20updated%202.2018.pdf.

57. New York City Housing Authority, "NYCHA Office of Recovery and Resilience 2017 End of Year Report," 2018, www1.nyc.gov/assets/nycha/downloads/pdf/Sandy2017EOYReport.pdf.

58. Regional Plan Association, "NYCHA's Crisis: A Matter for All New Yorkers," 2018, http://library.rpa.org/pdf/RPA-NYCHAs_Crisis_2018_12_18_.pdf.

59. Leigh Graham, "Public Housing Participation in Superstorm Sandy Recovery: Living in a Differentiated State in Rockaway, Queens," *Urban Affairs Review* (May 29, 2018), https://doi.org/10.1177/1078087418776438.

60. Hurricane Sandy Rebuilding Task Force, *Hurricane Sandy Rebuilding Strategy: Stronger Communities, a Resilient Region* (Washington, DC: U.S. Department of Housing and Urban Development, 2013).

61. Robert Puentes and Bruce Katz, "A Statement on the Hurricane Sandy Rebuilding Task Force Report," *Brookings.edu*, August 19, 2013, www.brookings.edu/blog/the-avenue/2013/08/19/a-statement-on-the-hurricane-sandy-rebuilding-task-force-report/.

62. See www.hud.gov/sandyrebuilding/rebuildbydesign.

63. Hurricane Sandy Rebuilding Task Force, *Hurricane Sandy*, 46.

64. John Bisker, Amy Chester, and Tara Eisenberg, eds., *Rebuild by Design* (New York: Rebuild By Design, 2016).

65. Amy Chester and Tom Wright, "The City's Odd Storm Splurge: Mayor de Blasio Wants to Spend $700 Million More on a Resiliency Plan. Why?" *New York Daily News*, October 29, 2018, www.nydailynews.com/opinion/ny-oped-the-citys-odd-storm-splurge-20181025-story.html.

66. Bill de Blasio, "My New Plan to Climate-Proof Lower Manhattan," *New York Magazine.com*, March 13, 2019, http://nymag.com/intelligencer/2019/03/bill-de-blasio-my-new-plan-to-climate-proof-lower-manhattan.html.
67. Annie Karni and Patricia, "Trump Lashes Out Again at Puerto Rico, Bewildering the Island," *NYTimes.com*, April 2, 2019, www.nytimes.com/2019/04/02/us/trump-puerto-rico.html.
68. City of New York, "One New York: The Plan for a Strong and Just City," 2015, https://onenyc.cityofnewyork.us/wp-content/uploads/2019/04/OneNYC-Strategic-Plan-2015.pdf.
69. City of New York, "Housing New York 2.0," 2017, www1.nyc.gov/assets/hpd/downloads/pdf/about/hny-2.pdf.
70. Cynthia Rosenzweig and William Solecki, "Hurricane Sandy and Adaptation Pathways in New York: Lessons from a First-responder City," *Global Environmental Change* 28 (2014): 395–408.

5

HURRICANE HARVEY
ISSUES FOR URBAN DEVELOPMENT

Ashley D. Ross

Hurricane Harvey made its first landfall on the middle Texas coast Friday, August 25, 2017. As a Category 4 hurricane, wind and storm surge damages in the area of impact were substantial. However, Harvey's biggest imprint on the state of Texas was the flooding it caused in the metropolitan area of Houston. Dumping nearly the amount of Houston's annual rainfall, Harvey was an unprecedented rainfall event. The region was inundated with over 48 inches of rain in just four days. With its sprawling impervious surfaces, Houston's urban landscape was unable to absorb this onslaught, overwhelming drainage and flood control infrastructure. An estimated 30 percent of households in Houston sustained some form of flood damage to their home or personal property, 10 percent of which had floodwater inside their homes.[1]

Houston's experience with Hurricane Harvey underscores the relationship between land use and disaster impacts. Located in a coastal plain, Houston is a city built on swamp and prairie land. Unchecked by zoning laws, runaway development and low-density urban sprawl have replaced naturally occurring wetlands in the region and created one of the largest expanses of impervious surfaces in the nation. At the same time, aging drainage infrastructure has not been replaced and storm water infrastructure has not been improved to manage changes in hydrology associated with population growth. The result is higher vulnerability to flooding further exacerbated in areas with concentrated race and ethnic minority populations where government and private investment in infrastructure and flood control has been historically neglected.[2]

Actions taken since Hurricane Harvey by the City of Houston and Harris County have centered on heightening floodplain regulations and housing recovery and supported by a $2.3 billion allocation from the U.S. Department of Housing and Urban Development.[3] Of these funds, Harris County has designated 74 percent for housing recovery while the City of Houston has set aside 89 percent for this purpose. Housing recovery plans developed by both local governments focus on assistance to homeowners, home buyouts, rental assistance, and increasing the stock of single-family homes in the area. Additionally, both authorities have passed stricter home elevation requirements. In part, these policy changes and recovery programs were interpreted as attempts to remedy past land use and development failures brought to light by Harvey. Until the implementation of these policies is complete and their outcomes made apparent, the effectiveness of these actions is uncertain.

An estimated 68 percent of homes flooded during Hurricane Harvey were outside the Federal Emergency Management Agency (FEMA) designated 100-year floodplain,[4] and Houston's elevation requirements and buyout programs only apply to properties within floodplains. Home buyouts are voluntary, typically resulting in piecemeal mitigation across flood-prone neighborhoods. Thus, government programs only address a portion of the area's vulnerable land and population, and private property owners must take their own action to mitigate risk outside the floodplain. Houston long ago chose development over regulation, which may not be sufficient to shift the trajectory of this growing urban center away from severe flood events in the future. Whether Houston addresses this issue depends on the implementation and outcomes of the new floodplain regulations and disaster recovery programs. It will also depend on Harvey's impact in shifting prevailing public thinking about land use and flood risk, a challenge for such a large area whose socioeconomic boom has been fueled by the ethos of free market development.

A Rainfall Event Unrivaled in U.S. History

Hurricane Harvey intensified within 40 hours from a scattered tropical depression in the Gulf of Mexico to a Category 4 hurricane. Models of the storm's path and intensity were fraught with uncertainties from the beginning, primarily due to weak steering currents in the upper atmosphere. The storm re-formed after making landfall in the Yucatán Peninsula of Mexico and then re-intensified in the Gulf of Mexico. Initially, there was uncertainty about the amount and location of the heaviest rainfall. It was only 36 hours before the storm that computer models began to predict that precipitation totals would be exceptionally high, with peak totals from 40 to 60 inches.[5]

Although weather models of Hurricane Harvey were accurate and timely, communication of the predicted impacts was muddled. Many local public officials and residents did not heed the warnings, and there was miscommunication among state and local officials. This led to subsequent confusion among the public about what to do. The governor of Texas, Greg Abbott, encouraged Houston residents to retreat while City of Houston Mayor Sylvester Turner cautioned that the best action was to stay home. Mixed messages were also rampant in other parts of the state. While coastal and inland towns, including Rockport and Port Aransas, issued mandatory evacuations with dire warnings to the public, the City of Corpus Christi, in the direct line of the storm, called for only voluntary evacuations.[6]

Hurricane Harvey made its initial landfall in Texas at Rockport, located on the middle Texas coast, around 10 p.m. on Friday, August 25, 2017. Harvey was the first major hurricane in the area since Celia in 1970. Peak wind gusts were recorded at 132 mph, and the highest storm surge levels were more than 12 feet above ground level in some areas. In addition to wind and storm surge, Harvey produced torrential rainfall and flash flooding. Behaving differently than typical hurricanes that move inland and away from the coast, Harvey stalled over southeast Texas for days (see Figure 5.1). Dumping unprecedented amounts of precipitation, Harvey rainfall totals peaked at 51.88 inches in the Houston area and at 60.58 inches across the state.[7]

In scope and peak rainfall totals, Harvey is the most significant tropical cyclone rainfall event in U.S. history. The magnitude of the precipitation

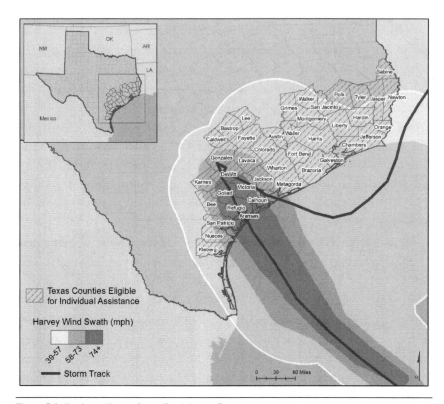

Figure 5.1 Hurricane Harvey Storm Track Across Texas

Source: Data from National Hurricane Center and FEMA. Graphic reproduced by Erika Pham, University of South Carolina

event was unrivaled: 20 inches of rain fell over an area of nearly 29,000 square miles and 30 inches of rain fell over an area of approximately 11,000 square miles. The National Weather Service had to revise its traditional methods of representing storms in order to map it effectively. Harris County Flood Control District estimates that approximately 70 percent of the county (1,300 square miles), including the City of Houston, was covered with up to 1.5 feet of water, prompting thousands of swift water rescues.[8]

The excessive precipitation Hurricane Harvey dumped on Texas resulted in reservoir and riverine flooding throughout the state.[9] Nine of 19 rain gauges in Harris County registered record-setting flood levels, with several

of the rivers flooding so high that the gauges were damaged. To prevent failure and uncontrolled releases, the U.S. Army Corps of Engineers (USACE)
opened dams at Addicks and Barker Reservoirs in Harris County, flooding about 4,000 homes downstream.[10] East of Houston, Jefferson, Orange,
Hardin, and Tyler counties all experienced record rainfall (approximately
40 inches), and subsequent river and bayou flooding.[11] The Lower Neches
River topped previous water level records, and flooding in several counties
were attributed to the extreme levels reached in the Colorado, Brazos, and
San Bernard Rivers.

After meandering across the state and offshore for days, Harvey made
its final landfall on August 29, 2017, just east of the Texas-Louisiana border. Rainfall totals that day set records. Harvey dumped about 26 inches
of rain in 24 hours on the Port Arthur/Beaumont area. Many cities in the
area experienced historic flooding, in part due to releases from reservoirs
on the Sabine and Neches Rivers.[12]

Disaster Impacts

Hurricane Harvey affected 268,597 square miles across the states of
Texas and Louisiana, threatening 25.2 million people, over 30 percent of
the population.[13] Forty-nine counties were eligible for FEMA Community Development Block Grant–Disaster Recovery (CDBG-DR) assistance; these counties comprise a land area roughly the size of the state of
Kentucky.[14] Areas in southern Texas were affected more by wind, while
Houston, Port Arthur/Beaumont, and surrounding areas were flooded
through record-breaking precipitation.

Harvey caused $125 billion in damages across the states of Texas and
Louisiana, making it the second costliest disaster in U.S. history behind
Hurricane Katrina's $161 billion in damages. More than 204,000 homes
and apartment buildings in Harris County alone were damaged. Pay-
ments made through FEMA's Individual Assistance program, Small
Business Administration (SBA) loans to individuals and businesses, and
claims filed with the National Flood Insurance Program (NFIP) and
Texas Wind Insurance Association (TWIA) totaled nearly $15 billion.
Insured flood losses, through NFIP, accounted for $8.8 billion alone.[15]

Hurricane Harvey resulted in 103 direct and indirect fatalities. More than 80 percent of the fatalities associated with the event were due to drowning and occurred in the greater Houston area where heavy rainfall and dam releases caused unprecedented urban flooding. Surprisingly, most fatalities occurred outside the designated 100- and 500-year floodplains. In addition to loss of life, almost 780,000 Texas evacuated their homes. At its peak, nearly 43,000 evacuees were in shelters, with approximately 1,400 individuals remaining in shelters 30 days after Hurricane Harvey made landfall.[16]

Disaster Response

The public sector agency response to Hurricane Harvey was massive.[17] The Coast Guard and National Guard deployed, and FEMA coordinated search and rescue across Texas that involved the National Park Service, U.S. Fish and Wildlife Service, Customs and Border Patrol, and the Department of Defense. First responders from local, state, and federal agencies rescued a reported 122,331 people and 5,234 pets. The American Red Cross provided $45 million to more than 100,000 disaster survivors to help them with immediate needs, and the Red Cross organized more than 3,000 staff and volunteers to operate shelters throughout the impacted counties. The Department of Health and Human Services deployed medical staff and equipment, and U.S. Geological Survey sent scientists to assist the National Weather Service. The Department of Energy supported the Texas Division of Emergency Management and utility companies to restore power to more than 300,000 customers, and the Environmental Protection Agency worked with the Texas Commission on Environmental Quality to complete over 1,000 water assessments and assessments of dozens of superfund sites.

Harvey Reveals Legacy Issues in Houston

Houston, also known as the "Bayou City," is located in the upper Gulf coastal plain of the state of Texas, approximately 50 miles from the Gulf of Mexico. The city, initially built on swamp land, expanded bayous to allow for drainage and subsequent development. This created relatively flat terrain – the city is about 50 feet above sea level – that is prone to flooding. Research has shown that the city's geography and its history of low-density, sprawling urban development contributed to flood losses in the area. Harris County ranks among the top counties in the nation for rates of repetitive flood losses. Flood losses are not isolated to one area in Harris County. Rather, flooding is a problem across the across the region. An estimated 68 percent of the homes flooded by Hurricane Harvey were outside the 100-year floodplain. When the floodwaters receded, two issues came into sharp focus: Houston's legacy of land (mis)use and the related perpetuation of socioeconomic vulnerabilities of the city's race and ethnic minority communities.[18]

Land (Mis)Use in the Houston Metroplex

Fueled by population growth, affordable housing, and availability of jobs, Houston and Harris County have experienced a development boom in the past several decades. In favor of economic gain and property rights, this development has been largely unchecked by local government. Rather, land use in Houston is governed by a patchwork of regulations stitched together by local special districts. As a result, low-density urban development has spread across prairie land, contributing to significant wetland loss, and developers have been allowed to erect communities in areas vulnerable to flooding. Urban sprawl in the Houston area has created one of the largest expanses of impervious surfaces in the nation; yet the area is not equipped to deal with flooding caused by this development. Many neighborhoods continue to rely on aging and poorly maintained drainage systems, and storm water infrastructure has not improved to manage changes in hydrology associated with population growth.[19]

While residential areas concentrated in Houston before the 1960s, today the city is far less densely populated than are most others of similar size. Sprawl can compromise hydrological functions and increase surface runoff by dispersing impervious surfaces across a watershed. Impervious surfaces reduce water absorption and infiltration, and runoff from impervious surfaces overwhelms discharge systems, leading to more incidences of flooding. Low-density urban development in the Houston area has increased the runoff ratio, thereby increasing flooding and associated damages. A study of 7,900 properties that claimed flood insurance losses from 1999–2009 found that a percentage increase in low-intensity development translates into, on average, $1,734 in additional property damage caused by floods.[20] Such patterns of development place more structures and people at risk from flooding, over a larger area, and require substantial storm water infrastructure to manage persistent floods. Further, sprawl is more likely to encroach on flood-prone areas that were previously left untouched, including in wetlands.[21]

Harris County has experienced considerable degradation of wetlands since the 1990s.[22] A study of Harris County from 1992 to 2010 found that the region lost 30 percent of its freshwater wetlands, and losses have been more severe in specific areas including White Oak Bayou river watershed, northwest of Houston, with 70 percent wetland loss.[23] These losses, taken together, have reduced the region's storage capabilities by four billion gallons of storm water, the equivalent to $600 million worth of floodwater detention capacity, according to the study. Further, research s established that such alteration of wetlands significantly increases flooding events and associated property damage. A study of 37 Texas coastal counties from 1997 to 2001 found a single wetland permit translates to an average of over $200 in additional property damage per flood.[24] Houston's pattern of low-density urban sprawl has not only resulted in loss of wetlands, it has also led to development of land highly exposed to flood risk.

Flood mitigation measures taken in areas that are vulnerable to flood hazards, ranging from channelization to flood embankments, often create a "safe development paradox."[25] In Houston, this false sense of security, further bolstered by NFIP coverage, has increased development in risky areas.[26] These misguided development practices were revealed during Hurricane Harvey in many ways, but especially with the flooding of homes adjacent to Addicks and Barker Reservoirs.

Addicks and Barker Dams located in northwest Houston, were designed by USACE in the 1940s to specifically protect downtown Houston and the Houston Ship Channel from flooding. At that time, Houston was 20 miles downstream with a population of 400,000. Decades later, the reservoirs created by Addicks and Barker Dams now sit in the middle of an urban population of six million. At the time of dam construction,

USACE purchased land only within the 100-year flood pool, leaving 8,000 acres with a high potential for flooding as private land. Significant development of this private land began in the 1990s and 2000s with large, planned communities with no disclosure that these neighborhoods were in the flood pool required by Houston or Harris County.[27]

During Hurricane Harvey, Addicks and Barker Reservoirs reached record heights; they impounded approximately 126 billion gallons of water. The extreme levels of precipitation Harvey dumped, however, overwhelmed the dams. To prevent uncontrolled releases and dam failure, USACE opened the floodgates on both dams, allowing water to flow at more than 13,000 cubic feet per second into Buffalo Bayou.[28] Local governments issued evacuation orders, and more than 150,000 people fled the floodwaters. More than 10,000 homes and businesses built within the reservoirs' flood pools were inundated, many of which are now part of lawsuits filed against the government.[29] Figure 5.2 shows the parcels surrounding the reservoirs that were flooded by Harvey.

For homeowners in Addicks and Barker Reservoirs flood pool, neither developers nor public officials gave any warnings. Many homeowners were unaware of the risk because these privately owned properties were outside the 100-year floodplain. The danger posed by development around Addicks and Barker Reservoirs, however, was known. As part of USACE's Dam Safety Program, inspection of the two dams between 2009 and 2013 led to a rating of "extremely high risk." In 2015, the USACE launched a $75 million project to fortify the dams to prevent failure in high rainfall events. In the meantime, the thousands of residents (many without flood insurance) flooded by Harvey continue to recover. Risky development, such as the neighborhoods around Addicks and Barker Reservoirs, continues in Houston.[30]

The City of Houston is notorious for being the only major city in North America without zoning laws, largely attributed to the region's pro-development values that favor private enterprise and economic growth.[31] The authority for land-use controls, ranging from deed restrictions to building codes, reside with a multitude of local special districts. Municipal utility districts, local improvement districts, and homeowners' associations, among others, are responsible for creating the rules that

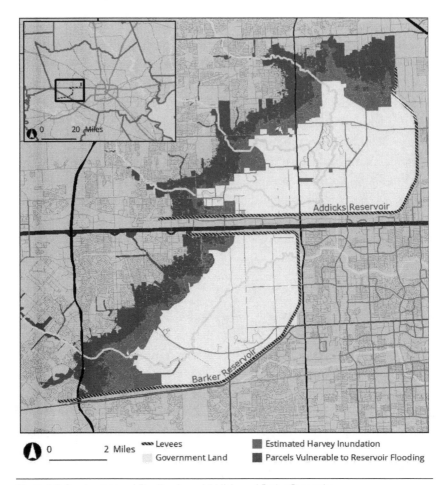

Figure 5.2 Development and Flooding Around Addicks and Barker Reservoirs

Source: Data obtained from Greater Houston Flood Mitigation Consortium. Graphic reproduced by Erika Pham, University of South Carolina

govern development and land use.[32] This ad hoc system of land-use regulation has satisfied development demands as the population grows. It also reflects prevailing free market values that place the responsibility of hazard protection on individuals and private firms.[33] This system, however, failed in major ways during Hurricane Harvey, as evidenced by the damages to homes in the areas surrounding Addicks and Barker Reservoirs. It has also reinforced and perpetuated racial and economic segregation in the city.

Socioeconomic Vulnerabilities in Houston

Although Houston has no zoning ordinances, there are quite a few regulations, including deed and covenant restrictions and conditions that limit land use. These restrictions have distributive consequences that exclude moderate- and low-income families from neighborhoods. From an economic perspective, restricting land use is beneficial in that it increases property values for those residential neighborhoods where commercial development is limited. However, it increases overall housing costs that place more burdens on low-income households, who have a higher proportion of their income dedicated to housing costs.[34]

From a social perspective, deed restrictions draw class and racial lines across communities. In Houston, these divisions were created deliberately following the oil and gas boom of the early 1900s. Developers designed neighborhoods within the city center to accommodate a range of incomes, divided into block groups. Using lot size and deed restrictions, communities within communities became separated by race and class. As the city grew in population and territory, some neighborhoods in the city center saw racial transformations. Connected by newly constructed highways, many affluent, white families migrated to emerging neighborhoods developed outside the city center. Investment in infrastructure and municipal services flowed out of the city center and away from minority communities. African Americans, also experiencing a population boom, moved into the neighborhoods that had previously excluded minorities. As the petrochemical industry further developed, the land in the city center was less desirable and, therefore, less valuable for residential purposes. Such property is more affordable for lower income families but also a target for commercial and industrial use. Minority neighborhoods also became Houston's dumping ground – from the 1920s through the 1970s, 85 percent of city-owned landfills and incinerators were built in black neighborhoods. Mixed-use neighborhoods where moderate- and low-income and minority families concentrate have had less success adopting and enforcing land-use restrictions that might protect them from the negative consequences of industrial development. Given this trend, many scholars point to Houston's land-use system as one captured by private interests and political elites that perpetuates socioeconomic vulnerability of minority populations, within a system of institutionalized racism.[35]

Segregation has not been the only issue reinforcing socioeconomic vulnerability in Houston. The areas where the majority of racial and ethnic minority populations have settled have been and continue to be more vulnerable to flooding. A study of 2,400 miles of Houston roadside found that communities of color are more likely to have open-ditch systems while higher income white neighborhoods often have closed, underground storm drainage systems.[36] Open ditches are problematic because they are limited in their ability to discharge storm water, thereby putting people and property in harm's way. A study commissioned in 2014 by Houston's Housing and Community Development Department found that 88 percent of drainage ditches are located in Houston's majority–minority neighborhoods; 43 percent of all drainage ditches are inadequate.[37] Due to the mixed land use of this area and the predominance of petrochemical industry, flooding has the potential to create natural hazard-induced technological failures (or na-tech events). Such was the case following Hurricane Harvey when superfund and industrial sites leaked contaminants and toxins into surrounding neighborhoods, putting the health of communities, including many minority communities, at risk.[38]

Infrastructure investment that would mitigate flood vulnerability in the most vulnerable areas of Houston is limited. A *Houston Chronicle* article, titled "Why Houston Remains Segregated," asserted "neighborhoods where subsidized housing is overwhelmingly concentrated lack the basic services and investment that majority white neighborhoods take for granted."[39] The inequity in infrastructure investment can be traced back to the 1950s when the city began to incorporate communities, including many communities of color, that were developed outside of city limits. The annexed communities had very limited infrastructure – lack of drainage, sidewalks, streetlights, and other basic infrastructure – which has since not been sufficiently addressed.[40] One such neighborhood, Sunnyside, asserts on its community website:

> The predominantly white part of west Houston identified as the city's strongest market, receive a disproportionate amount of public funding for infrastructure while low income communities of color like Sunnyside remain ignored. Even though Sunnyside's

needs are much greater, and its issues are a direct result of public disinvestment and discrimination, the neighborhood receives far less infrastructure funding.[41]

Research has shown that lack of infrastructure investment along race and class lines is also problematic in other cities. In a survey of racial biases evident in floods and disasters, Bullard and Wright note in their book *The Wrong Complexion for Protection*: "If a community happens to be poor or black or is located on the 'wrong side of the tracks,' it receives less protection than communities inhabited largely by affluent whites in the suburbs."[42] This study of New Orleans following Hurricane Katrina found there was no increase in levee protection for the mostly African-American parts of towns, places that are the most exposed to hazards and the most socioeconomically vulnerable.[43] Neglect of public investment in flood protection is further exacerbated by the lack of household resources to enact private protective measures, such as elevation of homes above the floodplain.[44]

Action to Address Urban Flooding and Housing Recovery

Hurricane Harvey put into sharp focus the consequences of poor land use and the neglect of socioeconomically vulnerable communities. There are a number of policy actions underway in Houston and in Harris County since Hurricane Harvey to address reservoir capacity and flood control infrastructure needs, revise floodplain regulations, pursue home buyouts in areas vulnerable to flooding, and facilitate housing recovery throughout the affected region. While some projects were already in progress, Hurricane Harvey has called attention to the need for these and, in some cases, has accelerated action. Given the damages incurred to both public and private properties due to Hurricane Harvey, the scope of these policies and programs are considerable. To put it in perspective, Harris County, the third most populous county in the nation, supports a population of 4.65 million; the City of Houston, the fourth largest city in the nation, is home to 2.31 million. There are 1.77 million households in the county; 8.7 percent flooded by Harvey. Of the 700,000 households in Houston, an estimated 30 percent sustained some form of flood damage to their home or personal property; 10 percent of households had floodwater inside their homes. Of the top ten zip codes incurring the most direct losses from Harvey, six are located in Houston/Harris County; damages in these areas alone totaled approximately $2.25 million. Additionally, the metro area contains 2,500 miles of tributary channels and drainage ditches; Harvey caused about $74 million in damage to Harris County flood control infrastructure.[45]

To address these needs, the City of Houston and Harris County received an allocation of $2.3 billion from the U.S. Department of Housing and Urban Development (HUD). These funds were part of a $5.024 billion Community Development Block Grant–Disaster Recovery (CDBG-DR) administered by HUD to the State of Texas for recovery assistance. The funds were allocated on November 17, 2017 through the Continuing Appropriations Act 2018 and Supplemental Appropriations for Disaster Relief Act 2017 that earmarked $7.4 billion in response to the major disasters declared in 2017.[46] However, they were not available for use until ten months following Hurricane Harvey. Rather than put the funds to immediate use, the General Land Office (GLO) of Texas and HUD engaged in a multi-month planning process to designate the use of the funds; HUD approved the GLO's State Action Plan on June 25, 2018.[47]

CDBG-DR supports a range of disaster recovery activities, including housing redevelopment, business assistance, infrastructure repair, and economic development. At least 80 percent of the CDBG-DR funds must be used in the "most impacted and distressed" areas as identified by HUD, which in the case of Hurricane Harvey include Harris County, and priority should be given to support activities that benefit low- and middle-income persons.[48]

Harris County and the City of Houston elected to develop their own local recovery programs. The budgets for these plans appear by category of expenditure in Table 5.1. Harris County has allocated 74 percent of its funding to housing recovery while the City of Houston has set aside 89 percent for this purpose.[49] Taken together, housing recovery in the greater Houston area alone comprises over one-third of the funds allocated to the State of Texas for recovery from Hurricane Harvey.

Table 5.1 Harris County and City of Houston Recovery Budgets and Programs

	Harris County			City of Houston		
HOUSING RECOVERY						
Homeowners	Homeowner Assistance Program	$214,000,000	(18.9%)	Homeowner Assistance Program	$392,729,436	(33.4%)
	Single Family Affordable Housing Program	$25,000,000	(2.2%)			
	Reimbursement Program	$15,000,000	(1.3%)			
Buyouts	Buyout Program	$175,000,000	(15.5%)	Buyout Program	$40,800,000	(3.5%)
Rentals	Affordable Rental Program	$204,500,000	(18.1%)	Multifamily Rental Program	$321,278,580	(27.3%)
				Small Rental Program	$61,205,100	(5.2%)
Single Family Development	Single Family New Construction	$119,888,035	(10.6%)	Single Family Development Program	$204,000,000	(17.3%)
	Housing Project Delivery	$83,709,781	(7.4%)	Homebuyer Assistance Program	$21,741,300	(1.8%)
			73.9%			**88.6%**
INFRASTRUCTURE, PUBLIC SERVICES & ECONOMIC DEVELOPMENT						
	Commercial Buyout Program	$12,500,000	(1.1%)	Public Services	$60,000,000	(5.1%)
	Method of Distribution (Local)	$120,000,000	(10.6%)	Economic Revitalization Program	$30,264,834	(2.6%)
	Competitive Application	$76,668,492	(6.8%)			
	Instructure Project Delivery	$13,351,180	(1.2%)			
			19.7%			**7.7%**
PLANNING & ADMINISTRATION						
	Planning	$55,769,342	(4.9%)	Planning	$23,100,000	(2.0%)
	Housing Administration	$16,741,956	(1.5%)	Housing Administration	$20,835,088	(1.8%)
			6.4%			**3.7%**
Total		$1,132,128,786		**Total**	$1,175,954,338	

Source: Texas Government Land Office, State of Texas Plan for Disaster Recovery, 2018

Housing Recovery

The housing recovery plans for Harris County and the City of Houston include four primary activities: 1) assistance to homeowners; 2) home buyouts; 3) rental assistance; and 4) single family home development. Assistance to homeowners is offered in a variety of ways, including but not limited to rehabilitation or reconstruction of damaged homes on behalf of homeowners; reimbursement to homeowners for completed partial or full repairs; home demolition; and temporary mortgage assistance. Single-family home development promotes efforts to increase the stock of homes in areas less at-risk to flooding and offers programs to assist low- and middle-income families with the purchase of new homes. As a separate initiative under this program, Harris County will also identify low- and middle-income areas in need of community revitalization that have been damaged by Hurricane Harvey or previous disaster events.[50] The county will undertake projects in these areas to improve drainage and other forms of infrastructure that serve neighborhoods.

In addition to assistance to homeowners, both county and city plans address rental assistance and multifamily housing projects, areas that often fall through the cracks in housing recovery from disasters.[51] Harris County allocations include support for an Affordable Rental Housing Program that provides for the acquisition, rehabilitation, reconstruction, and new construction of affordable multifamily housing projects. Similarly, the City of Houston's Multifamily Rental Program provides for the acquisition and/or rehabilitation of flood-damaged multifamily rental housing. It also scopes and acquires land for multifamily development in areas that are less prone to flooding. Given that renters comprise over 46 percent of the housing market in Houston and that low- and middle-income families have higher rates of denial for federal disaster assistance and slower recovery to disasters,[52] these programs are critical for reducing inequalities across race and class lines. Programs such as these recognize that housing is a critical component of overall economic recovery. As urban planning scholar, Anuradha Mukherji puts it:

> A house, whether it is an owner-occupied property, a rental unit, or
> an informal dwelling, it is more than just a shelter. It is often a place

for economic activities and deeply impacts the earning capacity of a household. It is thus not just the economic recovery of households that is critically tied to housing, but the economic recovery of an urban region is also inextricably linked to its housing recovery. It includes renter households and informal housing residents because these groups are an important part of the urban economy.[53]

Houston has a mixed track record of restoring public, multifamily housing from damages incurred in previous disasters. A decade after Hurricane Ike (2008), Houston still has not spent tens of millions in assistance dollars it received to build affordable housing.[54] Furthermore, many public housing complexes in the city are located in areas exposed to flood risk. Tenants in one Houston apartment complex flooded by Hurricane Harvey sued HUD for intentional discrimination in June 2018, citing specifically that the complex puts residents at risk.[55] The complex has a contract with HUD to rent units to families that qualify for housing assistance as long as standards of safety and sanitation are met. Residents claim the units are not safe or sanitary given that the apartments have flooded twice since 2016, are in a floodway, and pose health hazards due to mold issues caused by Harvey flooding. Following through with housing recovery plans to construct multifamily housing on land not exposed to flood risk will not only provide safe, affordable housing for low-income families but also take strides in restoring public trust in government.

Beyond multifamily housing and renters' assistance, the recovery plans for both Harris County and the City of Houston also include programs for the acquisition of homes located deep in the floodplain as well as the elevation of homes to reduce flood risk. Elevation of homes is an issue that local governments in the area took up following Hurricane Harvey. Both the county and city have enacted new floodplain regulations that require elevation of homes two feet above the 500-year floodplain. Additionally, both governments have expanded existing home buyout programs to remove repetitive loss properties from the floodplain. These two policies – floodplain regulations and home buyout programs – address gaps created by Houston's legacy of runaway development and take strides to reduce risk in this urban center.

Floodplain Regulations

Harris County acted quickly following Hurricane Harvey to revise building codes, passing rules that require new buildings in the 100-year floodplain be built two feet above the 500-year floodplain elevation.[56] Other regulations prohibit fill as a means of elevating structures within the 100-year floodplain. Rather, builders must use open foundations, including piers or continuous foundation walls with appropriate openings. These building codes went into effect January 1, 2018, but only apply to county jurisdictions; municipalities within the county maintain authority over building codes in their city bounds.

On April 4, 2018, the Houston City Council approved, by a 9–7 vote, the modification of the city's floodplain regulation.[57] The ordinance expanded existing rules that require homeowners in the 100-year floodplain to have flood insurance and build new homes one foot above the floodplain. The new ordinance increases the freeboard requirement to two feet and extends it to homes in the 500-year floodplain. Additionally, the regulation applies to new construction and existing homes that are significantly improved (defined as expanding the structural footprint by 33 percent or more). Existing homes without significant improvements are grandfathered and do not have to be elevated. The revised ordinance, according to a city study, would have prevented 84 percent of the homes in the 100- and 500-year floodplains that flooded during Harvey to avoid damage.[58] The city change to building codes went into effect September 1, 2018.

While these heightened regulations aim at reducing flood risk in the City of Houston and Harris County, they do not address flooding outside the floodplain. Studies show that 47 percent of flood losses in Harris County and 55 percent in the Clear Creek watershed (south of Houston) occurred outside the FEMA-mandated 100-year floodplain.[59] An analysis using a spatially distributed hydrologic model of the Armand Bayou watershed, southeast of Houston, found that 75 percent of insured losses from 1999 to 2009 were outside the 100-year floodplain.[60] Studies thus highlight that flooding is prevalent outside of floodplains in the Houston area and that FEMA floodplains have failed to account accurately for flood risk and impacts.

Furthermore, the studies of flood losses outside the FEMA-designated floodplain offer a more accurate method for modeling flood risk that incorporates land-use changes, including loss of wetlands and the addition of impervious surfaces resulting from development. Using these models would greatly expand the extent of the floodplains in the fast-growing Houston metropolitan. The potential expansion of the floodplain is important because it would curtail current risky development just outside of floodplain boundaries. Additionally, because flood insurance is not required by lenders and mortgage companies for homes outside the floodplain, it would force residents in these vulnerable areas to be insured. An estimated 70–80 percent of homeowners that experienced severe flooding during Hurricane Harvey did not have flood insurance primarily because it was not required.[61] Updating floodplain maps to more accurately align with flood realities and promoting mitigation in areas that are at true risk – not simply outside the FEMA floodplain – is critical to reduce flood losses and promote safer development.

Although stricter building codes reduce flood risk, they may also have negative consequences for homeowners in floodplains by making recovery more expensive for those residing in these areas. Because FEMA requires structures be compliant with local regulations, building codes mandating increased elevation can burden already financially strapped homeowners. Studies have shown that elevating a 2,000-square-foot house higher than the base-flood elevation costs between $890 and $4,470 per square foot, depending on the foundation type. Other concerns include the cost of compliance with new regulations among low-income and race and ethnic minority subpopulations, groups that have predominantly settled in Houston's areas most exposed to flood risk. Research demonstrates a connection between local hazard damages and wealth inequality. Since Hurricane Harvey, the City of Houston has used federal disaster assistance to elevate 40 homes and applied for an additional FEMA grant to cover the costs of elevating another 80 homes. This assistance, however, does not cover all costs; homeowners participating in the program must carry flood insurance and must provide matching funds, averaging more than $13,000 per property.[62] The homes targeted by these programs are severe repetitive loss properties, where more than $5,000 in flood assistance claims were filed or where two separate claims add up to more than the total value of the home. This assistance, therefore, does little to alleviate the costs of mitigation to the broader population of homeowners, a policy action criticized as "passing the buck" from the city to homeowners.[63] Requiring responsibility for individual flood risk is a step in the right direction, but the new building codes will likely disproportionately hurt poorer, older, and minority families in the economic burden they carry.

Home Buyout Programs

Home buyouts are used to reduce flood risk in areas that are deep – often several feet – in the floodplain and where structural projects, such as channel modifications or storm water detention basins to reduce flooding, are not cost effective.[64] Harris County and the City of Houston have designated 70 priority areas for home acquisitions, including for low-income and predominately race and ethnic minority communities.[65] Participation in these programs is voluntary, and local government agencies may exchange homeowners' storm-damaged homes for newly constructed homes or the damaged homes may be rehabilitated then offered for sale or further exchange. However, the buyout programs of both the county and city prioritizes acquisition of properties that may be converted for flood control – e.g., green space, detention areas – and not be redeveloped for residential or commercial use.[66]

Harris County has actively pursued home buyouts since the 1980s.[67] From 1985 to 2017, HCFCD spent $342 million in federal, state, and county funds to acquire over 3,100 properties, restoring a total of 1,060 acres to the floodplain. Since Hurricane Harvey, Harris County has secured more than $50 million from FEMA's Hazard Mitigation Grant Program for home buyouts. Additionally, the $2.5 billion bond passed by Harris County in 2018 allocates funding to support acquisition projects totaling $736.5 million. As of December 2018, Harris County received 4,000 voluntary requests for home buyouts. Of these, 1,000 were eligible properties and approved for the buyout program. Nearly 135 properties have been purchased, and another 597 are in the appraisal and sale process. Further, Harris County has set aside 15.5 percent of its

CDBG-DR allocation for home buyouts; the City of Houston has allocated 3.5 percent.[68]

Even though acquisitions reduce flood risk and potential losses to homeowners and the community, they are fraught with challenges. The buyout process is complicated and long; funding for acquisitions from federal sources takes several months to years to secure. Most homeowners do not benefit from a buyout for between 12 and 24 months after volunteering. During that time, many homeowners who might have considered a buyout have already completed repairs and continue to live in high-risk areas. To counter this, acquisition programs often allow homeowners to use disaster assistance funds to make repairs on their home while waiting for a potential buyout offer. The total amount of insurance claims and disaster assistance is deducted from the price offered for the home. Since the cost of repairs is non-recoverable, however, homeowners participating in a buyout must relocate with diminished resources.[69]

Although the pace of the acquisition process can be daunting, research following Hurricanes Katrina and Sandy shows that buyout program participants are particularly concerned about getting information throughout the process. Of specific concern is the "ability (or inability) to access coherent, accurate, and timely information needed to make important decisions."[70] Buyout programs need to be transparent and inclusive of the homeowner. Additionally, buyout decisions and offers to the homeowner should be made quickly to help families move out of high-risk areas.

There are other concerns focused on equity and future risk surrounding acquisition programs. Home buyout programs often rely on Benefit-Cost Analysis (BCA) showing that the estimated cost of future flood damage surpasses the cost of purchasing and demolishing a structure. This is a difficult requirement to satisfy in neighborhoods with low property values. Because residents in these areas are typically racial and ethnic minorities and/or low-income households, race and class inequalities may emerge in home buyout programs.[71] Such inequities may perpetuate vulnerabilities by trapping families in homes located in areas exposed to flood risk that only decrease in value. This will only further exacerbate the slow recovery often found tied not to disaster damages but to economic and social inequalities.[72]

Additionally, there are concerns that home buyout programs may result in loss of social capital – the social ties that generate norms of reciprocity and trust, allow collective action, and foster information and resource flows among people.[73] When homes are bought out, households must relocate, disrupting established social networks and breaking social ties. Because social capital plays a critical role in disaster recovery for both individuals and communities,[74] home buyouts may be detrimental to the social resources that individuals draw upon. A study examining home acquisitions in New York after Hurricane Sandy found that buyouts not only result in loss of social capital but also that these losses endure for years after relocation.[75]

Furthermore, buyout programs cannot ensure that households relocate to areas of reduced risk. A study of New York's home buyout program following Hurricane Sandy suggests that 20 percent of households moved to an area exposed to flood risk.[76] While financial incentives encouraging participants to relocate within city bounds are vital for maintaining fiscal bases supporting the community, requirements guiding the purchase of new homes – in this case, out of the floodplain – are also important. Furthermore, because participation in home buyout programs is voluntary, reduction of future risk for entire neighborhoods is limited unless cluster buyouts are pursued. More typically, patchworks of buyouts emerge, pocking a neighborhood with empty lots but not reducing aggregate flood exposure.[77] Taken together, these concerns raise important questions about the efficacy of home buyout programs. The specific actions taken during implementation of these programs by local government agencies in Houston will be critical to ensuring inequities, preserving social capital, and halting the perpetuation of place-based vulnerability.

Conclusion: Sociopolitical Challenges for Urban Recovery and Development

Disaster recovery must navigate a complex web of interdependent social, political, economic, and environmental factors that is only made more complicated by past legacies that condition the range of current options. In Houston's case, understanding the scope of recovery from the damages of Hurricane Harvey requires an honest look at its history of land use. Unchecked development over decades created one of the nation's largest areas of flood risk. Low-density urban sprawl resulted in the dispersion of impervious surfaces at the cost of wetland preservation. Safe development paradoxes have justified development in areas prone to flooding, and the neglect of infrastructure has created inefficient drainage systems, particularly in communities of color. Addressing these poor land-use choices within the context of widespread disaster damages is difficult. Housing stocks are low while pressures for quick recovery are high. By passing stricter floodplain regulations, the City of Houston and Harris County have demonstrated political will sufficient to tackle tough decisions. However, this political will is dynamic. It may fluctuate with public sentiment and is prone to change by political turnover and competing political agendas.

Will the effects of Hurricane Harvey serve as a sufficiently powerful wake-up call to shape Houston's and the state's urban development agenda going forward? A 2018 survey conducted by Rice University's Kinder Institute for Urban Research found that of approximately 1,500 Houston area residents, 66 percent agree that "if local government had imposed more stringent regulations on development, this would have significantly reduced the damage caused by Hurricane Harvey." More than 75 percent responded "it is almost certain that the Houston region will experience more severe storms during the next ten years compared to the past ten years." And the majority are willing to support action to reduce flood risk: 72 percent favor using public money to protect industries along the Ship Channel from hurricane surge flooding, and 56 percent are in favor of increasing local taxes to enable government to buy out more of the homes that have repeatedly flooded.[78]

It is uncertain how local, state, and national politics will frame the issues and what elected leaders will pursue in relation to Houston's disaster recovery and future development. In 2018, Harris County experienced considerable turnover in elected offices on the municipal and county levels.[79] In the political arena, there are critical issues at stake, including revenue streams for local governments. There has been a push for the state legislature to tap its "rainy-day" (savings account) fund to cover local matches of federal assistance dollars and to compensate Harvey-affected school districts for lost revenue resulting from decreases in property values and per-student funding.[80] Also of concern is legislative action to cap property tax growth at 2.5 percent.[81] Because property taxes are the central source of revenue for counties, caps on property taxes severely undercut the ability of counties to raise additional revenue for infrastructure and other disaster recovery projects.

Another critical issue that has emerged on the political agenda is a coastal storm protection system, comprised of floodwalls, floodgates, seawall improvements, and beach and sand dune restoration, put forward in 2018 by the Texas General Land Office and U.S. Army Corps of Engineers.[82] The system, which borrows concepts of the "Ike Dike" developed after Hurricane Ike by Texas A&M University at Galveston professor Bill Merrell, would protect the Houston Ship Channel, the Houston metroplex, and the entire region from potentially devastating impacts of storm surge. The project, however, is estimated to cost $31 billion, a high price tag for the state and local governments.

In the aftermath of Hurricane Harvey, one journalist commented, "Harvey is gone but Houston still faces Texas-sized problems."[83] So far, Houston and Harris County have risen to the challenge of making floodplain policy changes and establishing recovery programs that attempt to meet the needs of homeowners and renters and address flood-prone areas. Big ideas like the Ike Dike are being explored across the state to address hazard vulnerabilities. And the majority of the public is supportive of flood protection and regulated development. Only time will tell if current sociopolitical forces are strong enough to create a change in Houston's urban development trajectory and its Texas-sized problem of future flood risk. In the meantime, Hurricane Harvey's impact on the Houston metroplex serves as a cautionary tale about unchecked urban development and unaddressed socioeconomic inequities. As urban populations across the nation grow and natural hazards intensify and become more frequent, may we all learn from it.

Notes

The author would like to acknowledge the following individuals for their assistance with preparation of this manuscript, including the creation of the initial maps: Dr. Russell Blessing (Center for Texas Beaches and

Shores), Ryan Eddings (Center for Texas Beaches and Shores), Abbey Hotard (Master of Marine Resource Management Program, Texas A&M University at Galveston), Mary Lee (Master of Marine Resource Management Program, Texas A&M University at Galveston), and Dr. William Mobley (Center for Texas Beaches and Shores).

Notes

1. Harris County Flood Control District, "Harris County Has Never Seen a Storm Like Harvey," last updated January 29, 2019, www.hcfcd.org/hurricane-harvey/; National Weather Service, "Major Hurricane Harvey – August 25–29, 2017," www.weather.gov/crp/hurricane_harvey; City of Houston, "Fact Sheet: City of Houston Releases Updated Needs Assessment for Hurricane Harvey," October 16, 2018, http://houstontx.gov/housing/Fact_Sheet_Needs_Assessment.pdf.
2. Commission to Rebuild Texas, *Eye of the Storm: Report of the Governor's Commission to Rebuild Texas* (Texas A&M University System, November 2018), www.rebuildtexas.today/wp-content/uploads/sites/52/2018/12/12-11-18-EYE-OF-THE-STORM-digital.pdf; Elizabeth K. Julian, Ann Lott, Demetria McCain, and Chrishelle Palay, "Why Houston Remains Segregated," *The Houston Chronicle*, February 16, 2017, www.houstonchronicle.com/local/gray-matters/article/Why-Houston-remains-segregated-10935311.php; Christina Rosales, "Houston Knew Neighborhoods of Color Were Inadequately Protected from Even Modest Storm Events," *Texas Houser*, August 31, 2017, https://texashousers.net/2017/08/31/houston-knew-neighborhoods-of-color-were-inadequately-protected-from-even-modest-storm-events/.
3. Texas General Land Office, "State of Texas Plan for Disaster Recovery: Amendment 1, Hurricane Harvey – Round 1," September 6, 2018, http://recovery.texas.gov/files/hud-requirements-reports/hurricane-harvey/harvey-5b-sap-amend1.pdf.
4. Harris County Flood Control District, "Immediate Report – Final: Hurricane Harvey – Storm and Flood Information," June 4, 2018, www.hcfcd.org/media/2678/immediate-flood-report-final-hurricane-harvey-2017.pdf.
5. National Weather Service, "Major Hurricane Harvey"; Linus Magnusson, Ivan Tsonevsky, and Fernando Prates, "Predictions of Tropical Cyclones Harvey and Irma," *European Centre for Medium-Range Weather Forecasts Newsletter* 157, no. Autumn (2017), www.ecmwf.int/en/newsletter/153/news/predictions-tropical-cyclones-harvey-and-irma; Eric S. Blake and David A. Zelinsky, "National Hurricane Center Tropical Cyclone Report: Hurricane Harvey," May 9, 2018, www.nhc.noaa.gov/data/tcr/AL092017_Harvey.pdf; Jason Samenow, "Forecasts for Harvey Were Excellent but Show Where Predictions Can Improve," *The Washington Post*, August 28, 2017, www.washingtonpost.com/news/capital-weather-gang/wp/2017/08/28/forecasts-for-harvey-were-excellent-but-show-where-predictions-can-improve/?utm_term=.f812b6f828a9.
6. Brandon Formby and Edgar Walters, "Ahead of Hurricane Harvey, Officials Send Texans Mixed Messages on Evacuations," *The Texas Tribune*, August 25, 2017, www.texastribune.org/2017/08/25/officials-send-texans-mixed-messages-hurricane-evacuations/; Ashley Ross, "Why Texans Heard Conflicting Messages About Evacuating Ahead of Hurricane Harvey," *The Conversation*, August 31, 2017, https://theconversation.com/why-texans-heard-conflicting-messages-about-evacuating-ahead-of-hurricane-harvey-83203.

7. Allison Ehrlich, "What Was the Last Hurricane to Hit Corpus Christi?" *Corpus Christi Caller Times*, August 23, 2017, www.caller.com/story/news/local/2017/08/23/what-last-hurricane-hit-corpus-christi-hurricane-celia-1970/590150001/; National Weather Service, "Major Hurricane Harvey"; Bob Henson, "Harvey Slams Ashore in Texas: Catastrophic Flood Threat Still to Come," *Weather Underground*, August 26, 2017, www.wunderground.com/cat6/harvey-slams-ashore-texas-catastrophic-flood-threat-still-come; Robert Morast, "Hurricane Harvey by the Numbers," *The Houston Chronicle*, September 4, 2017, www.houstonchronicle.com/life/article/Hurricane-Harvey-by-the-numbers-12172287.php; Blake and Zelinsky, *National Hurricane Center Report*.

8. Jason Samenow, "Harvey Is a 1,000-year Flood Event Unprecedented in Scale," *The Washington Post*, August 31, 2017, www.washingtonpost.com/news/capital-weather-gang/wp/2017/08/31/harvey-is-a-1000-year-flood-event-unprecedented-in-scale/?utm_term=.2ea2f33d7a48; Bill Chappell, "National Weather Service Adds New Colors So It Can May Harvey's Rain," *National Public Radio*, August 28, 2017, www.npr.org/sections/thetwo-way/2017/08/28/546776542/national-weather-service-adds-new-colors-so-it-can-map-harveys-rains; Harris County Flood Control District, "Immediate Report – #1: Hurricane Harvey – Storm and Flood Information," September 5, 2017, www.hcfcd.org/media/2678/immediate-flood-report-final-hurricane-harvey-2017.pdf; Colin Dwyer, "The Goal is Rescue': Harvey's Historic Deluge Met with Equally Massive Response," *National Public Radio*, August 28, 2017, www.npr.org/sections/thetwo-way/2017/08/28/546714612/-the-goal-is-rescue-harvey-s-historic-deluge-met-with-equally-massive-response.

9. Harris County Flood Control District, "Immediate Report-Final."

10. Commission to Rebuild Texas, "Eye of the Storm."

11. Blake and Zelinsky, *National Hurricane Center Report*.

12. National Weather Service, "Major Hurricane Harvey"; Jason Samenow, "Harvey Is a 1,000-year Flood Event Unprecedented in Scale"; Blake and Zelinsky, *National Hurricane Center Report*; Steve W. Stewart, "Corps of Engineers Issue Dire Warning to Jefferson County Regarding Historic Dam B Release," *KJAS*.com, August 30, 2017, www.kjas.com/news/local_news/article_1b1ae0ce-8de5-11e7-a538-dbad63c36d1a.html.

13. Federal Emergency Management Agency, *2017 Hurricane Season FEMA After-Action Report* (Washington, DC, 2018), www.fema.gov/media-library/assets/documents/167249.

14. Texas General Land Office, *State of Texas Plan*.

15. FEMA, *2017 Hurricane Season*; David Hunn, Matt Dempse and Mihir Zaveri, "Harvey's Floods: Most Homes Damaged by Harvey Were Outside Flood Plain, Data Shows," *The Houston Chronicle*, March 30, 2018, www.houstonchronicle.com/news/article/In-Harvey-s-deluge-most-damaged-homes-were-12794820.php; Commission to Rebuild Texas, "Eye of the Storm."

16. FEMA, *2017 Hurricane Season*; Sebastiaan N. Jonkman, Maartje Godfroy, Antonia Sebastian, and Bas Kolen, "Brief Communication: Loss of Life due to Hurricane Harvey," *Natural Hazards and Earth System Sciences* 18, no. 4 (2018): 1073–1078.

17. Federal Emergency Management Agency, "Historic Response to Hurricane Harvey in Texas," September 22, 2017, www.fema.gov/news-release/2017/09/22/historic-disaster-response-hurricane-harvey-texas.

18. Russell Blessing, Antonia Sebastian, and Samuel D. Brody, "Flood Risk Delineation in the United States: How Much Loss Are We Capturing?" *Natural Hazards Review* 18, no. 3 (2017), https://doi.org/10.1061/(ASCE)NH.1527-6996.0000242;

Samuel D. Brody, Sammy Zahran, Wesley E. Highfield, Himanshu Grover, and Arnold Vedlitz, "Identifying the Impact of the Built Environment on Flood Damage in Texas," *Disasters* 32, no. 1 (2008): 1–18; Samuel D. Brody, Russell Blessing, Antonia Sebastian, and Philip Bedient, "Examining the Impact of Land Use/Land Cover Characteristics on Flood Losses," *Journal of Environmental Planning and Management* 57, no. 8 (2014): 1252–1265; Federal Emergency Management Agency; Harris County Flood Control District, "Immediate Report-Final."

19. Harris County Budget Management Department, "Population Report – January 2017," 2018, https://budget.harriscountytx.gov/doc/Budget/fy2018/reports/FY18_Population_Report.pdf; Lars Lerup, *One Million Acres & No Zoning* (London, UK: Architectural Association Publications, 2011); Antonia Sebastian, Kasper T. Lendering, Baukje Kothuis, Nikki Brand, Sebastiaan N. Jonkman, Pieter van Gelder, Maartje Godfroij, Bas Kolen, Tina Comes, and Step Lhermitte, *Hurricane Harvey Report: A Fact-Finding Effort in the Direct Aftermath of Hurricane Harvey in the Greater Houston Region* (Delft: Delft University Publishers, 2017), https://pure.tudelft.nl/portal/files/31283193/TU_Delft_Texas_Hurricane_Harvey_Report_Phase_I_20171108.pdf.; Kim McGuire, "Houston's Development Boom and Reduction of Wetlands Leaves Region Flood Prone," *The Houston Chronicle*, July 22, 2016, www.houstonchronicle.com/news/houston-texas/houston/article/Houston-s-development-boom-and-reduction-of-8403838.php; Michael Kimmelman, "Lessons from Hurricane Harvey: Houston's Struggle is America's Tale," *The New York Times*, November 11, 2017, www.nytimes.com/interactive/2017/11/11/climate/houston-flooding-climate.html; Commission to Rebuild Texas, "Eye of the Storm."

20. Samuel Brody, Heeju Kim, and Joshua Gunn, "Examining the Impacts of Development Patterns on Flooding on the Gulf of Mexico Coast," *Urban Studies* 50, no. 4 (2013): 789–806.

21. Zhu Qian, "Without Zoning: Urban Development and Land Use Controls in Houston," *Cities* 27, no. 1 (2010): 31–41; Michael J. Paul and Judith L. Meyer, "Streams in the Urban Landscape," *Annual Review of Ecology and Systematics* 32 (November 2001): 333–365; Shuhab D. Khan, "Urban Development and Flooding in Houston Texas, Inferences from Remote Sensing Data Using Neural Network Technique," *Environmental Geology* 47, no. 8 (2005): 1120–1127; Brody et al., "Impact of Land Use/Land Cover."

22. Brody et al., "Impact of Built Environment."

23. John S. Jacob, Kirana Pandian, Ricardo Lopez, and Heather Biggs, *Houston-Area Freshwater Wetland Loss, 1992–2010* (College Station, TX: Texas A&M Agrilife Extension and Texas Sea Grant at Texas A&M University, ERPT-002/TAMU-SG-14-303, 2015), http://agrilife.org/urbannature/files/2015/06/WetlandLossPub.pdf.

24. Brody et al., "Impact of Built Environment."

25. Raymond J. Burby, "Hurricane Katrina and the Paradoxes of Government Disaster Policy: Bringing about Wise Governmental Decisions for Hazardous Areas," *The ANNALS of the American Academy of Political and Social Science* 604 (2006): 171–191.

26. Commission to Rebuild Texas, "Eye of the Storm."

27. Harris County Flood Control District, "Controlled Releases on Addicks and Barker Reservoir Increase Flooding Threat Along Buffalo Bayou," August 29, 2017, www.hcfcd.org/press-room/current-news/2017/08/controlled-releases-on-addicks-and-barker-reservoir-increase-flooding-threat-along-buffalo-bayou/; Kimmelmann, "Lesson from Hurricane"; Commission to Rebuild Texas, "Eye of the Storm."

28. Harris County Flood Control District, "Immediate Report-Final"; Harris County Flood Control District, "Controlled Releases."

29. Lise Olsen, "Record Reservoir Flooding Was Predicted Even Before Harvey Hit Houston," *The Houston Chronicle*, February 21, 2018, www.houstonchronicle.com/news/houston-texas/houston/article/barker-addicks-dams-flooding-predicted-army-corps-12632041.php; Lise Olsen, "Lawmaker Calls for Probe of What Corps Knew of Harvey Flooding Risks," *The Houston Chronicle,* February 23, 2018, www.houston chronicle.com/news/houston-texas/houston/article/Lawmaker-calls-for-probe-of-whether-Corps-knew-of-12705152.php.

30. Olsen, "Record Reservoir"; Commission to Rebuild Texas, "Eye of the Storm"; US Army Corps of Engineers, "Dam Safety Program," n.d., www.swg.usace.army.mil/Missions/Dam-Safety-Program/.

31. Lerup, *One Million Acres.*

32. Sebastian et al., *Hurricane Harvey Report.*

33. Zhu Qian, "Without Zoning: Urban Development and Land Use Controls in Houston," *Cities* 27, no. 1 (2010): 31–41.

34. Edwin Buitelaar, "Zoning, More than Just a Tool: Explaining Houston's Regulatory Practice," *European Planning Studies* 17, no. 7 (2009): 1049–1065; Zhu Qian, "Shaping Urban Form without Zoning: Investigating Three Neighbourhoods in Houston," *Planning Practice & Research* 26, no. 1 (2011): 21–42; Sanford Ikeda and Emily Washington, *How Land-Use Regulation Undermines Affordable Housing* (Arlington, VA: Mercatus Research Center at George Mason University, November 2015), www.mercatus.org/system/files/Ikeda-Land-Use-Regulation.pdf.

35. Barry J. Kaplan, "Race, Income, and Ethnicity: Residential Change in a Houston Community, 1920–1970," *The Houston Review* winter (1981): 178–202, https://houstonhistorymagazine.org/wp-content/uploads/2014/06/race-income-ethnicity-HR-3.1.pdf; Qian, "Shaping Urban Form"; Robert D. Bullard, *Invisible Houston: The Black Experience in Boom and Bust* (College Station, TX: Texas A&M University Press, 1987); Timothy Collins, Sara Grineski, and Jayajit Chakraborty, "Environmental Injustice and Flood Risk: A Conceptual Model and Case Comparison of Metropolitan Miami and Houston, USA," *Regional Environmental Change*, no. 18 (2018): 311–323; Robert D. Bullard and Beverly Wright, *The Wrong Complexion for Protection: How the Government Response to Disaster Endangers African American Communities* (New York, NY: New York University Press, 2012); Christopher Berry, "Land Use Regulation and Residential Segregation: Does Zoning Matter?" *American Law and Economics Review* 3, no. 2 (2001): 251–274.

36. Marccus D. Hendricks, *The Infrastructures of Equity and Environmental Justice* (College Station, TX: Texas A&M University, Unpublished doctoral dissertation, 2017).

37. Rosales, "Houston Knew Neighborhoods."

38. Tanvi Misra, "A Catastrophe for Houston's Most Vulnerable People," *The Atlantic,* August 27, 2017, www.theatlantic.com/news/archive/2017/08/a-catastrophe-for-houstons-most-vulnerable-people/538155/; Jennifer Horney et al., "Comparing Residential Contamination in a Houston Environmental Justice Neighborhood Before and After Hurricane Harvey," *PLoS ONE* 13, no. 2 (2018), e0192660.

39. Elizabeth K. Julian, Ann Lott, Demetria McCain, and Chrishelle Palay, "Why Houston Remains Segregated," *The Houston Chronicle*, February 16, 2017, www.houstonchronicle.com/local/gray-matters/article/Why-Houston-remains-segregated-10935311.php.

40. Rosales, "Houston Knew Neighborhoods."

41. Sunnyside, Community Development, "Housing and Infrastructure," February 2017, https://txlihis.wixsite.com/home/community-development-housing.

42. Bullard and Wright, *Wrong Complexion*, 50.

43. Robert D. Bullard and Beverly Wright, "Race, Place, and the Environment in Post Katrina New Orleans," in *Race, Place, and Environmental Justice after Hurricane Katrina: Struggles to Reclaim, Rebuild, and Revitalize New Orleans and the Gulf Coast*, edited by Robert D. Bullard and Beverly Wright (Boulder, CO: Westview Press, 2009), 19–49.

44. Florian Martin, "Is Houston's Floodplain Ordinance Bad for Low Income Communities?" *Houston Public Media*, August 28, 2018, www.houstonpublicmedia.org/articles/news/in-depth/2018/08/28/301910/is-houstons-floodplain-ordinance-bad-for-low-income-communities/.

45. U.S. Census Bureau, "New Census Bureau Population Estimates Show Dallas-Fort Worth-Arlington Has Largest Growth in the United States," March 22, 2018, www.census.gov/newsroom/press-releases/2018/popest-metro-county.html; U.S. Census Bureau, "Census Bureau Reveals Fastest-Growing Large Cities," May 24, 2018, www.census.gov/newsroom/press-releases/2018/estimates-cities.html; U.S. Census Bureau, "Population and Housing Unit Estimates 2017," www.census.gov/programs-surveys/popest.html; Harris County Flood Control District, "Immediate Report-Final"; City of Houston, "Fact Sheet"; Commission to Rebuild Texas, "Eye of the Storm"; Harris County Flood Control District, "HCFCD Unit Numbering System," www.hcfcd.org/drainage-network/hcfcd-unit-numbering-system/; City of Houston, "Ditch Maintenance Section," www.publicworks.houstontx.gov/ditch-maintenance-section; Mihir Zaveri, "Harvey Caused More than $74M in Damage to Flood Control Infrastructure," *The Houston Chronicle*, October 31, 2017, www.houstonchronicle.com/news/politics/houston/article/Hurricane-Harvey-caused-more-than-74-million-in-12317778.php.

46. Texas General Land Office, *State of Texas Plan*.

47. Paul Cobler, "Federal Government Approves Texas Plan for Long-Term Harvey Recovery Funds," *The Texas Tribune*, June 25, 2018, www.texastribune.org/2018/06/25/hurricane-harvey-long-term-recovery-funds-approved-federal-government/.

48. Commission to Rebuild Texas, "Eye of the Storm"; Texas General Land Office, *State of Texas Plan*; Mike Morris, "Houston Releases Harvey Recovery Plan for $1B in Housing Aid," *Houston Chronicle*, June 7, 2018, www.houstonchronicle.com/news/houston-texas/houston/article/Houston-releases-Harvey-recovery-plan-for-1B-in-12975337.php.

49. Texas General Land Office, *State of Texas Plan*.

50. Ibid.

51. Anuradha Mukherji, "Post-Earthquake Housing Recovery in Bachhau, India: The Homeowner, the Renter, and the Squatter," *Earthquake Spectra* 26, no. 4 (2010): 1085–1100; Jie Ying Wu and Michael K. Lindell, "Housing Reconstruction after Two Major Earthquakes: The 1994 Northridge Earthquake in the United States and the 1999 Chi-Chi Earthquake in Taiwan," *Disasters* 28, no. 1 (2004): 63–81.

52. Texas General Land Office, *State of Texas Plan*; U.S. Department of Housing and Urban Development, *Comprehensive Housing Market Analysis: Houston, Texas* (Washington, DC: U.S. Department of Housing and Urban Development, August 1, 2017), www.huduser.gov/portal/publications/pdf/HoustonTX-comp-17.pdf; Robert Downen, "Vulnerable Houstonians Will be First in Line for Harvey Recovery Money, City Says," *The Houston Chronicle*, January 9, 2019, www.houstonchronicle.com/news/houston-texas/houston/article/Vulnerable-Houstonians-will-be-first-in-line-for-13520476.php; Walter G. Peacock, Shannon Van Zandt, Yang Zhang, and Wesley E. Highfield, "Inequities in Long-Term Housing Recovery after Disasters," *Journal of the American Planning Association* 80, no. 4 (2014): 356–371.

53. Anuradha Mukherji, "Post-Disaster Housing Recovery," *Oxford Research Encyclopedia of Natural Hazard Science*, April 2017, https://doi.org/10.1093/acrefore/978019938 9407.013.82; quote is from p. 16.

54. Neena Satija, "A Decade After Ike, Houston Still Hasn't Spent Tens of Millions it Got to Build Affordable Housing," *The Texas Tribune*, March 29, 2018, www.texastribune. org/2018/03/29/houston-texas-affordable-housing-hurricane-ike-harvey/.

55. Christina Rosales, "Tenants at Houston's Flooded, Distressed Arbor Court Apartments Sue HUD for Intentional Racial Discrimination," *Texas Housers*, July 19, 2018, https://texashousers.net/2018/07/19/tenants-at-houstons-flooded-distressed-arbor-court-apartments-sue-hud-for-intentional-racial-discrimination/.

56. Juan A. Lozano, "Texas' Harris County Oks Post-Harvey Flood Construction Rules," *Insurance Journal*, December 7, 2017, www.insurancejournal.com/news/southcentral/ 2017/12/07/473470.htm/.

57. Cat Cardenas and Brandon Formby, "Houston Council Approves Changes to Floodplain Regulations in Effort to Reduce Flood Damage," *The Texas Tribune*, April 4, 2018, www.texastribune.org/2018/04/04/houston-city-council-approves-changes-floodplain-regulations-narrow-vo/.

58. City of Houston, "Houston Public Works Floodplain Management Data Analysis," March 2018, www.houstontx.gov/council/g/chapter19/Floodplain-Mgmt-Data-Analysis.pdf.

59. Wesley E. Highfield, Sarah A. Norman, and Samuel D. Brody, "Examining the 100-year Floodplain as a Metric of Risk, Loss, and Household Adjustment," *Risk Analysis: An International Journal* 33, no. 2 (2013): 186–191; Brody et al., "Impact of Land Use."

60. Blessing, "Flood Risk Delineation."

61. Lyle Adriano, "Majority of Harvey Victims Did Not Have Flood Insurance: Experts," *Insurance Business Magazine*, January 2, 2018, www.insurancebusinessmag.com/us/ news/catastrophe/majority-of-harvey-victims-did-not-have-flood-insurance-ex perts-88416.aspx.

62. Association of State Floodplain Managers, *The Costs & Benefits of Building Higher*, February 2018, www.floods.org/ace-images/BenefitsCost-FreeboardFlyerFinalFeb2018. pdf; Martin, "Is Houston's Floodplain"; Junia Howell and James R. Elliott, "Damages Done: The Longitudinal Impacts of Natural Hazards on Wealth Inequality in the United States," *Social Problems* 66, no. 3 (2019): 448–467, https://doi.org/10.1093/ socpro/spy016; Mike Morris, "Houston City Council Clears Way for Another 40 Flood-Prone Homes to Elevate," *The Houston Chronicle*, February 15, 2018, www. chron.com/news/politics/houston/article/Houston-City-Council-clears-the-way-for-another-12614204.php; Jasper Scherer, "Houston Council Approves FEMA Grant Application for Home Elevations, Buyouts," *The Houston Chronicle*, January 23, 2019, www.houstonchronicle.com/news/politics/houston/article/City-Council-approves-FEMA-grant-application-for-13556422.php.

63. Joel Kotkin, "The Battle for Houston," *City Journal*, August 15, 2018, www.city-journal.org/html/battle-houston-16113.html.

64. Harris County Flood Control District, "Home Buyout Program," www.hcfcd.org/ hurricane-harvey/home-buyout-program/.

65. Laura Thompson, "Buyouts Bring Promise and Challenges to Flood Affected Homeowners," *Urban Edge Rice University Kinder Institute for Urban Research*, August 21, 2018, https://kinder.rice.edu/2018/08/20/buyouts-bring-promise-and-challenges-flood-affected-homeowners.

66. Texas General Land Office, *State of Texas Plan*.

67. Grant Patterson, *Case Studies in Floodplain Buyouts* (Houston, TX: Rice University Kinder Institute for Urban Research), www.houstonconsortium.com/graphics/GHFMC_KI_2018_Buyout_Report.pdf.
68. Jen Para, "Update: FEMA Approves Another $51M for Harris County Home Buyouts," *Houston Business Journal*, June 5, 2018, www.bizjournals.com/houston/news/2018/06/05/fema-approves-26m-for-harris-county-home-buyouts.html; Harris County Flood Control District, "2018 Bond Projects," August 6, 2018, www.hcfcd.org/media/3065/2018bondprojectlist2018-08-06-1130.pdf; Harris County Flood Control District, "Home Buyout Program"; Texas General Land Office, *State of Texas Plan*.
69. Patterson, *Case Studies*; Thompson, "Buyouts Bring Promise"; Charlene K. Baker, Sherri B. Binder, Alex Greer, Paige Weir, and Kalani Gates, "Integrating Community Concerns and Recommendations into Home Buyout and Relocation Policy," *Risk, Hazards & Crisis in Public Policy* 9, no. 4 (2018): 455–479.
70. Sherri B. Binder and Alex Greer, "The Devil Is in the Details: Linking Home Buyout Policy, Practice, and Experience after Hurricane Sandy," *Politics and Governance* 4, no. 4 (2016): 97–106; quote from p. 103.
71. Patterson, *Case Studies*.
72. Walter Peacock and Chris Girard, "Ethnic and Racial Inequalities in Hurricane Damage and Insurance Settlements," in *Hurricane Andrew: Ethnicity, Gender, and the Sociology of Disasters*, edited by Walter Peacock, Betty Hearn Morrow, and Hugh Gladwin (New York: Routledge, 1997), 171–190; Alice Fothergill, Enrique G.M. Maestas, and JoAnne D. Darlington, "Race, Ethnicity and Disasters in the United States: A Review of the Literature," *Disasters* 23, no. 2 (1999): 156–173; Rebekah Green, Lisa K. Bates, and Andrew Smyth, "Impediments to Recovery in New Orleans' Upper and Lower Ninth Ward: One Year after Hurricane Katrina," *Disasters* 31, no. 4 (2007): 311–335.
73. Alejandro Portes, "Social Capital: Its Origins and Applications in Modern Sociology," *Annual Review of Sociology* 24, no. 1 (1998): 1–24; Robert Putnam, *Bowling Alone: The Collapse and Revival of American Community* (New York: Simon and Schuster, 2000); Daniel P. Aldrich, Michelle A. Meyer, and Courtney M. Page-Tan, "Social Capital and Natural Hazards Governance," *Oxford Research Encyclopedia Natural Hazard Science* (February 2018), https://doi.org/10.1093/acrefore/9780199389407.013.254.
74. Daniel P. Aldrich, *Building Resilience: Social Capital in Post-Disaster Recovery* (Chicago, IL: University of Chicago Press, 2012); Robin S. Cox, and Karin-Marie Elah Perry, "Like a Fish Out of Water: Reconsidering Disaster Recovery and the Role of Place and Social Capital in Community Disaster Resilience," *American Journal of Community Psychology* 48, no. 3–4 (2011): 395–411; Liesel A. Ritchie and Duane A. Gill, "Social Capital Theory as an Integrating Theoretical Framework in Technological Disaster Research," *Sociological Spectrum* 27, no. 1 (2007): 103–129.
75. Sherri B. Binder, John P. Barile, Charlene K. Baker, and Bethann Kulp, "Home Buyouts and Household Recovery: Neighborhood Differences Three Years after Hurricane Sandy," *Environmental Hazards* 18, no. 2 (2019): 127–145.
76. Devon McGhee, *Were the Post-Sandy Staten Island Buyouts Successful in Reducing National Vulnerability* (Durham, NC: Duke University, Unpublished master's thesis, 2017).
77. Heather Saucier, "Buyouts Bring Despair to Those Left," *Houston Chronicle*, May 22, 2003, www.chron.com/news/article/Buyouts-bring-despair-to-those-left-2112807.php.
78. Stephen Klineberg, *2018 Kinder Houston Area Survey: Tracking Responses to Income Inequalities, Demographic Transformations, and Threatening Storms* (Houston, TX: Rice

University Kinder Institute for Urban Research), https://kinder.rice.edu/sites/g/files/bxs1676/f/documents/Kinder%20Houston%20Area%20Survey%202018.pdf.

79. Brian Rogers, "Republican Judges Swept Out by Voters in Harris County Election," *The Houston Chronicle*, November 10, 2018, www.chron.com/news/houston-texas/houston/article/GOP-Free-Zone-Republican-judges-swept-out-by-13376806.php.

80. Kiah Collier, "How Will Texas Help Harvey-Ravaged Communities?" *The Texas Tribune*, February 13, 2019, www.texastribune.org/2019/02/13/how-will-texas-help-communities-ravaged-hurricane-harvey/.

81. Brandon Formby, Aliyya Swaby, and Arya Sundaram, "Texas Leaders Want Voters to OK Property Tax Revenue Growth Over 2.5 Percent. They Couldn't Get 4 Percent in 2017," *The Texas Tribune*, January 31, 2019, www.texastribune.org/2019/01/31/texas-leaders-want-let-voters-cap-local-property-tax-revenues/.

82. Juan A. Lozano, "Officials Propose Texas Coastal Protection Plan," *Insurance Journal*, November 5, 2018, www.insurancejournal.com/magazines/mag-features/2018/11/05/506223.htm.

83. Miles O'Brien, "Hurricane Harvey Leaves Houston with Texas-Sized Problems," *PBS News Hour*, August 31, 2018, www.pbs.org/newshour/show/hurricane-harvey-leaves-houston-texas-sized-problems.

6

HURRICANE IRMA AND CASCADING IMPACTS

Christopher T. Emrich, Sergio Alvarez,
Claire Connolly Knox, Abdul A. Sadiq, and Yao Zhou

Hurricane Irma stands as one of the strongest and costliest Atlantic hurricanes in recorded history.[1] Hurricane Irma made landfall in the Florida Keys as a Category 4 hurricane on September 10, 2017, and affected all counties in the state of Florida,[2] causing 42 deaths and about $50 billion in damages so far.[3] In addition, Hurricane Irma caused widespread power outages, flooding, and downed trees and power lines.[4] Irma capped an active hurricane season by affecting nearly the entire Florida peninsula with strong winds, rain, and storm surges. There were many reports of hurricane force winds in southeast and southwest Florida, through the center of the state, and Irma continued producing tropical storm force winds into the northern parts of the state and southern Georgia (Figure 6.1).

In the days prior to landfall, state and local authorities initially prepared for a direct landfall on the Miami–Fort Lauderdale–West Palm Beach metropolitan area in the state's east coast (Figure 6.2A; population 6.2 million). However, as Irma's projected path moved from east to west, pre-landfall preparations changed drastically with an expected direct landfall on the Tampa–St. Petersburg–Clearwater metropolitan area in the state's west coast (Figure 6.2C; population 3.1 million). Thus,

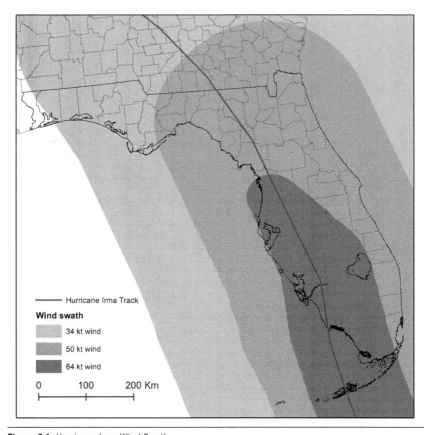

Figure 6.1 Hurricane Irma Wind Swath

Source: Data from the National Hurricane Center. Map produced by the authors

Irma's unprecedented size and strength, coupled with uncertainty in its projected path in the days leading to landfall (Figure 6.2), led to official evacuation orders across the state, including every coastal county east of the Apalachicola River in the Florida panhandle, and all the way to Nassau County in the Florida–Georgia line (Figure 6.3).

Irma produced moderate rainfall across much of western and central Florida (Figure 6.4). The maximum reported storm-total rainfall was nearly 22 inches between September 9 and September 12 in St. Lucie, located in Florida's southeastern coast.[5] The entire southwestern seaboard of Florida received between 6–14 inches of rain and localized heavy

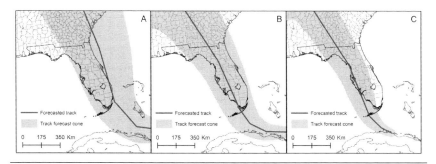

Figure 6.2 Hurricane Irma Projected Path and Cone of Uncertainty

Source: Data from the National Hurricane Center. Map produced by the authors

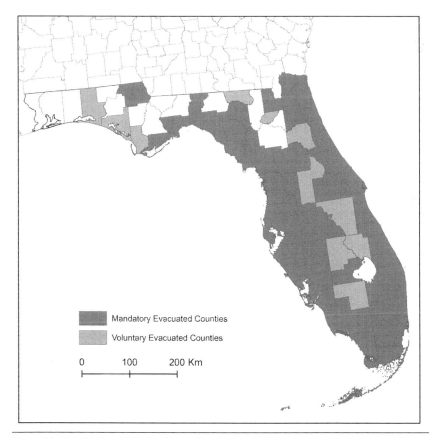

Figure 6.3 Mandatory and Voluntary Evacuations During Hurricane Irma

Source: Data from http://fl-counties.com/sites/default/files/2018-02/Evacuations%20Report.pdf. Map produced by the authors

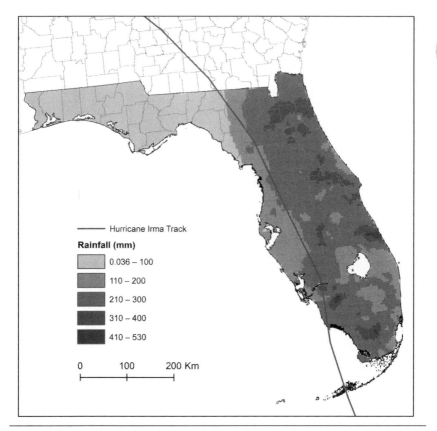

Figure 6.4 Total Precipitation From Hurricane Irma

Source: Parameter-elevation Regressions on Independent Slopes Model (PRISM), PRISM Climate Group, Oregon State University, http://prism.oregonstate.edu. Map produced by authors

rainfall across central Florida in Pasco and Polk counties produced localized flash flooding.

Irma produced moderate storm surge in coastal areas from the Keys north through Naples and along the eastern coast from North of Miami all the way through the northern border with the state of Georgia. South Florida counties saw storm surges in excess of eight feet with Monroe and Miami-Dade recording observed storm surges over 15 feet in some locations. Storm surges along the St. Johns River and its tributaries were also extreme as Irma's large rain bands extended into the Atlantic, driving water up toward the mouth of the St. Johns River. Here, fresh water outflows from rivers slowed the retreat of the storm surges in Jacksonville, elongating the flooding period over the days following Irma. With each rise of the tides, residents along the tributaries of the St. Johns River experienced repeat flooding events for numerous days following the storm, making initial response and recovery efforts very difficult. The convergence of wind, rain, and surges produced significant widespread damage to homes, businesses, infrastructure, and agriculture.

While not the most powerful hurricane in U.S. history, a combination of factors made Irma a record-shattering storm. A path over the most densely populated areas in the third most populous state in the United States threatened more than 18 million people, bringing life-threatening conditions to both coasts and significant inland flooding to rivers and creeks in the central regions of the state. A hurricane of Irma's size and strength will inevitably create serious challenges for impacted local governments. But, as seen during Hurricane Irma, when a storm of this magnitude cuts through a heavily populated state during an already busy hurricane season, underlying vulnerabilities will be exposed, and the ability of the state and federal governments to provide an effective response will be significantly strained. This chapter provides an overview of losses and impacts associated with Hurricane Irma, and through cascading and compounding effects how these impacts exacerbated and exposed even greater vulnerabilities. In addition, we outline how the lessons learned can uncover future risks and vulnerabilities and improve planning for disaster resilience.

Losses and Impacts

This section provides an overview of Hurricane Irma's impacts to Florida's populations in both general terms and the specific losses to property, businesses, agriculture, and infrastructure across the state. It then explores specific challenges for evacuating populations, those requiring emergency shelters, and food needs following Hurricane Irma.

Impacts and Need for Individual Assistance

FEMA's Individual Assistance (IA) Program provides a multitude of services for individuals in disaster-declared counties. More than 2.6 million applicants (12.4 percent of Florida's population) filed for FEMA IA statewide as a result of Hurricane Irma, making it the most widely impactful disaster on record since 2004 (Table 6.1). FEMA's IA program focuses primarily on homeowner-occupied housing repair and secondarily on personal property loss for anyone affected by the disaster. As such, FEMA's loss accounting for renter populations does not include real property losses – a severe deficit in disaster loss accounting. While FEMA has a reasonable understanding of damages to homeowners across the state, it knows very little about damages to rental housing including many low-moderate income rental properties.

Table 6.2 shows the FEMA Real Property Verified Loss (RPFVL) determinations for homeowners in Florida's disaster-declared counties.[6] FEMA Real Property Verified Losses are losses to real property (physical structures) identified by FEMA upon inspection. While every county in the declared disaster area has some applicants, counties in southwest, southeast, and central Florida bore the brunt of Irma's impacts to lives and livelihoods. Interestingly, inspection rates showing where FEMA

Table 6.1 FEMA Individual Assistance Registrants

Year	Disaster	Registrants to FEMA's Individual Assistance Program
2017	Hurricane Irma	2,637,167
2005	Hurricane Katrina	1,706,232
2017	Hurricane Maria	1,120,759
2016	Hurricane Harvey	890,296
2005	Hurricane Rita	792,864
2008	Hurricane Ike	784,431
2005	Hurricane Wilma	580,739
2004	Hurricane Jeanne	553,932
2012	Hurricane Sandy	544,728

Source: OpenFEMA Dataset: "Registration Intake and Individuals Household Program – V1," FEMA, accessed December 10, 2018, www.fema.gov/openfema-dataset-registration-intake-and-individuals-household-program-v1

performed in-person verification of damages varied significantly across the state. Some counties had fewer than 10 percent of damaged homes inspected whereas others had near 30 percent inspection rates. Furthermore, the average FEMA verified loss amounts are indicative of differences in housing types, quality, and impacts across the disaster area. Hendry county, for example, located in southwest Florida and directly in the front right quadrant of Irma, had an average FEMA loss amount of just over $450 whereas the more north central Okeechobee County had more than double that with an average loss of over $1,000.

Housing funds, made available through FEMA's Individual Assistance (IA) program, help to bridge the gap between sheltering/interim housing and permanent housing. These funds are granted to homeowners for limited basic home repairs and both renters and owners for replacement of essential household items as well as rental payments for temporary housing. FEMA IA grant limits aim to bring the home back to a basic level of "safe and sanitary living or functioning condition"[7] and may not account for the full extent of the home's damage or need. Utilizing FEMA's IA program data consisting of information on losses and federal assistance for rebuilding/repairs, rent, and personal property enables a comprehensive view of losses across the impact area. Although comprehensive geographically, FEMA's IA dataset may not be capturing all housing damages caused by Hurricane Irma.

There were more than 2.6 million applicants to FEMA's Housing Assistance Program across the 49 presidentially declared counties. Of these, only 7.3 percent had a FEMA Real Property Verified Loss (RPFVL) assessment; however, this does not mean that the applicant received funding (Table 6.3). Of the applicants with a RPFVL, 18.5 percent (35,645 out of 192,928) received FEMA housing assistance in the form of repair or replacement funds. An estimated $360,956,426 in damage was assessed. For the applicants with an FVL, assessed damages were around $361 million, which resulted in nearly $183 million in received housing assistance to date. Interestingly, an additional $288 million in housing assistance was provided to nearly 260,000 additional applicants who did not have a recorded FEMA property loss.[8]

Table 6.2 FEMA IA Applicant Summary

County	# of Applicants	Number Inspected	% Inspected	Number with Inspected Damage	% With Inspected Damage	Number Receiving Repair Assistance	Total FEMA Verified Loss Amount	Average FEMA Verified Loss Amount
Alachua	9,233	1,263	13.68%	558	44.18%	2,593	$1,674,007	$479
Baker	1,693	414	24.45%	273	65.94%	482	$659,703	$611
Bradford	2,158	561	26.00%	292	52.05%	615	$1,205,229	$688
Brevard	32,993	4,373	13.25%	2,838	64.90%	6,458	$9,540,450	$1,742
Broward	122,766	15,593	12.70%	7,479	47.96%	29,340	$14,146,651	$264
Charlotte	7,791	1,197	15.36%	601	50.21%	2,006	$1,584,170	$563
Citrus	8,340	964	11.56%	520	53.94%	2,373	$898,867	$253
Clay	9,108	1,393	15.29%	884	63.46%	2,183	$5,983,929	$653
Collier	37,613	5,979	15.90%	3,747	62.67%	9,447	$11,993,903	$1,374
Columbia	3,922	404	10.30%	161	39.85%	1,072	$391,758	$466
DeSoto	2,359	677	28.70%	482	71.20%	732	$1,682,032	$409
Dixie	1,275	264	20.71%	192	72.73%	362	$271,142	$299
Duval	42,176	5,921	14.04%	3,263	55.11%	11,287	$11,958,256	$638
Flagler	5,131	752	14.66%	427	56.78%	1,133	$2,632,468	$1,134
Gilchrist	960	128	13.33%	48	37.50%	219	$93,786	$346
Glades	1,180	393	33.31%	265	67.43%	267	$536,707	$646
Hardee	2,379	651	27.36%	497	76.34%	619	$1,492,439	$487
Hendry	4,791	1,362	28.43%	801	58.81%	1,203	$1,492,963	$469
Hernando	8,670	1,122	12.94%	602	53.65%	2,272	$1,532,894	$528
Highlands	14,273	3,073	21.53%	2,000	65.08%	3,077	$3,945,757	$419
Hillsborough	46,500	5,017	10.79%	2,287	45.59%	11,839	$5,394,589	$485
Indian River	5,730	1,146	20.00%	696	60.73%	1,340	$1,520,096	$425
Lafayette	616	73	11.85%	27	36.99%	200	$32,816	$206
Lake	21,194	2,574	12.14%	1,521	59.09%	4,296	$2,746,961	$365

County							
Lee	61,368	11,636	18.96%	6,857	58.93%	16,007	$16,963,748	$494
Leon	1	1	100.00%	—	0.00%	—	$0	$0
Levy	2,584	317	12.27%	146	46.06%	736	$163,140	$173
Manatee	14,111	1,704	12.08%	821	48.18%	3,339	$1,493,204	$325
Marion	25,574	2,221	8.68%	1,253	56.42%	7,616	$3,014,044	$462
Martin	4,257	835	19.61%	366	43.83%	923	$623,278	$295
Miami-Dade	213,532	29,657	13.89%	16,134	54.40%	55,673	$30,356,886	$315
Monroe	18,808	7,115	37.83%	4,467	62.78%	6,850	$38,704,370	$2,313
Nassau	3,992	628	15.73%	368	58.60%	1,055	$1,181,186	$765
Okeechobee	3,245	1,000	30.82%	627	62.70%	684	$1,321,601	$1,037
Orange	63,796	8,898	13.95%	4,864	54.66%	14,449	$9,598,248	$290
Osceola	18,100	2,522	13.93%	1,680	66.61%	2,615	$3,839,746	$309
Palm Beach	66,049	6,287	9.52%	2,952	46.95%	16,883	$5,264,168	$197
Pasco	23,312	2,344	10.05%	1,243	53.03%	5,523	$2,744,093	$384
Pinellas	67,635	7,638	11.29%	3,367	44.08%	19,199	$4,457,544	$272
Polk	53,051	8,420	15.87%	5,355	63.60%	12,695	$12,461,126	$390
Putnam	8,280	1,387	16.75%	868	62.58%	2,272	$1,961,535	$603
Sarasota	16,055	1,529	9.52%	649	42.45%	4,177	$1,203,818	$357
Seminole	26,121	2,428	9.30%	1,312	54.04%	6,315	$3,327,010	$336
St. Johns	7,365	1,034	14.04%	667	64.51%	1,963	$2,812,870	$1,040
St. Lucie	17,128	2,343	13.68%	1,404	59.92%	3,064	$3,651,879	$422
Sumter	4,249	848	19.96%	488	57.55%	1,132	$1,004,397	$439
Suwannee	2,918	479	16.42%	247	51.57%	912	$390,998	$280
Union	718	204	28.41%	116	56.86%	162	$178,447	$1,076
Volusia	30,286	2,638	8.71%	1,512	57.32%	7,566	$4,624,894	$677
Total	1,145,390	159,411	24.71%	88,224	50.75%	287,226	234,753,803	$513

Source: OpenFEMA Dataset: "Registration Intake and Individuals Household Program — V1," FEMA, accessed December 10, 2018, www.fema.gov/openfema-dataset-housing-assistance-data-owners-v1; "OpenFEMA Dataset: Housing Assistance Data Renters — V1," accessed December 10, 2018, www.fema.gov/openfema-dataset-housing-assistance-data-renters-v1

Table 6.3 FEMA Applicant Assessed Damage and Housing Assistance

Hurricane Irma Impact Areas	FEMA IA Applicants	Amount	Average Value
Universe	**2,639,876**	$470,872,021	$178
FEMA Verified Loss (FVL)	*192,928*	$360,956,426	$1,870.94
Received Housing Assistance (HA)	35,645	$182,774,184	$5,128
Received No Housing Assistance (HA)	157,283		
No FEMA Verified Loss (FVL)	*2,446,948*		
Received Housing Assistance (HA)	258,291	$288,097,837	$1,115.40
Received No Housing Assistance (HA)	2,188,657		

Source: Individual and Households Program Applicant Report, FIDA25761_4337 as of 12/22/2017. Received via personal communication on December 22, 2017

Economic Loss

The Small Business Administration (SBA) makes low-cost disaster loans available to qualified businesses. Utilizing SBA business data to understand the financial impact to livelihoods provides a robust and comprehensive understanding of impacts and recovery across the state. According to SBA business loan information, approximately 3,752 applicants had a verified total property loss of $944,498,448 and another 10,867 applicants either withdrew or had their loan applications declined. The average verified loss for all applicants was $251,933, and the median loss was $38,370. Overall, the SBA business data reported total losses exceeding $1.6 billion including verified real property losses of $944 million mentioned above. The additional loss estimates include roughly $417 million from applicants who either declined or withdrew from the program, verified reconstruction loss of $20 million, verified relocation (rebuild elsewhere) losses of $68,193, and verified and estimated losses to furniture, machinery, inventory, and business operating expenses ($314 million).[9]

Impact to Agribusiness and Florida's Crops

Hurricane Irma's path coincided with some of Florida's most productive agricultural landscapes and consequently caused major losses to all segments of production agriculture. The impact of a hurricane on production agriculture goes beyond wind ripping crops from live plants and breaking fruit trees, storm surge flooding aquaculture ponds, and floods drowning animals. Hurricanes disrupt field preparation and planting, destroy critical farm infrastructure such as irrigation equipment and pumps used to provide animals with water, and result in blackouts that deem much of the equipment that remains unusable. Agriculture in Florida is quite diverse, and while many crops were not in season when Hurricane Irma made landfall, all crops were adversely affected. As shown in Figure 6.5, the commercial avocado harvest was underway as usual in south Florida when Irma came through on September 11, with little left to salvage after Irma's winds caused massive fruit drop and tree damage. Winter vegetables like tomatoes and bell peppers were not even planted at the time, but most of the field preparation – fertilizer and pesticide soil treatments, set up of irrigation pipes, and lay down of protective plastic mulch – had already taken place when Irma's winds came through ripping plastic and blowing away treated soil. Growers had to act fast not to miss the profitable winter vegetable season, and used non-treated soil to plant their crops, which resulted in significantly lower yields. Production of oranges faced a combination of these impacts: the harvest was due to begin early in October, just a few weeks after Irma's winds caused massive fruit drop and citrus trees, which were already under pressure from citrus greening disease, were further stressed by flooding in groves. Thanks to Hurricane Irma, the 2017–2018 Florida citrus season made history as the worst on record, with harvest levels as low as they were in the 1944–1945 season, when the industry was just beginning to grow (FDACS 2018).[10]

Agricultural losses totaled over $2.5 billion, 79 percent coming from reduced crop sales (e.g., wind or flood induced product losses, decreased yields, spoiled product, and dead livestock). The remaining sources of loss experienced by agricultural commodity producers included debris cleanup, additional feed or harvest costs, and damage to land, infrastructure, and equipment. As mentioned above, the citrus sector had the most damage (30 percent of the total), followed by greenhouse, nursery, and floriculture (24 percent) and sugar (15 percent).[11]

Infrastructure Loss and FEMA Public Assistance

Infrastructure systems affected by Hurricane Irma included mainly roadways, bridges, and state beaches with little reported damage to wastewater

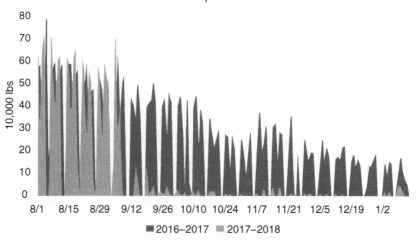

Fresh Avocado Shipments from Florida

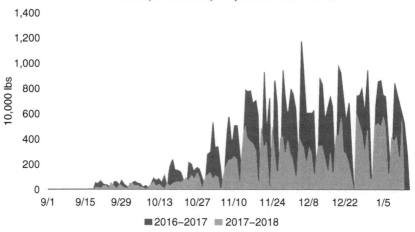

Fresh Tomato (all varieties) Shipments form Florida

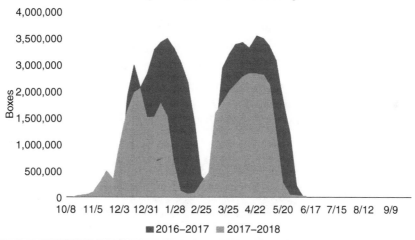

Oranges Reported for Processing

Figure 6.5 Comparison of Weekly Harvests Before and After Hurricane Irma

Source: Data from USDA Agricultural Marketing Service, and Florida Department of Citrus. Graphic produced by the authors

treatment systems or drinking water. The immediate recovery efforts were well documented by the individual recovery support functions and by the initial project worksheets being submitted for Public Assistance by cities and counties across the state.[12]

The FEMA Public Assistance (FEMA PA) program provides immediate assistance to affected jurisdictions for emergency protective measures and permanent repairs to infrastructure and community facilities. The federal share of assistance is generally not less than 75 percent of the eligible project cost, requiring the state or local governments to contribute the remaining 25 percent in cost share. In some instances, the federal cost share can be as high as 100 percent.

FDEM has preliminarily identified more than 35,000 damaged infrastructure sites with a total estimated repair cost of $4.3 billion across all public assistance categories.[13] The federal share of funding was for debris removal and emergency measures. The applicant share of infrastructure damage minus the debris removal and emergency measures categories comes to roughly $387 million for allowable public assistance projects related to roads and bridges, water control facilities, buildings and equipment, utilities, and other.

On a county-by-county basis, there are differences in FEMA PA funding levels (Figure 6.6). Although some counties in south Central Florida were in the direct path of Hurricane Irma, they received notably less federal public assistance funds for disaster response and infrastructure recovery than surrounding counties. This difference in spending highlights inequity in federal recovery fund distribution possibly linked to underlying socioeconomic characteristics of the counties.

Evacuations and Their Impact on Fuel

The Florida Division of Emergency Management (FDEM) estimated that 6.8 million Floridians evacuated.[14] The massive evacuation, considered the largest displacement of people in the history of the United States,[15] led to severe fuel shortages throughout the state. Reports indicate that a large percentage of fueling stations in many areas were out of fuel: 58 percent in Gainesville; 40 percent in Palm Beach; 38 percent in Fort Myers–Naples; 35 percent in Tampa–St. Petersburg; and 32 percent

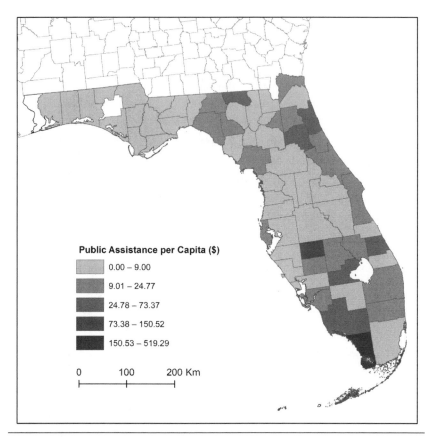

Figure 6.6 FEMA Public Assistance Spending Per Capita

Source: Data on public assistance spending from FEMA, population estimates from the U.S. Census Bureau's American Community Survey. Map produced by the authors

in Orlando.[16] While fuel demand was unprecedented due to the scale of the evacuation, supply factors also contributed to the fuel shortage. Florida has no oil refineries and instead relies on shipments of refined oil products that arrive in barges and tankers at its ports.[17] Hence, port closures and shipment delays resulting from hurricane conditions complicated transportation of additional fuel supplies into the state.

Emergency Shelters and Food

While many evacuees were able to leave the state entirely, a large number of people opted to shelter in place in one of the state's designated shelters.

Pre-landfall shelter counts by the FDEM indicate that 341,258 people registered in official shelters throughout the state before Irma's landfall. Of these, 18,227 people registered as special needs, while 1,516 registered as having some type of medical need. In addition, 21,667 individuals registered as bringing a pet along with them to the emergency shelter, highlighting the need for pet-related capability for emergency shelters. Data from the American Red Cross indicates that by September 16, nearly five days after Irma's landfall, 680 shelters were open throughout Florida. Substantial supplies were required to sustain the population in these shelters. Statewide statistics compiled by FDEM indicate that these commodities included 6.7 million shelf-stable meals and 11.2 million liters of water. These numbers do not include the millions of hot meals and additional aid distributed by relief agencies and the private sector.[18]

Exacerbating Vulnerabilities Through Cascading and Compounding Effects

An event of Irma's magnitude can be expected to cause financial hardship in even the most stable households and businesses, as costs of preparation, cleanup, repair, and rebuilding can add up to hundreds or thousands of dollars. In addition, households and businesses depending on industries particularly exposed to hurricane-related risks such as tourism, food service, and agriculture, may experience days, weeks, or even months without income due to power outages, floods, wind damage, and market shocks that result in temporary or permanent business closures. For individuals and households already experiencing financial hardship, an event like Hurricane Irma can be completely catastrophic and upend their livelihoods. For these vulnerable families, access to nutrition assistance can be the lifeline that puts them on the path to recovery.

Food Needs

Irma's aftermath revealed a massive need for post-disaster nutrition assistance. News outlets from across the state reported long lines as thousands of people waited to sign up for the United States Department of Agriculture's (USDA) Disaster Supplemental Nutrition Assistance Program (D-SNAP), which offers eligible households with one month of benefits.

In heavily populated Miami, demand for D-SNAP was so high that the Florida Department of Children and Families, which administers the program on behalf of USDA, was forced to open the sign-up period for a second round and allow disabled individuals to sign up through a telephone hotline.[19] By November 2017, nearly 1.9 million people had signed up to receive food assistance through D-SNAP.

The overwhelming demand for nutrition assistance after Hurricane Irma should come as no surprise. Prior to the implementation of D-SNAP, there were two major food assistance programs available for the needy in Florida. The first – The Emergency Food Assistance Program (TEFAP) – is a federal program that helps supplement the diets of low-income Americans, including elderly people, by providing them with food and nutrition assistance at no cost. In 2017, TEFAP served 691,854 households, or an estimated 1.8 million individuals. The second is the Commodity Supplemental Food Program (CSFP), which supplements diets of low-income elderly persons. In 2017, CSFP assisted 9,822 elderly individuals with their food needs.[20]

Special Needs Care: Tragedy at the Nursing Home

Irma's aftermath turned deadly as temperatures rose, but electricity blackouts kept air conditioning units off for several days. At The Rehabilitation Center of Hollywood Hills, 12 elderly residents died of environmental heat exposure. According to representatives of the nursing home, from September 10, when the blackouts began, to September 12, the staff monitored the facility's 150 patients, and none exhibited any sign of heat exhaustion. However, around 3 a.m. on September 13, several patients began showing signs of respiratory and cardiac distress. The nursing home's staff called 911 for assistance, and by 6 a.m., Hollywood police officers and paramedics declared a mass casualty situation. Three people died inside the facility and nine more perished hours after being transported to a nearby hospital.[21]

This tragedy resulted in legislation requiring nursing homes in Florida to have a backup power source capable of keeping residents cool during power outages. The legislation requires licensed nursing homes to maintain an alternative power source that can air-condition an area of no less than 20 sq. ft. per resident at a temperature of 81 degrees Fahrenheit or lower for at least 96 hours. Nursing homes must also keep fuel on-site or use piped natural gas.

Puerto Rican Evacuees From Hurricane Maria

Hurricane Maria's impact on Puerto Rico left a majority of the island without power and destroyed much of the infrastructure including schools, homes, and critical facilities. As a result, populations of evacuees headed to mainland USA to find schools, jobs, and safe living quarters. While data to capture this population influx is limited, there are indicators of these impacts. An estimated 300,000 evacuees from Puerto Rico came to Florida based on counts by Florida Department of Education's (FDOE) operations at airports between October 3, 2017, and January 8, 2018, and by FEMA Transitional Sheltering Assistance Program. As of March 20, 2018, up to 3,600 Maria evacuees still resided in hotels across the country with many of those receiving assistance in Florida. Utilizing true counts of enrolled student populations in association with census data on households with school-aged populations from Puerto Rico, estimates of the number of people residing in Florida was 59,196).[22] Evacuee populations are higher in central Florida, including Orange, Osceola, Polk, and Hillsborough, where more than 50 percent of the evacuees appear to be residing (Table 6.4). These evacuee populations may lead to fewer affordable housing units, decreased availability of public resources, and strains on local and regional response and recovery resources.

Uncovering Future Risks and Vulnerabilities

This section explores the vulnerabilities of south Florida to climate change and discusses what Hurricane Irma taught us about south Florida's vulnerability to climate change. It also looks at how south Florida is adapting to the challenges engendered by climate change and concludes with a few recommendations for reducing these impacts.

Vulnerability of South Florida to Climate Change

Climate change continues to pose significant threats to communities all over the world.[23] In the United States, the impacts of climate change are

Table 6.4 Projected Resettlement From Hurricane Maria in Florida

County	Data Sources			Distribution of Estimated Population	Distribution of Estimated Households
	Dept. of Education Enrollment	FEMA Current Mailing Addresses	BEBR Population Migration Flow		
ALACHUA	0.71%	0.42%	0.40%	315	127
BAKER	0.00%	0.00%	0.00%	–	0
BAY	0.21%	0.25%	0.61%	181	73
BRADFORD	0.00%	0.02%	0.03%	8	3
BREVARD	0.79%	1.43%	1.01%	645	260
BROWARD	7.00%	5.70%	6.33%	3,758	1,515
CALHOUN	0.00%	0.01%	0.01%	3	1
CHARLOTTE	0.17%	0.13%	0.00%	71	29
CITRUS	0.02%	0.14%	0.20%	64	26
CLAY	0.33%	0.33%	0.62%	231	93
COLLIER	0.53%	0.23%	1.31%	335	135
COLUMBIA	0.07%	0.04%	0.07%	36	15
DESOTO	0.02%	0.00%	0.21%	29	12
DIXIE	0.00%	0.00%	0.04%	5	2
DUVAL	1.83%	1.74%	2.04%	1,085	438
ESCAMBIA	0.05%	0.04%	0.75%	109	44
FLAGLER	0.24%	0.19%	0.23%	129	52
FRANKLIN	0.00%	0.01%	0.01%	2	1
GADSDEN	0.00%	0.00%	0.02%	3	1
GILCHRIST	0.00%	0.01%	0.05%	7	3
GLADES	0.00%	0.00%	0.02%	3	1
GULF	0.00%	0.00%	0.01%	2	1
HAMILTON	0.00%	0.00%	0.03%	3	1

County					
HARDEE	0.02%	0.01%	26	0.17%	10
HENDRY	0.00%	0.01%	9	0.07%	4
HERNANDO	0.75%	0.62%	402	0.66%	162
HIGHLANDS	0.81%	0.58%	394	0.56%	159
HILLSBOROUGH	7.16%	7.79%	4,789	10.56%	1,931
HOLMES	0.00%	0.00%	7	0.06%	3
INDIAN RIVER	0.17%	0.17%	83	0.04%	33
JACKSON	0.00%	0.00%	5	0.04%	2
JEFFERSON	0.00%	0.00%	2	0.01%	1
LAFAYETTE	0.00%	0.00%	2	0.02%	1
LAKE	3.16%	2.06%	1,434	1.68%	578
LEE	0.00%	1.35%	481	1.37%	194
LEON	0.27%	0.09%	107	0.17%	43
LEVY	0.10%	0.05%	48	0.11%	19
LIBERTY	0.00%	0.00%	1	0.01%	0
MADISON	0.00%	0.00%	1	0.01%	0
MANATEE	0.00%	0.44%	165	0.51%	67
MARION	0.00%	1.30%	467	1.35%	188
MARTIN	0.08%	0.05%	75	0.37%	30
MIAMI-DADE	7.90%	8.11%	4,736	7.97%	1,910
MONROE	0.00%	0.06%	14	0.00%	6
NASSAU	0.01%	0.05%	13	0.00%	5
OKALOOSA	0.03%	0.09%	61	0.28%	25
OKEECHOBEE	0.04%	0.00%	18	0.07%	7
ORANGE	30.33%	27.40%	16,928	27.53%	6,826

(Continued)

Table 6.4 (Continued)

County	Data Sources		BEBR Population Migration Flow	Distribution of Estimated Population	Distribution of Estimated Households
	Dept. of Education Enrollment	FEMA Current Mailing Addresses			
OSCEOLA	13.62%	18.25%	10.60%	8,801	3,549
PALM BEACH	3.64%	2.54%	3.39%	1,865	752
PASCO	1.76%	1.47%	1.20%	905	365
PINELLAS	1.74%	1.73%	2.70%	1,140	460
POLK	7.29%	7.92%	4.86%	4,176	1,684
PUTNAM	0.12%	0.08%	0.14%	62	25
SANTA ROSA	0.13%	0.05%	1.33%	201	81
SARASOTA	0.43%	0.21%	0.69%	235	95
SEMINOLE	4.33%	4.02%	0.08%	1,987	801
ST JOHNS	0.26%	0.24%	0.26%	148	60
ST LUCIE	0.80%	0.49%	2.55%	606	244
SUMTER	0.05%	0.08%	0.45%	83	33
SUWANNEE	0.00%	0.01%	0.08%	10	4
TAYLOR	0.00%	0.00%	0.01%	1	0
UNION	0.00%	0.03%	0.01%	9	4
VOLUSIA	3.00%	2.01%	3.80%	1,636	660
WAKULLA	0.02%	0.00%	0.03%	7	3
WALTON	0.00%	0.00%	0.15%	18	7
WASHINGTON	0.02%	0.00%	0.07%	14	6
Total				**59,196**	**23,869**

Source: Florida Housing Finance Corporation. Projected Resettlement by Florida County of Puerto Rican and Virgin Islander Households from Hurricane Maria Impacts, July 2018. Received via personal communication on July 11, 2018

evident and expected to increase in the future.[24] Climate change impacts such as the warming of the oceans and thermal expansion, coupled with the melting of glacier ice, have resulted in sea level rise, which can have a significant effect on human and ecological systems.[25]

Vulnerability can be defined as the susceptibility to natural and human-made hazards. The vulnerability of south Florida hinges on the interaction between human systems and climate-change–induced natural hazards such as hurricanes.[26] In south Florida, climate change is expected to lead to sea level rise between 9 and 24 inches by 2060, causing impacts such as increased flooding, elevated ground water tables along the coast, salt-water intrusion, coral reef destruction, coastal inundation, and shore-line recession.[27] Where we live is an important factor in determining vulnerability. In south Florida, about 75 percent of the residents live in coastal counties, which account for 79 percent of Florida's annual economy.[28] South Florida has some of the nation's priciest as well as most vulnerable properties.[29] Such properties, especially those located along the coast in south Florida, are susceptible to the effects of climate-change–induced sea level rise.[30] In fact, according to Zillow Group, a housing database company, approximately half a million houses in south Florida could be under water by the end of the 21st century.[31] Furthermore, the warming of ocean waters could have a devastating effect on Florida's coral reefs through a phenomenon known as coral bleaching – when algae that live in a coral die due to high ocean water temperatures.[32] In sum, the combination of climate change-induced flooding and sea level rise, coupled with increased real estate development in south Florida, could serve as a recipe for disasters in the future.

What Hurricane Irma Taught Us About South Florida's Vulnerability to Climate Change

Although disasters have negative impacts on societies, when they occur, they provide communities the opportunity to learn and improve their emergency management systems. Hurricane Irma was no different. This storm helped south Florida realize that is it highly vulnerable to not only hurricanes, but to climate change as well. First, Hurricane Irma exposed the gaps in current local emergency management plans that need filling. For example, the Miami-Dade County Office of Emergency Management's website did not update information regarding available shelters. In addition, the evacuation planning for Miami-Dade County residents, especially those with special needs, lacked effective implementation.

Second, Hurricane Irma revealed a lack of awareness about disaster preparedness among residents, schools, and business employees.[33] For instance, Miami-Dade residents were not sure about what to bring to shelters.

Third, Hurricane Irma showed that poverty is a major obstacle to disaster preparedness. According to a 2017 report by United Way of Florida,[34] 61 percent of the 857,712 households in Miami-Dade County live in poverty or are Asset Limited, Income Constrained, Employed (ALICE is United Way's acronym to describe a group of people who have limited access, constrained income but are employed). Poverty makes it difficult for families to prepare for disasters or to have the financial wherewithal to manage after disasters. In fact, Hurricane Irma exacerbated poverty issues as many Miami-Dade residents' working in industries such as childcare, food service, and retail, who temporarily or permanently lost their means of livelihood due to business closure.[35]

Fourth, the vulnerabilities of south Florida's power infrastructure were exposed. Specifically, Hurricane Irma downed myriad power lines in south Florida, putting a significant number of residents in the dark. As a result, critical facilities like nursing homes and adult living centers incurred fatal losses.

How South Florida Is Adapting to Climate Change

After discussing the impacts of climate change on south Florida, we now examine what adaptation strategies south Florida is using to cope with the challenges posed by climate change. Adaptation refers to the adjustments made by the natural and social systems to moderate changes to the affected systems caused by climate change.[36] The need for adaptation strategies is urgent, as experts have predicted that, on average, the State of Florida, including south Florida, will warm up by 5 degrees (Fahrenheit) and 10 degrees in 2050 and 2100, respectively.[37] When adapting to climate change, there is no one-size-fits-all strategy; the adaptation strategy should be contextual since no two communities are exactly alike. For example, communities differ on their vulnerability to climate change, the resources they have to deal with climate change, and the scale and scope of climate change impacts.[38] Adaptation strategies can promote human systems' ability to adjust and adapt to the negative impacts resulting from climate change.[39]

In response to the threat posed by climate change, counties in southeast Florida – Palm Beach, Broward, Miami-Dade, and Monroe – established a compact to create a Regional Climate Action Plan in 2012. This plan emanates from a significant level of collaboration among these counties to reduce the impacts of climate change. These counties worked together to establish a method for mapping sea level rise that is consistent for the southeast region. In addition, the plan consists of a framework for establishing a sustainable transportation system and resilient communities, strategies to reduce the vulnerabilities of water supply systems, the management of infrastructures, and the preservation of natural systems and agricultural resources. Finally, the plan provides a common set of vocabularies for communicating risk and resilience initiatives to various stakeholders such as the public, elected officials, and decision makers.[40]

Planning for Disaster Resilience

This section provides an overview of emergency management planning in Florida, highlighting specific pre-event planning efforts focused specifically on long-term recovery. It links progress made after Hurricane Andrew with outcomes from Hurricane Irma and portends Florida's future disaster response and recovery process with examples from 2018's Hurricane Michael.

Who Plans for Disasters and How?

Planning is a critical element of the preparedness phase of emergency management. Ideally, all county emergency management offices will have a Comprehensive Emergency Management Plan that includes all hazards and incorporates the whole community. This aligns with the goals of the National Planning Frameworks. Strong interorganizational and governance systems are essential for effective planning and response efforts.[41] For example, in Florida, the Emergency Management Act (Chapter 252 of the State Statutes) requires each county to prepare a Comprehensive Emergency Management Plan and have a designated emergency manager.

Recommendations and lessons learned during the response and short-term recovery phases link directly to long-term planning efforts. Long-term recovery planning is an essential element of a community's resilience, but is often underutilized because of a lack of capacity at the local government level. This was evident in Hurricane Katrina in 2005 when all levels of government failed in their response.[42] This lack of capacity has led to repeated failures in disaster response and repeated policy and organizational recommendations during and after natural disasters.[43]

What Is the Case in Florida?

Florida has a long history of learning from previous disasters and making substantial policy and organizational changes. Most notable was the *Governor's Disaster Planning and Response Review Committee Final Report* (commonly referred to as the Lewis Report) following Hurricane Andrew in 1992. The Category 5 hurricane devastated southeastern Florida and the local governments were quickly overwhelmed with response efforts. Similar to Hurricane Katrina in 2005, Andrew not only brought to light the need to make substantial policy and organizational changes at the local, state, and federal levels of government, but also ushered in a new era of professionalism in emergency management in Florida. Some of the 94 recommendations implemented from the Lewis Report included:

- Restructuring and redefining some emergency support functions to include designated primary and support agency roles;
- Establishing the Florida Division of Emergency Management under the Department of Community Affairs;
- Increasing flexibility in communication options to keep up with changing technology;

- Strengthening building codes and regulations;
- Passing the Emergency Management Act/Chapter 252 of the Florida Statutes;
- Requiring gas stations, hospitals, and supermarkets to have generators; and
- Educating the public regarding donations.[44]

Most importantly, Hurricane Andrew marked the shift from the command-and-control approach in emergency management to a networked approach in Florida and later throughout the United States.[45]

Yet, even with these recommendations implemented at each level of government, we have continued to experience repeated failures in responding to natural and human-made disasters. While planning and preparedness efforts have dramatically increased since Hurricane Andrew and again following Hurricane Katrina, fully implementing them at the local government level has lagged.[46] During the 2004 hurricane season, Florida experienced four hurricanes within six weeks – Charley, Frances, Ivan, and Jeanne – that tested the new policy and organizational changes following Andrew. While many of the changes benefited the response and recovery efforts during those hurricanes (e.g., interorganizational networks established and institutionalized), there remained issues concerning special needs and pet shelters, Emergency Operations Center (EOC) and shelter staff training, and incorporating the private and nonprofit sectors in the Emergency Support Functions.[47]

Hurricane Irma once again tested Florida's emergency management system, especially the new policy and organizational changes from the 2004 hurricane season. In fact, Hurricane Irma was the first major hurricane to make landfall in Florida since 2004, so there were real concerns among many officials that the public had hurricane amnesia. Therefore, emergency managers across the state made an increased effort for public education and reinforced informal and formal network relationships through memorandums of understanding, mutual aid agreements, etc.

In a recent analysis of Hurricane Irma after action reports from 21 central and south Florida counties (68 percent response rate), Knox et al. found strength among multiple resiliency factors across the counties including shelter capacity, health/well-being of internal employees, internal local government collaboration, formal education of staff, and communication capacity.[48] Most of these indicators were policy and organizational recommendations from the 2004 Hurricane Season and were strategic initiatives within the county offices of emergency management. Yet, sheltering remained a concern as a few shelters turned away evacuees. As discussed previously, this was largely because the hurricane's path varied greatly prior to landfall. Many counties were the weakest in referencing the county's land use plans, external institutional change recommendations, long-term relocation of vulnerable populations, and collaboration with faith-based and private sector organizations. Since the 2004 Hurricane Season, emergency managers have strengthened their relationships with the faith-based and private organizations; however, the after-action reports detailed gaps, which led to increased efforts among EOC staff to address community needs. The Florida House Select Committee on Hurricane Response and Preparedness Report raised similar issues.[49]

What Is the Outlook for the Next Disaster?

While there are similarities among human-made and natural disasters that allow jurisdictions the ability to plan and prepare, we must remember that each disaster is unique; as a profession and as a society, we are repeating mistakes. We need a concerted effort to build and sustain the local government's capacity to prepare, respond, recover, and mitigate from a disaster. For example, communication technology continues to evolve, and local governments include redundancies within its communication systems; yet, gaps remain. On October 10, 2018, Category 4 Hurricane Michael, the strongest hurricane ever to make landfall in Florida's panhandle, devastated communities and strained communications between some counties and the state EOC. The backup system was destroyed, requiring the National Guard to escort emergency management liaisons from Tallahassee to the affected area.[50] Additionally, as witnessed in hurricanes Harvey and Irma, four nursing homes did not evacuate residents prior to Michael's landfall.[51]

Summary and Conclusions

Hurricane Irma had a major effect on the Florida peninsula and damaged homes, businesses, agriculture, and infrastructure. Irma represented the first real test of emergency management plans and procedures developed more than a decade ago following the 2004–2005 hurricane seasons. State and local preparedness operations as well as Irma's impacts across Florida's peninsula both highlighted lessons learned and exposed existing weaknesses in policies, plans, and emergency management procedures, heavily testing local government response capacity.

No plan is perfect; however, the planning process is an essential element for a disaster resilient community. Each disaster provides an opportunity to learn and improve, make institutional changes, modify existing policies and plans, strengthen networks, and educate the public. Yet, there remains a lack of capacity at the local government level to implement these changes and execute plans.

Hurricane Irma exposed challenges in planning for, responding to, and recovering from large scale and complex disasters not unique to Florida but rather ubiquitous among disaster impact areas across the nation. Among these challenges remain the following critical areas of needed improvement across the state and the nation:

1. Vulnerable populations should be the focus of preparedness, response, and recovery operations. Plans must more adequately account for vulnerabilities manifesting themselves in a variety of ways across the landscape. Failure to account for social, demographic, economic, and infrastructure vulnerabilities will continue to result in negative impacts to lives and livelihoods.

2. Risky areas will only increase in hazardousness with an uncertain climate future. The time is now to turn plans into actions in the most vulnerable and risky areas of the nation. All mitigation options, including managed retreat from hazardous areas, are viable if we are to successfully build toward a collective sustainable future.

3. Leveraging societal resilience is perhaps more important now than ever before. Options for risk reduction, mitigation, and

adaptation must account for and leverage a growing understanding of and confidence in community resilience as part of an equation for a safe and secure society.

Notes

1. National Hurricane Center, *National Hurricane Center Tropical Cyclone Report: Hurricane Irma* (Miami, FL, 2018), www.nhc.noaa.gov/data/tcr/AL112017_Irma.pdf.
2. Jenna Tyler and Abdul-Akeem Sadiq, "Business Continuity and Disaster Recovery in the Aftermath of Hurricane Irma: Exploring Whether Community-Level Mitigation Activities Make a Difference," *Natural Hazards Review* 20, no. 1 (2019), https://doi.org/10.1061/(ASCE)NH.1527.6996.0000323.
3. "Billion Dollar Weather and Climate Disasters: Overview," National Centers for Environmental Information (NCEI), 2018, www.ncdc.noaa.gov/billions/.
4. Daniella Levine Cava, *Hurricane Irma: Report and Recommendations* (Miami, FL, n.d.), www.miamidade.gov/district08/library/irma-after-report.pdf.
5. John P. Cangialosi, Andrew S. Latto, and Robbie Berg, *National Hurricane Center Tropical Cyclone Report – Hurricane Irma* (Miami, FL, 2018), www.nhc.noaa.gov/data/tcr/AL112017_Irma.pdf.
6. Federal Emergency Management Agency (FEMA), *Individual Assistance Applicant Data Report – FIDA 25761_4337* (FEMA Joint Field Office Individual Assistance Branch, 2017); "OpenFEMA Dataset: Housing Assistance Data Owners – V1," Federal Emergency Management Agency (FEMA), 2018, www.fema.gov/openfema-dataset-housing-assistance-data-owners-v1.
7. Federal Emergency Management Agency (FEMA), "Fact Sheet – Assistance to Individuals and Households," 2011, www.fema.gov/pdf/media/factsheets/2011/dad_asst_indv_households.pdf.
8. FEMA, *Individual Assistance Applicant Data Report.*
9. Small Business Administration (SBA), *Business Applicant Loan Report* (September 10, 2018).
10. Florida Department of Agriculture and Consumer Services (FDACS), *Florida Citrus Statistics 2016–2017* (Tallahassee, FL, 2018).
11. Ibid.
12. "Irma Recovery," Florida Division of Emergency Management (FDEM), 2017, www.floridadisaster.org/info/irma-recovery/; "OpenFEMA Dataset: Public Assistance Funded Projects Details – V1," Federal Emergency Management Agency (FEMA), 2018, www.fema.gov/openfema-dataset-public-assistance-funded-projects-details-v1.
13. FDEM, "Irma Recovery."
14. Greg Allen, "Lessons from Hurricane Irma: When to Evacuate and When to Shelter in Place," *National Public Radio*, June 1, 2018, www.npr.org/2018/06/01/615293318/lessons-from-hurricane-irma-when-to-evacuate-and-when-to-shelter-in-place.
15. Florida Association of Counties, *Hurricane Irma Evacuations Report* (Tallahassee, FL, 2018), http://fl-counties.com/sites/default/files/2018-02/Evacuationspercent20Report.pdf.
16. Nathan Bomey and Alexandra Glorioso, "Hurricane Irma Triggers Gas Shortages as Panicking Florida Motorists Evacuate," *USA Today*, September 8, 2017, www.usatoday.com/story/money/2017/09/08/hurricane-irma-gas-shortages-florida/645747001/.

17. Reuters, "There's a Fuel Shortage in Florida as Hurricane Irma's Path Gets Closer," *Fortune Magazine*, September 7, 2017, http://fortune.com/2017/09/06/florida-fuel-shortages-irma/.

18. Personal communication between authors and Emergency Support Function personnel at the State Emergency Operations Center during the Hurricane Irma response. FDEM data is from ESF 5 Information and Planning and ESF 8 Health and Medical, September 6–2, 2017.

19. Elizabeth Koh and Alex Harris, "It Hasn't Been Easy to Get Food Aid After Irma: You Now Have a Second Chance," *Miami Herald*, November 7, 2017, www.miamiherald.com/news/local/article183221681.html.

20. Personal communication between authors and Emergency Support Function personnel at the State Emergency Operations Center during the Hurricane Irma Response. Data on D-SNAP and other food distribution was provided by FDEM ESF 11-Food and Water, September 9–October 21, 2017.

21. Associated Press, "Deaths of 12 Patients at Hollywood Nursing Home After Hurricane Irma Ruled Homicides," *NBC Miami*, November 22, 2017, www.nbcmiami.com/news/local/Deaths-of-12-Patients-at-Hollywood-Nursing-Home-After-Hurricane-Irma-Ruled-Homicides-459417243.html.

22. Edwin Melendez, Jennifer Hinojosa, and Nashia Roman, *Research Brief: Post-Hurricane Maria Exodus from Puerto Rico and School Enrollment in Florida* (New York, 2017), https://centropr.hunter.cuny.edu/research/data-center/research-briefs/post-hurricane-maria-exodus-puerto-rico-and-school-enrollment.

23. Intergovernmental Panel on Climate Change (IPCC), "Summary for Policymakers," in *Climate Change 2014: Impacts, Adaptation, and Vulnerability. Part A: Global and Sectoral Aspects*, edited by C.B. Field, V.R. Barros, D.J. Dokken, K.J. Mach, M.D. Mastrandrea, T.E. Bilir, M. Chatterjee, K.L. Ebi, Y.O. Estrada, R.C. Genova, B. Girma, E.S. Kissel, A.N. Levy, S. MacCracken, P.R. Mastrandrea, and L.L. White (Cambridge and New York: Cambridge University Press, 2014), 1–32;

24. Fourth National Climate Assessment (NCA4), *Impacts, Risks, and Adaptation in the United States* (Washington, DC, 2018), www.globalchange.gov/nca4; Jerry M. Melillo, Terese C. Richmond, and Gary W. Yohe, *Climate Change Impacts in the United States: The Third National Climate Assessment* (Washington, DC, 2014), www.nrc.gov/docs/ML1412/ML14129A233.pdf; Southeast Regional Assessment Project (SERAP), "Assessing Global Change Impacts on Natural and Human Systems in the Southeast," n.d., https://casc.usgs.gov/projects/#/project/4f8c6557e4b0546c0c397b4c/54c2c1c5e4b043905e018557.

25. Anny Cazenave and Robert S. Nerem, "Present-day Sea Level Change: Observations and Causes," *Reviews of Geophysics* 42, no. 3 (2004): 1–20.

26. Susan L. Cutter, Laurie A. Johnson, Christina Finch, and Melissa Berry, "The U.S. Hurricane Coasts: Increasingly Vulnerable?" *Environment: Science and Policy for Sustainable Development* 49, no. 7 (2007): 8–21.

27. Robert E. Deyle, Katherine C. Bailey, and Anthony Matheny, *Adaptive Response Planning to Sea Level Rise in Florida and Implications for Comprehensive and Public-Facilities Planning* (Tallahassee, FL: Florida State University, 2007), https://biotech.law.lsu.edu/climate/docs/adaptiveresponseplanningsealevelrise.pdf; Environmental Protection Agency, "What Climate Change Means for Florida," 2006, https://19january2017snapshot.epa.gov/sites/production/files/2016-09/documents/climate-change-fl.pdf.

28. Florida Oceans and Coastal Council, *Climate Change and Sea Level Rise in Florida: An Update of the Effects of Climate Change on Florida's Ocean and Coastal Resources*

(Tallahassee, FL, 2010), https://floridadep.gov/sites/default/files/Climate percent-t20Change percent20and percent20Sea-Level percent20Rise percent20in percent-20Florida_1.pdf.

29. Christopher Flavelle, "South Florida's Real Estate Reckoning Could Be Closer than You Think," *Bloomberg*, December 29, 2017, www.bloomberg.com/news/features/2017-12-29/south-florida-s-real-estate-reckoning-could-be-closer-than-you-think.

30. *Climate Crisis: National Security, Public Health, and Economic Threats*, Hearing before the Subcommittee on Energy and Commerce House of Representatives, 111th Cong. 3 (2009) (Testimony of Frank Ackerman).

31. Flavelle, "South Florida's Real Estate Reckoning Could Be Closer than You Think."

32. Environmental Protection Agency, 2016.

33. Cava, *Hurricane Irma*.

34. United Way of Florida, *ALICE Report* (New Jersey, 2017), www.uwof.org/sites/uwof.org/files/17UW percent20ALICE percent20Report_FL percent20Update_2.14.17_Lowres.pdf.

35. Cava, *Hurricane Irma*.

36. Torsten Grothmann and Anthony Patt, "Adaptive Capacity and Human Cognition: The Process of Individual Adaptation to Climate Change," *Global Environmental Change* 15, no. 3 (2005): 199–213.

37. *Climate Crisis*, 2009.

38. National Research Council, *Disaster Resilience: A National Imperative* (Washington, DC: The National Academies Press, 2012), https://doi.org/10.17226/13457.

39. Abdul-Akeem Sadiq, Meredith Ollier, and Jenna Tyler, "Employees' Perceptions of Workplace Preparedness for Climate Change-Related Natural Hazards," *Risk, Hazards & Crisis in Public Policy* 7, no. 2 (2016): 62–78.

40. Southeast Florida Climate Compact, *A Region Responds to a Changing Climate: Southeast Florida Regional Climate Change Compact Counties* (Florida, 2012), www.southeastfloridaclimatecompact.org/wp-content/uploads/2014/09/regional-climate-action-plan-final-ada-compliant.pdf.

41. Thomas A. Birkland, Raymond J. Burby, David Conrad, Hanna Cortner, and William K. Michener, "River Ecology and Flood Hazard Mitigation," *Natural Hazards Review* 4, no. 1 (2003): 46–54.

    Thomas A. Birkland and Sarah Waterman, "Is Federalism the Reason for Policy Failure in Hurricane Katrina?" *Publius: The Journal of Federalism* 38, no. 4 (2008): 692–714.

    Naim Kapucu, Christopher V. Hawkins, and Fernando I. Rivera, "Disaster Resiliency: Interdisciplinary Perspectives," in *Disaster Resiliency* (New York: Routledge, 2013), 23–36.

42. William L. Waugh Jr, "EMAC, Katrina, and the Governors of Louisiana and Mississippi," *Public Administration Review* 67 (2007): 107–113.

43. Qian Hu, Claire Connolly Knox, and Naim Kapucu, "What Have We Learned Since September 11, 2001?: A Network Study of the Boston Marathon Bombings Response," *Public Administration Review* 74, no. 6 (2014): 698–712.

    Claire Connolly Knox, "Analyzing After-action Reports from Hurricanes Andrew and Katrina: Repeated, Modified, and Newly Created Recommendations," *Journal of Emergency Management* 11, no. 2 (2013): 160–168.

44. Lizette Álvarez, and Marc Santora, "After Andrew, Florida Changed Its Approach to Hurricanes," *New York Times*, September 6, 2017, www.nytimes.com/2017/09/06/us/hurricane-andrew-miami.html; See 41, Knox 2013.

45. Christopher Hawkins, and Claire Connolly Knox, "Disaster events and policy change in Florida," in *Disaster and Development* (Switzerland: Springer International Publishing, 2014) 111–127.
46. Hu et al., "What Have We Learned Since September 11, 2001?"
47. Ibid.
48. Claire Connolly Knox, Jasmine Blais, and Juan Lugo, *Resiliency after Hurricane Irma: Analysis of After Action Reports*, American Society for Public Administration Conference (Washington, DC, 2019).
49. Florida House of Representatives, *Select Committee on Hurricane Response and Preparedness: Final Report* (Tallahassee, FL, 2018), www.myfloridahouse.gov/Sections/Documents/loaddoc.aspx?PublicationType=Committees&CommitteeId=2978&Session=2018&DocumentType=General percent20Publications&FileName=SCHRP percent20- percent20Final percent20Report percent20online.pdf.
50. Florida State Emergency Response Team, *Hurricane Michael After Action Report and Implementation Plan* (Tallahassee, FL, 2019), https://portal.floridadisaster.org/SERT/AfterActionReports/Real-World percent20AARs/Hurricane percent20Michael percent20AAR-IP percent201-7-19.pdf.
51. News Service of Florida, "Hurricane Michael Forces Nursing Home, Hospital Evacuations," *WFSU News*, October 12, 2018, https://news.wfsu.org/post/hurricane-michael-forces-nursing-home-hospital-evacuations.

7

CALIFORNIA WILDFIRES

David Calkin, Karen Short, and Meg Traci

The social, economic, and ecological impacts of wildfire are an increasing concern in many areas of the world. In North America, the U.S. state of California stands out in terms of recent – 2017 and 2018 – high-loss fire events. California provides an interesting case study to examine the social, economic, and ecological conditions that influence and are affected by wildfire. California is the most populated U.S. state with an estimated 2018 population of over 39 million, or 12 percent of the total U.S. population. The California population is highly urbanized – 94 percent – with 1.8 million Californians distributed across rural areas. If California were an independent nation, it would rank as the world's fifth largest economy.[1] California has a range of fire-dependent ecosystems – landscapes that have evolved with varying frequency and intensity of wildfire – from Mediterranean chaparral, oak savanna, and conifer-dominated systems.[2] These ecosystems span differently managed geographies, including 100 federally recognized reservations or rancherias, seven other tribal areas, eight national parks, one national seashore, three districts of the Bureau of Land Management, and 18 national forests. Further, development patterns vary considerably from expansive suburban sprawl in southern and central coastal California to relatively rural isolated development in the forested northern portions of the state.

Historically, wildfires occurred throughout California from natural ignitions, such as lightning and extensive use of fire by indigenous people.[3] This fire history had a significant impact in defining the fire-adapted ecosystems of the state.[4] However, beginning in the early twentieth century, forest management largely eliminated the intentional use of fire and lightning-caused fires were suppressed to reduce potential wildfire losses to timber and human development, resulting in increased fuel loading and uncharacteristically dense forest and shrub conditions in many parts of the state.[5] Despite the near elimination of intentional fire use, human ignitions – both accidental and arson – are the predominant source of wildfire in the state.[6] Human-caused fires were positively correlated with population density for most of the twentieth century, with a peak around 1980, but the correlation between population density and wildfires reversed in recent decades, likely due in large part to increasing effectiveness of fire prevention programs.[7] However, increased population density can still exacerbate the overall wildfire problem, with increased probability of ignitions under the most extreme weather conditions, often from arson or by powerline failures.[8]

Anthropogenic climate change has increased the frequency and intensity of weather conditions under which extreme wildfire events can occur across most areas of the globe.[9] The impacts of increased wildfire potential can be mitigated or exacerbated by complex social (e.g., development patterns, wildfire management) and ecological (e.g., expansion of insect and disease in forested landscapes) processes.[10] Indeed, prior to the modern fire-suppression era, the amount of winter precipitation strongly and negatively correlated with the severity of the subsequent fire season. However, that relationship broke down as fire control efforts began to be successful in largely excluding fire under all but the most extreme fire weather conditions.[11]

Future climate scenarios for California include more wet-season moisture as rainfall and less from snow, followed by longer, hotter fire seasons. Thus, in contrast to historical scenarios in which wet winters decreased the likelihood of extreme fire years, such precursor conditions appear to have a diminished mitigating influence on fire season severity in current and future scenarios. Indeed, the 2017 and 2018 fire seasons and concomitant wildfire disasters both followed wet-winter extremes.[12] Moreover, because wet winters tend to increase the production of fine-flashy fuels – fuels that ignite readily and are consumed rapidly when dry – in grass-dominated ecosystems, including power-utility rights-of-way, they appear to increase the hazard from powerline fires.[13]

Emerging housing expansion into or adjacent to fire-dependent ecosystems creates the potential for wildfire disasters. This human expansion into what is termed the Wildland-Urban Interface (WUI) has been influenced by a range of factors, including increasingly expensive urban housing stock and a desire for environmental attributes associated with living near natural areas. WUI development has played a central role in the increased occurrence of wildfire disasters by both increasing the likelihood of accidental ignition or arson and increasing the potential consequences if a wildfire ignites. Although viewed primarily as a western U.S. phenomenon, the eastern United States is also experiencing increased wildfire risk. For example, the 2016 Chimney Tops 2 fire outside Gatlinburg, Tennessee killed 14 people and destroyed over 2000 structures.[14] Martinuzzi et al. estimates that 4.46 million housing units in California were located in the WUI as of 2010.[15] Haas et al. estimate that nine of the top 25 high wildfire risk (high burn probability and high development) counties in the coterminous United States are in California.[16] Wildfire disasters are currently impacting housing availability and affordability through increased building code requirement, restricted zoning, and increased insurance rates better reflective of relative structure risk. Given the devastating events of 2017 and 2018 (Table 7.1), these impacts appear only likely to worsen.

Wildfire Management

Wildfires are unique relative to other natural disasters such as hurricanes, floods, and tornados with respect to the role human activities and response have over these events. In many areas of the world, human-caused ignition – both arson and accidental – are the primary sources of wildfire.[17] Humans are currently the source of more than 80 percent of wildfire ignitions in the United States, but that figure varies by region.[18]

Table 7.1 Ten California Wildfires Included in Major Disaster Declarations of 2017 and 2018

Fire Year	Start Month	Disaster Declaration	Name	Cause	Area (ha) Burned	Structures Destroyed	Fatalities
2017	October	DR-4344	Atlas	Powerline	20,650	783	6
2017	October	DR-4344	Nuns[a]	Powerline	22,622	1,355	3
2017	October	DR-4344	Tubbs	Electrical equipment	14,723	5,636	22
2017	October	DR-4344	Redwood Valley	Powerline	14,609	546	9
2017	December	DR-4353	Thomas	Under investigation	112,757	1,063	23[b]
2018	July	DR-4382	Carr	Vehicle	91,860	1,604	8
2018	July	DR-4382	Ranch	Under investigation	164,081	280	1
2018	July	DR-4382	River	Under investigation	19,568	264	
2018	November	DR-4407	Camp	Under investigation	61,334	18,804	85
2018	November	DR-4407	Woolsey	Under investigation	38,780	1,643	3

Notes:
[a] Six fires that merged together
[b] Twenty-one fatalities were from post-fire debris flows

Source: The causes of five of the fires were still under investigation at press time, but they are believed to be human-caused and likely related to power transmission or related equipment use.

Federal Emergency Management Agency, Disaster declarations by year. Available at www.fema.gov/disasters/year; www.fire.ca.gov/communications/downloads/fact_sheets/Top20_Destruction.pdf

In the higher-elevation forested-mountain ecoregions of California (Figure 7.1) and the Intermountain West, for example, humans are only responsible for around 45 percent of ignitions, accounting for just 25 percent of burned area.[19] However, in the Mediterranean ecoregion of California with predominantly chaparral/brush fires (Figure 7.1), humans are the source of approximately 97 percent of the contemporary ignitions and 89 percent of the area burned.[20] Under most conditions when wildfires ignite, responders can extinguish them; however, under extreme fire weather conditions, such as high wind or aridity, wildfires are more likely to spread and cause significant damage.[21]

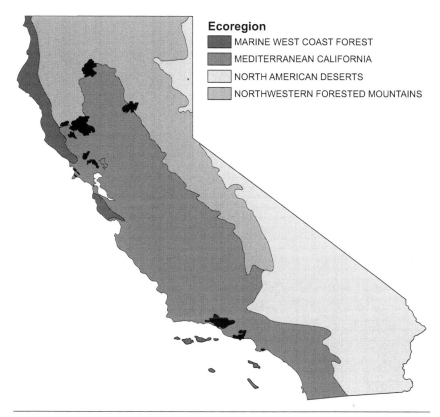

Figure 7.1 Ecoregions of California

Source: Authors. Map redrafted by Erika Pham, University of South Carolina

In response to the increasing damage over the last several decades, the state of California, local and county fire departments, and federal land management agencies including the U.S. Forest Service and Department of Interior have built up the largest coordinated wildfire response system in the world. Several studies have demonstrated that relative to wildfires in other U.S. states, wildfires in California are managed with significantly more suppression resources[22] and at higher cost[23] even after accounting for variation in fire size, environmental conditions, and values at risk. This increased response has had a major impact on governmental agencies charged with wildfire management. Within the California Department of Forestry, now known as Cal Fire to represent the agency's primary focus on wildfires, fire management costs have been continually increasing in response to fire response commitments. Emergency fund fire response expenditures in California reached $773 million in the fiscal year (FY) 2017–2018. Fire management costs for Forest Service Region 5 (California) are consistently higher than other regional expenditures and totaled over $600 million in both fiscal years 2017 and 2018. The rising cost of wildfire response on the Forest Service budget has had a major impact on the agency's ability to meet its core mission.[24] In 2018, Congress addressed the impacts of these rising costs on the Forest Service. Beginning in 2020, wildfire management costs in excess of the historical average will be covered through emergency funding similar to how other natural disaster relief is funded through FEMA.

Box 7.1 Wildland Fire Funding Fix

The FY 2018 Omnibus Spending Package included new budget authority for the United States Department of Agriculture (USDA) Forest Service and Department of the Interior (DOI) agencies to address the increasing scale and uncertainty of wildfire suppression spending. This budget authority begins in FY2020 and lasts through 2027. A total of $2.25 billion of new budget authority is available to USDA and DOI increasing by $100 million each year, ending at $2.95 billion in by FY2027. For the duration of the 8-year fix, the Forest Service suppression account will be funded at the FY 2015 President's Budget request of $1.0 billion. As a reference, in FY 2018, Forest Service wildfire suppression was budgeted at $1.6 billion but total spending was $2.6 billion.

Source: United States Department of Agriculture, *FY2020 Budget Justification*, March 2019, www.fs.fed.us/sites/default/files/media_wysi wyg/usfs-fy-2020-budget-justification.pdf

---

Humans have the ability to significantly alter the amount and arrangement of flammable vegetation through mechanical means (e.g. tree harvest), introduction of fire under controlled conditions (known as prescribed burning), and livestock grazing. Much of what we think of as historical landscapes (pre-Columbian in the United States) were largely shaped by indigenous peoples' use of fire.[25] Current fuel conditions in many areas are influenced by the decisions on how best to respond to emerging wildfires – either aggressively suppressing them when they are small or managing them in a manner to promote beneficial fire effects. Our ability to suppress wildfires when small played a major part in setting the stage for the current uncontrollable wildfire disasters being experienced in California and other parts of the globe. Essentially, the more effort that is put toward suppressing wildfires, the more likely that future fires will burn under conditions where suppression efforts do not work. Brown explained this "wildfire paradox" as being primarily driven by the accumulation of fuels that would have burned had fires not been suppressed.[26]

Beyond the physical accumulation of fuels, there is growing recognition that other systemic factors are leading to increasing suppression demands and associated costs.[27] Calkin et al. explored several additional factors driving the ever-increasing demands of wildfire suppression focusing on systemic feedbacks including public expectations, development subsidies, management agency budget influences, misalignment of fire manager incentives, and climate factors.[28] Collins et al. identified the tendency to underinvest in mitigation since it is difficult to clearly identify and take credit for actions when a disaster does not occur. Thus, the increasing cost of reactive suppression response can crowd out investment of preventive actions such as fuels reduction activities, resulting in the wildfire management organization caught in a "firefighting trap." This concept of a trap comes from business management literature and refers to conditions where a shortsighted focus on addressing immediate problems keeps organizations from addressing core problems that are at the root of these incidents. Further, this mentality of reactive response can become culturally ingrained in how we respond to wildfire that may be inconsistent with our societal goals and intentions.[29] Addressing core drivers of increasing wildfire loss will require an improved understanding of the structure and complexity of the existing fire management system and the role of suppression response as a limiting factor in addressing systemic change.[30] Fischer et al. describe this phenomenon as a socioecological pathology: "a nearly intractable problem . . . that is, a set of complex and problematic interactions among social and ecological systems across multiple spatial and temporal scales."[31]

Wildfire management is complicated as fire transitions from wildlands to areas of human development. Responding to wildfires in the WUI involves considerably more complexity, typically requiring coordination among local, state, and federal fire and emergency management responders. Not surprisingly, management costs for fires within the WUI are significantly greater than for wildfires burning in undeveloped lands.[32] WUI wildfire disasters, fires that destroy hundreds to thousands of homes, occur when wildfire in natural vegetation transitions to developed areas. These fire disasters share several common characteristics.[33] A landscape with high wildfire potential from the combination of burnable fuels and topography experiences an ignition under extreme fire weather conditions – particularly high winds – creating conditions for rapid fire spread. The wildfire then transitions into a community of homes susceptible to ignition, overwhelming both wildland and structure fire suppression efforts. In most WUI fire disasters, the majority of home loss occurs within several hours. Further, under mass-loss events, home-to-home ignition frequently plays a critical role (see, for example, the Coffey Park subdivision in Santa Rosa destroyed by the Tubbs fire). Despite the large geographic scale of recent WUI disasters such as the Camp and Tubbs fires (Table 7.1), home destruction is a localized phenomenon largely determined by what Cohen termed the Home Ignition Zone (HIZ).[34] The HIZ is defined as the characteristics of the home and the vegetation characteristics of the surrounding area only out to 100–150 feet. However, it is important to note that in most urban and suburban settings an individual homeowner may not have ownership of their HIZ.

Recent High-loss Events

Fire has been a pervasive natural disturbance in California's ecosystems for millennia. Ignited by lightning and Native Americans, wildland fires are estimated to have burned at least 1.8 million ha (4.5 percent of the land area) annually in California prior to nineteenth-century Anglo-European settlement.[35] As native populations dwindled and Anglo-European foresters embraced near-wholesale fire control (suppression) practices that became applied across the entire landscape well into the twentieth century, the area burned by wildfire fell to an average of around 100,000 ha per year – at least until recent decades.[36] Increased fuel loadings from long-standing fire-exclusion efforts, in conjunction with weather and climate conditions increasingly conducive to large fire-spread events, have set the stage for fires capable of burning over 100,000 ha – what was previously an average year's total burned area – in a single event.[37] Five such fires have occurred since 2003.[38] Wildfire area burned averaged approximately 265,000 ha per year between 2000 and 2018.[39] However, wildfires do not have to be extremely large to have massive impacts in terms of casualties and property loss. The Oakland Hills fire of 1991, which killed 25 people and destroyed 2,900 structures, grew to just 640 ha.[40]

First introduced in 1953, major disaster declarations have been issued for wildfires in 14 U.S. states.[41] However, they are most commonplace in California. Major wildfire disasters were declared in California during 16 of the 66 years from 1953 to 2018, while the other 13 affected states averaged only two disaster years each in the same 66-year period.[42] California's first major wildfire disaster was declared in 1956, in response to incendiary fires that burned 15,200 ha and spread into the community of Malibu, killing one person and destroying 120 structures.[43] Although brush and forest fires had threatened developed areas in California since Spanish mission days and burned into communities like Malibu repeatedly prior to the onset of formal disaster declarations, the events of 1956, including an earlier wildfire in San Diego County that killed 11 firefighters, brought national attention to the likelihood of even higher loss incidents.[44] The National Board of Fire Underwriters cautioned in the fires' aftermath that "with the encroachment into these areas [mountain brushfields] of more homes without a corresponding increase in the amount of quickly available fire protection, even greater losses are probable."[45]

Indeed, with fires continuing to burn into an increasingly populous Malibu on the average of two-and-a-half times per decade, additional wildfire disasters were inevitable.[46] The community's second major wildfire disaster was declared in 1970, when the 12,000-ha Wright fire consumed 403 structures and killed 10. A third occurred in 1993, when three lives and 350 structures were lost to two fires that burned 22,000 ha.[47] Then, in 2018, the 38,780 ha Woolsey fire prompted a fourth disaster declaration, with three fatalities, 1,643 structures destroyed, and nearly 300,000 people evacuated.[48]

Box 7.2 Disaster Declaration Types

When state and local emergency response resources are overwhelmed by a disaster or emergency, pending or realized, the governor may request aid from the federal government. The decision to provide federal assistance for such an incident is referred to as a "declaration." The Robert T. Stafford Disaster Relief and Emergency Assistance Act authorizes three types of declarations related to wildfires.

Major Disaster Declaration: A decision to provide federal assistance in response to an incident of such magnitude to cause severe damage, loss, suffering, or hardship. It can provide for a wide range of aid, including to individuals or households, state and local governments, and disaster relief organizations. Assistance can be provided for emergency work, temporary housing, crisis counseling, repair or replacement of damaged infrastructure, and other recovery programs. A major disaster declaration must be issued by the president.

Emergency Declaration: A decision to provide federal assistance to protect lives, property, and public health during or in anticipation of a catastrophic incident. Assistance is intended to supplement state and local emergency services (e.g., evacuation assistance, fire control resources) and does not extend to repair or replacement of affected facilities or infrastructure. An emergency declaration must be issued by the president.

Fire Management Assistance Grant (FMAG) Program Declaration (formerly Fire Suppression Authorization Declaration):

A FMAG declaration is intended to prevent a wildfire from developing into a major disaster. It authorizes federal assistance to state and local government entities for fire control and mitigation. It does not provide aid to individuals or households. A FMAG declaration can be issued by the President or a FEMA Regional Director.

Source: Bruce R. Lindsay and Francis X. McCarthy, *Stafford Act Declarations 1953–2014: Trends, Analyses, and Implications for Congress*, Congressional Research Service Report 7-5700 (Washington, DC: Congressional Research Service, 2015), available at https://fas.org/sgp/crs/homesec/R42702.pdf

In terms of structures destroyed, the Woolsey fire joined the Oakland Hills fire to rank among the top 20 most destructive California wildfires on record (Figure 7.2). Notably, 16 of those 20 occurred in the past two decades, with eight occurring in just the two most recent years, 2017 and 2018. All of those eight prompted major disaster declarations, as did the Ranch and River fires of northern California's Mendocino Complex in 2018 (Table 7.1). While not among the 20 most destructive in terms of structure loss, the Ranch fire became California's largest single fire on record, with a final size of 164,081 ha. Currently coming in second on the list of California's largest wildfires is the 2017 Thomas fire, which burned 112,757 ha and killed two people, with post-fire debris flows claiming another 21 lives.[49] California's deadliest and most destructive wildfire came in 2018 when the 61,334-ha Camp fire killed 85 people and destroyed 18,804 structures in the community of Paradise.[50]

Wildfire disasters and other high-loss fire events in California and elsewhere are generally the result of fires that spread rapidly into developed areas under extreme burning conditions that defy most suppression efforts.[51] Given an ignition, the resulting fire behavior, including spread rate and intensity, is a function of fuel conditions, weather, and topography. Unless recently burned or otherwise denuded, the shrublands and savannas of Mediterranean California and the state's forested mountains (Figure 7.1) generally provide ample fuel to carry fire under seasonally dry conditions, with higher fuel loadings leading to higher spread rates and

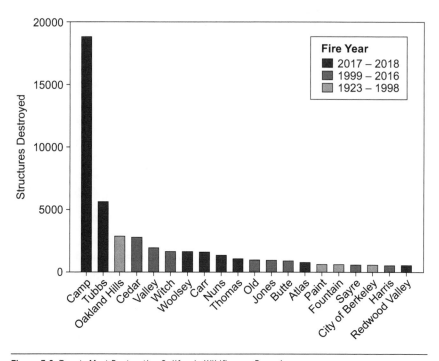

Figure 7.2 Twenty Most Destructive California Wildfires on Record

Source: www.fire.ca.gov/communications/downloads/fact_sheets/Top20_Destruction.pdf

intensities.[52] Moreover, seasonally dry conditions in the brushy Mediter-ranean ecoregion often co-occur with very strong easterly winds known – from south to north – as Santa Ana, Sundowner, or Diablo events. Any ignitions during those events can lead to intense, fast-spreading fires that can accelerate through rugged terrain (e.g., canyons). The vast majority – 97 percent – of wildfire ignitions in the Mediterranean region of Califor-nia are human-caused, including from incendiarism (arson) and downed powerlines.[53] Arsonists have been known to set their fires during these high wind events, which rarely occur in conjunction with lightning, and the winds themselves can be sources of tree strikes to powerlines or other electrical equipment failures that start wildfires.[54] The typical proximity of such ignitions to developed areas increases the likelihood that even a relatively short-duration (e.g., 12 hour) high-speed wind event could spread fire into areas of concern.[55] Under high winds, this includes fire spread through ember transport far ahead of the flaming fire front. Lofted embers can ignite vegetation and structures well ahead of the main fire, even in areas with impediments to surface fire spread (e.g., roads, defensible space) that should be effective barriers under more moderate conditions.[56] As structures begin to burn, they become an additional source of heat and embers and in densely developed areas can result in home-to-home ignition, and, ultimately, urban conflagrations (e.g., in the 2017 Tubbs fire).[57]

California has seen these wildfire disaster and high-loss scenarios play out repeatedly in recent decades (see Figure 7.2),[58] with increasing impacts in terms of property destruction that culminated in 2017 and 2018, when insured losses reached $13 billion in back-to-back years.[59] According to the National Fire Protection Association, the only "fire" – wildland or urban – on record with higher property damage totals than the combined California wildfire events of either 2017 or 2018 was the terrorist attack on the World Trade Center in New York City on September 11, 2001.[60] Moreover, the $13 billion in California fire losses in 2017 was more than all U.S.–insured wildfire losses from the previous decade combined.[61]

The level of devastation from these recent events is largely associated with massive increases in development in and near California wildlands. The 2017 Tubbs fire, for example, burned similarly to and in much of the same footprint the 1964 Hanley fire.[62] However, limited suburban development at the time of the 1964 blaze precluded the level of home losses seen in the Tubbs fire, including those destroyed in the newer Santa Rosa neighborhood of Fountaingrove.

The worst WUI wildfire disaster to date was the 2018 Camp fire, when a wind-driven wildfire grew to 40,000 ha in its first two days, engulfing the forested town of Paradise, in Butte County, California.[63] Butte County's population has grown by 60 percent since 1980, with much expansion into the forested foothills of the Sierra Nevada Mountains, where large wildfires have been historically prevalent.[64] The town of Paradise was one of Butte's rapidly growing foothills communities, expanding from a population of about 8,000 in the 1960s to more than 26,000 at the time of the Camp fire.[65] Its transportation infrastructure had not kept up with the needs of its growing – and relatively older – population. With limited points of egress from the ridgetop town, the extremely fast-moving fire not only destroyed 80 percent of the town's buildings but also claimed 85 lives, many of whom were trapped in their vehicles as they tried to evacuate.[66]

Table 7.2 shows the disproportionately high percentages of persons over the age of 65 who died in the fires. The percentages of seniors ranged from 30.4 percent to 81.7 percent among the fire and post-fire event fatalities. Older age groups and other population groups – children, pregnant women, people with disabilities and chronic health conditions – may give rise to more access and functional needs (AFN) during emergency. Indeed, most of the young adults who perished in the mudslides following the Thomas fire were caregiving for young children or had an older spouse. Without comprehensive emergency planning and preparedness,

Table 7.2 Higher Proportion of Seniors in Fire-Related Fatalities Than Expected

Event	Counties	Percent Elderly Population (> 65 yrs.)	Percent Elderly Fatalities (> 65 yrs.)	No. treated for injury/ hospitalized
Camp	Butte	18.2 (n=229,294)	81.7[a] (n=85)	>60
North Bay	Napa, Lake, Sonoma, Mendocino, Butte, and Solano	17.9 (n=140,973)	70.5[b] (n-44)	>192
Thomas	Ventura, Santa Barbara	15.0 (n=1,302,373)	50.0[c] (n=2)	At least 2 firefighters
Montecito Mudslides	Santa Barbara	14.9 (n=448,150)	30.4 (n=23[d])	>163

Notes:
[a] Percentage is of identified Camp Fire victims (n =71) as of 1/31/2019, available at: www.kqed.org/news/11710884/list-of-those-who-died-in-butte-county-paradise-camp-fire.
[b] Percentage is of identified North Bay Fire victims (n =44) reported 11/28/2017, (accessed 3/13/2019 Identified victims reported here (11/28/2017), available at: www.kqed.org/news/11633757/october-fires-44th-victim-a-creative-globetrotting-engineer-with-the-kindest-heart).
[c] www.latimes.com/local/lanow/la-me-thomas-fire-contained-20180112-story.html.
[d] Number includes with the 21 identified bodies the two missing children whose bodies have not been recovered.

Source: Authors compiled based on U.S. Census Bureau County Population Estimates, 2017

AFNs cannot be adequately supported during an emergency when people may be performing complex evacuation activities for the first time or after a repeated number of times with "evacuation fatigue." Information for individuals hospitalized or injured was unavailable, but it is likely that persons with AFNs were disproportionately represented in these groups as well.

Reflections on the 2017 and 2018 Wildfire Seasons

Reflecting on the wildfire disasters of 2017 and 2018, key takeaways include the following: 1) large, destructive wildfires are not unprecedented and future disasters are to be expected; 2) the current fire management paradigm is not effective at preventing high-loss events; and 3) communities need to plan for wildfires and incorporate engineering solutions much the way that earthquakes and other natural disasters are planned for.[67] Furthermore, Keeley et al. emphasized that "fire management needs to do more to convey to the public their limitations in stopping massive Santa Ana[-type] wind-driven fires."[68] The Thomas fire, for example, grew more than 25,000 ha on two days, December 4–5 and December 9–10, 2018, when it had nearly 2,000 and over 5,000 firefighting personnel, respectively, working to suppress it. It continued to grow by 4,000 ha on eight separate days when there were as many as 8000 firefighting personnel assigned.[69] Fires burning under the types of extreme weather conditions witnessed during the Thomas fire and other high-loss events are typically "controlled" only after those conditions moderate, e.g., after winds subside, rains come, or both.[70] As argued by Calkin, et al. to lessen the inevitable impacts of future events, it is crucial to overcome "perceptions of WUI fire disasters as a wildfire control problem" when they are better framed as a "home ignition problem, determined by home [exposure and] ignition conditions."[71]

The back-to-back high loss years of 2017 and 2018 caused the insurance industry to reconsider wildfire risk as a serious peril in league with hurricanes, earthquakes, and floods.[72] Insurers are increasingly investing in development of fire behavior and catastrophe models that allow them to better plan for and reduce exposure to future high-loss events, including those potentially exacerbated by further climate change. Such mitigating actions can take place in the core business of underwriting, as well as in asset management. California, for example, is one of the few states in which insurers have given premium credits on policies for homes that comply with NFPA's Firewise USA® guidance.[73] However, Firewise status does not necessarily confer disaster resistance under extreme burning conditions. Referring to Fountaingrove's status as a Firewise USA® Community, the NFPA declared that the Tubbs fire – which caused the largest urban conflagration since the 1906 San Francisco Earthquake fire[74] – "could not have encountered a more prepared community."[75] In addition to insured property claims, industry exposure includes losses from business interruption claims associated with wildfire smoke, and impacts to power grids, communications networks, transportation systems, and supply chains.[76] The utility industry is also heavily impacted by wildfire disasters, which in many cases they are suspected or confirmed to have caused.

Many of the recent catastrophic wildfires in California including the Wine Country fires of 2017 and the 2018 Camp fire, appear to have been caused by failure of the power transmission grid. Conditions where electric transmission system failure due to extreme wind events – specifically electric arcing due to tree limbs or fatigue failure of transmission poles – frequently align with conditions conclusive to rapid wildfire growth.[77] Shutting off electricity on high fire risk days could obviously reduce likelihood of catastrophic home loss. However, temporarily shutting off power on high fire risk days could have significant impact to communication networks necessary for effective evacuation, could disrupt local water supply, and ultimately affect vulnerable community members. Prophetically, Collins et al. stated "if powerlines are found to be the ignition source of a destructive wildfire, then it is highly likely that network operators will face substantial claims for damages and compensation."[78] Mitigation actions such as burying cables underground or enhancing the structural integrity of poles and lines along with enhance inspection and maintenance are effective ways to reduce wildfire risk from the power transmission grid. However, the required investment to "fire-proof" the existing grid is likely to be quite expensive. Following the 2018 Camp fire, Pacific Gas and Electric Corporation (PG&E) submitted a wildfire safety plan to the California Public Utilities Commission outlining planned 2019 mitigation efforts totaling $2.3 billion.[79]

While the cause of the Camp fire is still under investigation, PG&E, California's largest power company, filed for bankruptcy in January 2019, asserting that insurance would not cover its costs if it was determined responsible for the Camp blaze. In 2019, the California state legislature grappled with the implications of the current liability statute and the potential impacts to electricity generation and home insurance afford-ability. Although the full implications of recent fire events have yet to play out, it is likely that not only will the cost of electricity and home insurance increase but also that housing markets and future development patterns will be profoundly affected.

Responding to the New Wildfire Reality

Over the last several decades, the impact of wildfire on human and eco-logical communities has increased around the globe. Mass-loss wildfire events are not isolated to the state of California; however, many of the most significant events in North America have occurred there in recent years. Record-breaking wildfires appear to be the new norm with 2018 breaking records for fire size – Mendocino Complex – and community destruction – Camp fire, which broke the previous record set by the Tubbs fire the prior year. Despite the massive increase in fire manage-ment response, it does not appear that the trajectory of losses will likely change unless we fundamentally change how we build and maintain our communities, manage the landscapes, and respond to fire.[80] The diversity of the geography, development, and economic drivers in California are mirrored in the diversity of wildfire behavior and impacts. Community safety and ecological health are challenging problems that will require a comprehensive solution involving land-use planning, fire-safe construc-tion, property maintenance, active forest and rangeland management, promotion of naturally occurring wildfire where feasible, and effective suppression response when necessary.

Climatic and environmental changes are a major factor in the recent levels of loss. Riley et al. demonstrate how complex climatic, environ-mental, and human management drivers determine wildfire potential and over time these factors can flip from driving increased wildfire to reduced wildfire in different social-ecological systems.[81] Over the near term it is largely accepted that we are in a period of increasing wildfire activity in California and most of the western United States and that social and ecological consequences will continue to worsen.[82]

In 2009, Congress' Federal Land Assistance, Management, and Enhancement Act directed the Secretary of the Interior and the Secretary of Agriculture to submit a cohesive wildfire management strategy. From this directive, *the National Cohesive Wildfire Management Strategy* (NCWMS) was established. The strategy established a national vision for wildland fire management emphasizing collaborative work among stakeholders using best available science to achieve the following goals; 1) resilient landscapes; 2) fire adapted communities; and 3) safe and effective response.[83]

There is broad acceptance of the need for increased fuel reduction actions to improve ecological resilience to wildfire and reduce future wildfire risk. However, how fuel reduction goals are met is more contentious and the variety of ecotypes, land ownerships, and management objectives require a variety of management strategies. Increasing the pace of fuel reduction will require a combination of mechanical harvest, prescribed burning, and reduced suppression of wildfires that pose low risk to human development.[84] As argued by Keeley et al., fuel reduction efforts must be based on clearly defined objectives that do not rest on the expectation that even the largest practical fuel breaks will stop fast-moving, wind-driven fires.[85] But instead they may be strategically located, based on local or regional risk assessments, to provide defensible space for firefighting activities likely to mitigate those risks. Another challenge to address is our tendency to isolate the consideration of public land management, community mitigation, and wildfire management response; successful implementation of the NCWMS requires that we look at these goals using a systems approach that recognizes the interaction and feedback among wildlands, communities, and our response.[86] The transition between wildlands and communities defines the potential for WUI fire disasters. Coordinated management strategies in these areas is challenged by the multi-ownership nature of these areas, historic landscaping that has utilized highly flammable species such as Eucalyptus and Monterey Pine, the high cost of mechanical treatments, potential liability for prescribed burning and a lack of cross jurisdictional coordination. Recognizing these challenges, McBride and Kent make a call for implementation of regional commissions granted the authority to coordinate landscape planning, mitigation actions, and wildfire response coordination.[87]

Preparing at-risk communities for the eventuality of wildfire is a complex social and economic challenge. An integrated framework that recognizes wildfire as a necessary ecological process while addressing the vulnerability of communities is required.[88] However, severe wildland fire potential is a necessary but not sufficient condition for the occurrence of a WUI fire disaster. The condition of the structures and their immediate surrounding largely defines loss. Syphard et al. describe community wildfire safety as a complex, multi-variate problem requiring focus on home construction materials, home and landscape maintenance, and land use planning.[89] The state of California has implemented several land use planning and building material requirements to address home vulnerability to wildfire. In 2007 the state implemented the California Building Codes standards requiring the use of ignition resistant materials and design based on the classification system established in Fire Hazard Severity Zone mapping.[90] Additionally, California law requires the removal of all flammable vegetation within 30 feet with additional fire protection required up to 100 feet of all structures.[91] These efforts appear to influence structure loss as Syphard et al. demonstrated, finding that structure age and building material were particularly important in relatively high-density areas whereas defensible space was more critical for reducing home destruction in lower density areas.[92] Enforcement of existing WUI requirements is managed by the individual counties and therefore varies across jurisdiction.

A Shared Stewardship Vision for Future Wildfire Management

Although governmental agencies are currently playing a central role in wildfire risk mitigation and response it is likely that private industry will become an increasingly important actor. Potentially one of the biggest factors that could reverse the trajectory of increasing home loss is the insurance industry. As losses increase and our ability to predict the probability of a home burning due to wildfire improves, insurance rates may make development in high-risk areas unaffordable and require significant modifications of existing homes. Recent attempts to adjust federally subsidized flood insurance to better reflect new risk levels through modifications to the National Flood Insurance Program demonstrated the potential impacts of increasing natural disaster risk. However, unlike flood insurance, homeowner wildfire insurance is not subsidized and therefore potential actions by insurers and the re-insurance industry to fully account for wildfire risk may have a major influence on future development, the ability to rebuild burned structures after a wildfire, and the value and affordability of existing high-risk residence.

To date, the primary response to increased wildfire losses is an increased suppression response.[93] Wildfire suppression will remain a key component of any risk management strategy, with aggressive response to new wildfire starts the dominant response in areas near human development. Emerging research is helping to better understand how landscape conditions influence suppression opportunity to improve the effectiveness and efficiency of initial and large fire response.[94] Changing the way we respond to wildfires will require addressing systematic drivers of decision-maker behavior.[95] Improved understanding of suppression effectiveness that feed decision models to identify and address strategies to mitigate and respond to wildfire under critical conditions is necessary to achieve improved outcomes.[96] If communities in California and other areas with high wildfire potential adapt to become more resilient to wildfire there still will likely be wildfire disasters as the necessary transition occurs. The highest priority in fire response (wildfire and structural) is protection of human life.

More research is needed to understand wildfire impacts to communities. However, taking a whole community approach can help emergency managers learn from those who may be most sensitive to the impacts, and may have perspectives and solutions to integrate into emergency planning.[97] Local emergency management teams are coordinating with community organizations on these six whole community strategic themes: 1) understand community complexity; 2) recognize community capabilities and needs; 3) foster relationships with community leaders; 4) build and maintain partnerships; 5) empower local action; and 6) leverage and strengthen social infrastructure, networks, and assets. These strategies aim to address the disproportionately high rates of mortality and morbidity among certain population groups that not only define by geographic vulnerabilities (e.g., living in WUIs) as outlined previously, but also by a lack of representation and needed resources in emergency management.

As emergency managers take this approach, there is an increasing recognition that one in two community members falls into traditional "special needs population" categories.[98] Today, emergency managers no longer use these categories or the term "special populations" in planning; instead there is a growing focus on what access and functional needs a community might have during emergency preparedness, response, and recovery activities. With needs identified, resources and solutions are integrated into emergency plans with input from specific populations and community organizations.

In California's non-institutionalized population, 14 percent are over the age of 65, 6.3 percent are under the age of 5 years; 11 percent self-report disability (mobility, vision, hearing, cognitive, self-care, and/or independent living); 44 percent over age 5 speak a language other than English; and 17 percent live without broadband internet access.[99] California's institutionalized population includes people of all ages living in nursing homes, assisted living centers, large group homes, prisons, and other settings. Members of these populations are more likely to experience access and functional needs during wildfires; when involved in planning, stakeholders can help build governmental and certain private sector capabilities to perform emergency support functions (ESF) in ways that help the whole community. Planning for AFNs includes solutions in emergency management for evacuating and supporting persons living in poverty and with telecommunications and other communication problems; transportation challenges; caregivers and personal assistants; emotional support and service animals; and electricity for refrigerated medicines, air filters, and durable medical equipment. Community organizations affiliated with these populations usually can represent these needs and how they might be addressed in any scenario including wildfires. Such needs include early evacuation warnings and support to very young children and persons with mobility impairments and related disabilities; how to transport persons using wheelchairs; how to communicate with people who are deaf or blind; and how to make mass care shelters fully accessible to persons with disabilities and equipped for persons managing chronic conditions.

There are increasing occasions to broaden the partnership committed to mitigating the impacts of wildfire, post-fire events, and smoke. The challenges of coordinating across jurisdictions (federal, state, county, local, and tribal) and communicating strategies to reduce wildfire impacts to natural and human-made resources and human health impacts are extensive. Much more needs to be done to strengthen the partnerships between fire managers, emergency responders, and public health entities to plan for the inevitable future emergencies and increase the capacity of individuals and communities to weather these events. Taking a less-traditional approach of working with entities representing populations that are more vulnerable is one strategy consistent with emergency response traditions of worst case scenario planning. Data integration and use is one place to start with forging these partnerships in order to improve outcomes.[100]

Additional financial resources are being allocated at the federal and state level to address wildfire impacts. The NCWMS provides a structure under which cross-jurisdictional mitigation and response planning can achieve positive risk reduction goals. The power in the NCWMS comes from the recognition of the need for cross-jurisdictional coordination and the specific goals of resilient landscapes, fire adapted communities, and safe and effective response. The primary risk factors that are creating the increased wildfire losses we are experiencing vary across different communities and ecosystems. A uniform solution to address wildfire is unlikely to succeed and community wildfire preparation, risk mitigation, and event response will need to be tailored to the local reality. The additional attention and resources allocated to address wildfire are critical in achieving social and ecological resilience in the face of increasingly challenging wildfire conditions; however, new integrated strategies across ownership that identify and address dominant wildfire risk factors will be needed to achieving resilience. Success will be achieved by better learning to live with wildfire not by trying to win a fight with a natural and critical environmental process.

Notes

1. State of California Department of Finance (CDF), "Gross State Product: Comparison to Other Major Countries," 2019, www.dof.ca.gov/Forecasting/Economics/Indicators/Gross_State_Product/.
2. Neil G. Sugihara, Jan W. Van Wagtendonk, Joann Fites-Kaufman, Kevin E. Shaffer, and Andrea E. Thode, *Fire in California's Ecosystems* (Berkeley, CA: University of California Press, 2006).
3. Scott L. Stephens, Robert E. Martin, and Nicholas E. Clinton, "Prehistoric Fire Area and Emissions from California's Forests, Woodlands, Shrublands, and Grasslands," *Forest Ecology and Management* 251, no. 3 (2007): 205–216, https://doi.org/10.1016/j.foreco.2007.06.005.
4. Sugihara et al., *Fire in California's Ecosystems*.
5. Brandon M. Collins, Jay D. Miller, Eric E. Knapp, and David B. Sapsis, "A Quantitative Comparison of Forest Fires in Central and Northern California Under Early (1911–1924) and Contemporary (2002–2015) Fire Suppression," *International Journal of Wildland Fire* 28, no. 2 (2019): 138–148, https://doi.org/10.1071/WF18137.
6. Jon E. Keeley and Alexandra D. Syphard, "Historical Patterns of Wildfire Ignition Sources in California Ecosystems," *International Journal of Wildland Fire* 27, no. 12 (2018): 781–799, https://doi.org/10.1071/WF18026.
7. Ibid.
8. Ibid.; Kathryn M. Collins, Trent D. Penman, and Owen F. Price, "Some Wildfire Ignition Causes Pose More Risk of Destroying Houses than Others," *PLoS ONE* 11, no. 9 (2016): e0162083, https://doi.org/10.1371/journal.pone.0162083.
9. W. Matt Jolly, Mark A. Cochrane, Patrick H. Freeborn, Zachary A. Holden, Timothy J. Brown, Grant J. Williamson, and David M.J.S. Bowman, "Climate-Induced Variations in Global Wildfire Danger from 1979 to 2013," *Nature Communications* 6 (2015): 7537, https://doi.org/10.1038/ncomms8537.
10. Karin L. Riley, A. Park Williams, Shawn P. Urbanski, David E. Calkin, Karen C. Short, and Christopher D. O'Connor, "Will Landscape Fire Increase in the Future? A Systems Approach to Climate, Fire, Fuel, and Human Drivers," *Current Pollution Reports* 5, no. 2 (2019): 9–24, https://doi.org/10.1007/s40726-019-0103-6.
11. Eugene R. Wahl, Eduardo Zorita, Valerie Trouet, and Alan H. Taylor, "Jet Stream Dynamics, Hydroclimate, and Fire in California From 1600 CE to Present," *Proceedings of the National Academy of Sciences* 116, no. 12 (2019): 5393–5398, https://doi.org/10.1073/pnas.1815292116.
12. Ibid.
13. Keeley and Syphard, "Historical Patterns Wildfire Ignition."
14. Jonathan L. Case and Bradley T. Zavodsky, "Evolution of 2016 Drought in the Southeastern United States from a Land Surface Modeling Perspective," *Results in Physics* 8 (2018): 654–656, https://doi.org/10.1016/j.rinp.2017.12.029.
15 Sebastiín Martinuzzi, Susan I. Stewart, David P. Helmers, Miranda H. Mockrin, Roger B. Hammer, and Volker C. Radeloff, *The 2010 Wildland-Urban Interface of the Conterminous United States Research Map NRS-8* (Newtown Square, PA: US Department of Agriculture, Forest Service, Northern Research Station, 2015), https://doi.org/10.2737/NRS-RMAP-8.

16. Jessica R. Haas, David E. Calkin, and Matthew P. Thompson, "A National Approach for Integrating Wildfire Simulation Modeling into Wildland Urban Interface Risk Assessments within the United States," *Landscape and Urban Planning* 119 (2013): 44–53, https://doi.org/10.1016/j.landurbplan.2013.06.011.

17. Food and Agriculture Organization of the United Nations (FAO), *Fire Management Global Assessment 2006* (Rome, Italy: FAO Forestry Paper 151, 2007), www.fao.org/3/a0969e/a0969e00.htm.

18. Jennifer K. Balch, Bethany A. Bradley, John T. Abatzoglou, R. Chelsea Nagy, Emily J. Fusco, and Adam L. Mahood, "Human-Started Wildfires Expand the Fire Niche across the United States," *Proceedings of the National Academy of Sciences* 114, no. 11 (2017): 2946–2951, https://doi.org/10.1073/pnas.1617394114.

19. Ibid.

20. Ibid.

21. Collins et al., "Quantitative Comparison"; Jerry Williams, "Exploring the Onset of High-Impact Mega-Fires through a Forest Land Management Prism," *Forest Ecology and Management* 294 (2013): 4–10, https://doi.org/10.1016/j.foreco.2012.06.030.

22. Michael Hand, Hari Katuwal, David E. Calkin, and Matthew P. Thompson, "The Influence of Incident Management Teams on the Deployment of Wildfire Suppression Resources," *International Journal of Wildland Fire* 26, no. 7 (2017): 615–629, https://doi.org/10.1071/WF16126.

23. Krista M. Gebert, David E. Calkin, and Jonathan Yoder, "Estimating Suppression Expenditures for Individual Large Wildland Fires," *Western Journal of Applied Forestry* 22, no. 3 (2007): 188–196; Michael S. Hand, Krista M. Gebert, Jingjing Liang, David E. Calkin, Matthew P. Thompson, and Mo Zhou, *Economics of Wildfire Management: The Development and Application of Suppression Expenditure Models* (Berlin, Germany: Springer Science & Business Media, 2014); Michael S. Hand, Matthew P. Thompson, and David E. Calkin, "Examining Heterogeneity and Wildfire Management Expenditures Using Spatially and Temporally Descriptive Data," *Journal of Forest Economics* 22 (2016): 80–102, https://doi.org/10.1016/j.jfe.2016.01.001.

24. Sherry Devlin, "Former Forest Service Chiefs to Congress: Wildfire Funding Needs Immediate Fix," *Treesource*, January 23, 2018, https://treesource.org/news/management-and-policy/forest-service-chiefs-fire-funding/.

25. Stephen J. Pyne, *Fire in America: A Cultural History of Wildland and Rural Fire* (Seattle, WA: University of Washington Press, 1982).

26. Stephen F. Arno and James K. Brown, "Overcoming the Paradox in Managing Wildland Fire," *Western Wildlands* 17 (1991): 40–46.

27. David E. Calkin, Matthew P. Thompson, and Mark A. Finney, "Negative Consequences of Positive Feedbacks in US Wildfire Management," *Forest Ecosystems* 2, no. 1 (2015): 9, https://doi.org/10.1186/s40663-015-0033-8.

28. Ross D. Collins, Richard de Neufville, João Claro, Tiago Oliveira, and Abílio P. Pacheco, "Forest Fire Management to Avoid Unintended Consequences: A Case Study of Portugal Using System Dynamics," *Journal of Environmental Management* 130 (2013): 1–9.

29. Matthew P. Thompson, Donald G. MacGregor, Christopher J. Dunn, David E. Calkin, and John Phipps, "Rethinking the Wildland Fire Management System," *Journal of Forestry* 116, no. 4 (2018): 382–390, https://doi.org/10.1093/jofore/fvy020.

30. Matthew P. Thompson, Christopher J. Dunn, and David E. Calkin, "Systems Thinking and Wildland Fire Management," *Journal of the International Society for the Systems Sciences: Proceedings of the 60th Annual Meeting of the ISSS-2016 Boulder, CO, USA* 1, no. 1 (2016), http://journals.isss.org/index.php/proceedings60th.

31. A. Paige Fischer, Thomas A. Spies, Toddi A. Steelman, Cassandra Moseley, Bart R. Johnson, John D. Bailey, Alan A. Ager et al., "Wildfire Risk as a Socioecological Pathology," *Frontiers in Ecology and the Environment* 14, no. 5 (2016): 276–284, https://doi.org/10.1002/fee.1283. Quote is from p. 276.
32. Gerbert et al., "Estimating Suppression Expenditures"; Hand et al., *Economics of Wildfire*; Patricia H. Gude, Kingsford Jones, Ray Rasker, and Mark C. Greenwood, "Evidence for the Effect of Homes on Wildfire Suppression Costs," *International Journal of Wildland Fire* 22, no. 4 (2013): 537–548, https://doi.org/10.1071/WF11095.
33. David E. Calkin, Jack D. Cohen, Mark A. Finney, and Matthew P. Thompson, "How Risk Management Can Prevent Future Wildfire Disasters in the Wildland-Urban Interface," *Proceedings of the National Academy of Sciences* 111, no. 2 (2014): 746–751, https://doi.org/10.1073/pnas.1315088111.
34. Jack D. Cohen, "Preventing Disaster: Home Ignitability in the Wildland-Urban Interface," *Journal of Forestry* 98, no. 3 (2000): 15–21.
35. Stephens et al., "Prehistoric Fire Area."
36. Ibid.; Keeley and Syphard, "Historical Patterns Wildfire Ignition"; Collins et al., "Quantitative Comparison."
37. Collins et al., "Quantitative Comparison"; Nicholas Nauslar, John Abatzoglou, and Patrick Marsh, "The 2017 North Bay and Southern California Fires: A Case Study," *Fire* 1, no. 1 (2018): 1–17, https://doi.org/10.3390/fire1010018.
38. Cal Fire, "Top 20 Largest California Wildfires," California Department of Forestry and Fire Protection, accessed March 9, 2019, www.fire.ca.gov/communications/downloads/fact_sheets/Top20_Acres.pdf.
39. National Interagency Coordination Center, "Historical Year-End Fire Statistics by State," accessed March 9, 2019, www.nifc.gov/fireInfo/fireInfo_statistics.html.
40. Cal Fire, "Top 20 Most Destructive California Wildfires," California Department of Forestry and Fire Protection, accessed March 9, 2019, www.fire.ca.gov/communications/downloads/fact_sheets/Top20_Destruction.pdf.
41. Federal Emergency Management Agency (FEMA), "Disaster Declarations by Year," accessed March 9, 2019, www.fema.gov/disasters/year.
42. Ibid.
43. Pyne, *Fire in America*.
44. Ibid.; FEMA, "Disaster Declarations"; Mike Davis, "The Case for Letting Malibu Burn," *Environmental History Review* 19, no. 2 (1995): 1–36, https://doi.org/10.2307/3984830.
45. Pyne, *Fire in America*, 405.
46. Davis, "Letting Malibu Burn."
47. Ibid.; FEMA, "Disaster Declarations."
48. Cal Fire, "Most Destructive California"; FEMA, "Disaster Declarations."
49. Cal Fire, "Largest California."
50. Cal Fire, "Most Destructive California."
51. Tedim et al., "Defining Extreme Wildfire"; Nausler et al., "The 2017 North Bay"; Jon E. Keeley, C.J. Fotheringham, and Max A. Moritz, "Lessons from the October 2003 Wildfires in Southern California." *Journal of Forestry* 102, no. 7 (2004): 26–31, https://doi.org/10.1093/jof/102.7.26.
52. Keeley et al., "Lessons from October 2003."
53. Balch et al., "Human-Started Wildfires"; Keeley and Syphard, "Historical Patterns Wildfire Ignition"; Jacob Bendix and Justin J. Hartnett, "Asynchronous Lightning and Santa Ana Winds Highlight Human Role in Southern California Fire Regimes," *Environmental Research Letters* 13, no. 7 (2018): 074024.

54. Keeley and Syphard, "Historical Patterns Wildfire Ignition"; Bendix and Hartnett, "Asynchronous Lightning."
55. Nausler et al., "The 2017 North Bay."
56. Ibid.; Keeley et al., "Lessons from October 2003"; Caton et al., "Review of Pathways."
57. Caton et al., "Review of Pathways"; Nausler et al., "The 2017 North Bay."
58. Keeley et al., "Lessons from October 2003"; Jon E. Keeley, Hugh Safford, C.J. Fotheringham, Janet Franklin, and Max Moritz, "The 2007 Southern California Wildfires: Lessons in Complexity," *Journal of Forestry* 107, no. 6 (2009): 287–296.
59. Chris Folkman, *California Wildfires: The New Abnormal* (Newark, CA: Risk Management Solutions Catastrophe Review, 2018), www.rms.com/; California Department of Insurance (CDI), "Insurance Commissioner Reports Insured Losses from November 2018 Wildfires Up to $11.4 Billion – A 25 Percent Increase from Initial Report," Press release, January 28, 2019, www.insurance.ca.gov/0400-news/0100-press-releases/2019/release14-19.cfm.
60. Stephen Badger, "Large-Loss Fires and Explosions in 2017," *NFPA Journal*, November 1, 2018, www.nfpa.org/News-and-Research/Publications/NFPA-Journal/2018/November-December-2018/Features/Large-Loss-Fires-2017.
61. Insurance Information Institute (III), "Wildfire Losses in the United States, 2007–2016," 2019, www.iii.org/graph-archive/208963.
62. Nauslar et al., "The 2017 North Bay."
63. Incident Information System, "Final Posting of Inciweb for the Camp Fire," *Inciweb*, November 25, 2018, https://inciweb.nwcg.gov/incident/6250.
64. Folkman, *California Wildfires*; Paige St. John and Anna M. Phillips, "Despite Fire After Fire, Paradise Continued to Boom – Until California's Worst Wildfire Hit," *Los Angeles Times*, November 13, 2018, www.latimes.com/local/lanow/la-me-paradise-fire-development-warnings-20181113-story.html.
65. St. John and Phillips, "Despite Fire After Fire."
66. Ibid.; Folkman, *California Wildfires*.
67. Actually, these are the same three 'lessons learned' as paraphrased from Keeley et al. (2004), writing on the Southern California disaster fires of October 2003.
68. Keeley et al., "Lessons from October 2003." Quote from p. 30.
69. Nauslar et al., "The 2017 North Bay"; FAMWEB, "2017 SIT Data," accessed March 10, 2019, https://fam.nwcg.gov/fam-web/.
70. Mark Finney, Isaac C. Grenfell, and Charles W. McHugh, "Modeling Containment of Large Wildfires Using Generalized Linear Mixed-Model Analysis," *Forest Science* 55, no. 3 (2009): 249–255.
71. Calkin et al., "How Risk Management," p. 746.
72. Folkman, *California Wildfires*; Tom Sabbatelli, *Introduction*, in 2018 Catastrophe Review (Newark, CA: Risk Management Solutions, 2018), www.rms.com/.
73. Evan Mills, Ted Lamm, Sadaf Sukhia, Ethan Elkind, and Aaron Ezroj, *Trial by Fire: Managing Climate Risks Facing Insurers in the Golden State* (Berkeley, CA: UC Berkeley School of Law Center for Law, Energy and the Environment, and California Department of Insurance, 2018), www.law.berkeley.edu/research/clee/research/climate/california-climate-action/insurance/.
74. Ibid.
75. Lucian Deaton, "No Backing Down," *NFPA Journal*, July 2, 2018, www.nfpa.org/News-and-Research/Publications/NFPA-Journal/2018/July-August-2018/Columns/Wildfire.
76. Mills et al., *Trial by Fire*.

77. Joseph W. Mitchell, "Power Line Failures and Catastrophic Wildfires Under Extreme Weather Conditions," *Engineering Failure Analysis* 35 (2013): 726–735, https://doi.org/10.1016/j.engfailanal.2013.07.006.
78. Collins et al., "Some Wildfire Ignition," p. 12.
79. United States District Court Northern District of California San Francisco Division, "Memorandum Re 2019 Wildfire Safety Plan in Response to Court's January 30 2019 Order," February 6, 2019, https://assets.documentcloud.org/documents/5729391/PG-E-2019-Wildfire-Safety-Plan.pdf.
80. Calkin et al., "How Risk Management"; Thompson et al., "Rethinking Wildland Fire Management"; Max A. Moritz, Enric Batllori, Ross A. Bradstock, A. Malcolm Gill, John Handmer, Paul F. Hessburg, Justin Leonard et al., "Learning to Coexist with Wildfire," *Nature* 515, no. 7525 (2014): 58. https://doi.org/10.1038/nature13946; M.P. North, S.L. Stephens, B.M. Collins, J.K. Agee, G. Aplet, J.F. Franklin, and P.Z. Fule, "Reform Forest Fire Management," *Science* 349, no. 6254 (2015): 1280–1281, https://doi.org/10.1126/science.aab2356; Matthew Thompson, Christopher Dunn, and Dave Calkin, "Wildfires: Systemic Changes Required," *Science* 350, no. 6263 (2015): 920–920, https://doi.org/10.1126/science.350.6263.920-b.
81. Riley et al., "Landscape Fire Increase."
82. Calkin et al., "How Risk Management."
83. U.S. Departments of Interior and Agriculture, *The National Strategy: The Final Phase in the Development of the National Cohesive Wildland Fire Management Strategy* (Washington, DC: U.S. Government, April 2014), www.forestsandrangelands.gov/strategy/thestrategy.shtml.
84. North et al., "Reform Forest Fire."
85. Keeley et al., "Lessons from October 2003."
86. Thompson et al., "Wildfires: Systemic Changes."
87. Joe R. McBride and Jerry Kent, "The Failure of Planning to Address the Urban Interface and Intermix Fire-Hazard Problems in the San Francisco Bay Area," *International Journal of Wildland Fire* 28, no. 1 (2019): 1–3, https://doi.org/10.1071/WF18107.
88. Moritz et al., "Learning to Coexist."
89. Alexandra D. Syphard, Teresa J. Brennan, and Jon E. Keeley, "The Importance of Building Construction Materials Relative to Other Factors Affecting Structure Survival During Wildfire," *International Journal of Disaster Risk Reduction* 21 (2017): 140–147, https://doi.org/10.1016/j.ijdrr.2016.11.011.
90. Cal Fire, "Wildland Hazard and Building Codes: Fire Hazard Severity Zone Maps," California Department of Forestry and Fire Protection, 2012, www.fire.ca.gov/fire_prevention/fire_prevention_wildland_zones.
91. Cal Fire, "Homeowner's Summary of Fire Prevention and Loss Reduction Laws," California Department of Forestry and Fire Protection, September 2007, www.fire.ca.gov/about/downloads/preventionlaws.pdf.
92. Syphard et al., "Importance Building Construction."
93. Calkin et al., "Negative Consequences."
94. Christopher D. O'Connor, David E. Calkin, and Matthew P. Thompson, "An Empirical Machine Learning Method for Predicting Potential Fire Control Locations for Pre-Fire Planning and Operational Fire Management," *International Journal of Wildland Fire* 26, no. 7 (2017): 587–597, https://doi.org/10.1071/WF16135.
95. Thompson et al., "Rethinking the Wildland Fire."
96. Christopher J. Dunn, Matthew P. Thompson, and David E. Calkin, "A Framework for Developing Safe and Effective Large Fire Response in a New Fire Management

Paradigm," *Forest Ecology and Management* 404 (2017): 184–196, https://doi. org/10.1016/j.foreco.2017.08.039.

97. Federal Emergency Management Agency (FEMA), *A Whole Community Approach to Emergency Management: Principles, Themes, and Pathways for Action* (Washington, DC: FEMA, FDOC 104-008-1, 2011), www.fema.gov/media-library-data/20130726-1813-25045-0649/whole_community_dec2011__2_.pdf.

98. June Isaacson Kailes and Alexandra Enders, "Moving Beyond 'Special Needs' A Function-Based Framework for Emergency Management and Planning," *Journal of Disability Policy Studies* 17, no. 4 (2007): 230–237.

99. U.S. Census Bureau, "American Community Survey 5-Year Estimates 2013–2017," March 12, 2019, https://factfinder.census.gov/faces/nav/jsf/pages/index.xhtml.

100. Farshid Vahedifard, Alireza Ermagun, Kimia Mortezaei, Amir AghaKouchak, "Integrated Data Could Augment Resilience," *Science* 363, no. 6423 (2019): 134, https://doi.org/10.1126/science.aaw2236.

8

HURRICANE MARIA IN PUERTO RICO

PREEXISTING VULNERABILITIES AND CATASTROPHIC OUTCOMES

Jenniffer M. Santos-Hernández, Ashley J. Méndez-Heavilin, and Génesis Álvarez-Rosario

On September 2017, Puerto Rico was devastated by the impact of two hurricanes, Irma (Presidential Disaster Declaration FEMA-4336-DR) and Maria (Presidential Disaster Declaration FEMA-4229-DR).[1] These events made explicit the condition of social vulnerability to disasters of Puerto Rico and its residents. The situation in the immediate aftermath, and in months following the hurricanes, is one that has been socially produced over decades and with roots that extend beyond the emergency response phase.

At the heart of the current situation in Puerto Rico is the long-standing development challenge of reducing poverty while also creating a prosperous economy for those living on the island. In the last two decades, the main development challenge for Puerto Rico has been the North American Free Trade Agreement (NAFTA), signed in 1992. Under the terms of NAFTA, tax exemptions exclusively offered by the Internal Revenue Service to U.S. corporations operating in Puerto Rico were phased out. The results of policy changes compounded the multilevel vulnerabilities socially produced over decades, which directly influenced the outcomes of hurricanes Irma and Maria on the island. This chapter explores the preexisting vulnerabilities that led to the catastrophic outcomes of the storms.

Although the eye of Hurricane Irma skirted the island on September 6, 2017, and passed approximately 50 nautical miles north of Puerto Rico, the extreme event flooded many areas, resulting in significant damage to the eastern part of Puerto Rico, particularly the islands of Culebra and Vieques and the municipalities of Fajardo, Loíza, Canóvanas, and Luquillo. In the aftermath of Hurricane Irma, over a million residents of Puerto Rico were without electricity; many were still without the service when Hurricane Maria arrived.

The catastrophic situation in the U.S. Virgin Islands and the British Virgin Islands following Hurricane Irma called for a response from Puerto Rico. Aid drives organized throughout the island to collect supplies for neighboring islands. Voluntary groups coordinated the transportation of collected goods using private boats and vessels. The government of Puerto Rico responded by receiving evacuated patients, tourists, and residents at the San Juan Convention Center.

As Puerto Rico was responding to the emergency resulting from Hurricane Irma, the National Hurricane Center detected an atmospheric disturbance with potential for cyclonic development in the lower tropical latitudes of Cape Verde. On September 17, 2017, eight days after the Governor of Puerto Rico, Ricardo Rosselló Nevares, requested a presidential disaster declaration for Hurricane Irma to assist the island municipalities of Vieques and Culebra, tropical storm Maria intensified into a hurricane. The system developed very quickly; within twelve hours, Hurricane María became a Category 5 hurricane.

As the system was undergoing a process referred to as "eyewall replacement," Hurricane Maria hit Puerto Rico on September 20 at the southeast municipality of Yabucoa.[2] The eyewall touched the coast of Yabucoa at approximately 6:15 a.m. AST. The wind speed upon landfall averaged 155 miles per hour; residents in areas high above sea level felt stronger gusts.

Hurricane Maria resulted in extensive flooding and landslides, destruction of the electrical grid, loss of all telecommunications, collapse of many bridges in the interior part of the island, and flooding of low-lying coastal communities. For the first eight days following September 20, 2017, government officials struggled to provide an initial assessment of the damages, and it was not until September 28, 2017 through executive order that the governor provided a roadmap to guide the immediate response.[3] At the community level, coping with the limited capacity to fulfill the most basic needs was approached with solidarity. Admirable solidarity became the emergent social norm as assistance failed to reach communities, while thousands lost their lives.

Quarantelli points out at least six features of catastrophes that distinguish them from disasters:

1. The built environment is heavily impacted;
2. Local officials are unable to undertake their usual work role;
3. Help from nearby communities cannot be provided;
4. Everyday community functions are interrupted;
5. There is diffusion of rumors by the media, and the situation is framed as socially constructed; and
6. The political arena becomes paramount.[4]

The next sections seek to elucidate how the fragile condition of social vulnerability to disasters of Puerto Rico resulted in a major catastrophe that was very difficult to manage in the hurricane's immediate aftermath, requiring one of the largest emergency response operations in history.

Social Vulnerability to Disasters Before Hurricane Maria

The preexisting social vulnerability mapped in Figure 8.1 shows the distribution of the population living below poverty and the trajectory of hurricanes Irma and Maria. While the stronger winds were felt in the southeast and northern regions of the island, the interior and western region of the island also reported extensive damages, highlighting the fragility of infrastructure systems and the preexisting condition of social vulnerability that prevailed on the island.

The Puerto Rico Emergency Management Agency held a table exercise in May 2017 in which a scenario of a Category 2 hurricane identified areas for improvement.[5] A press conference held at the time emphasized

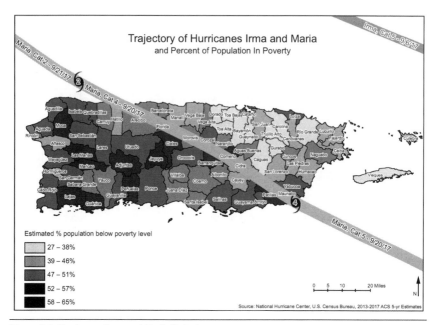

Figure 8.1 Hurricanes Irma and Maria Trajectory

Source: Data from U.S. Census, American Community Survey and the National Hurricane Center. Map produced by Erika Pham, University of South Carolina

the importance of family emergency planning. Alejandro de la Campa, former director of FEMA Caribbean, stated:

> We are ready to support the Government of Puerto Rico and its seventy-eight Municipalities. We hope that nothing happens this year but, if it does, all the governmental machinery [is ready]. Because when we respond to a disaster, we do so as a team: Municipal government, State, and Federal. And to emphasize what the Director of PREMA just did, that family planning is important. That family preparedness for an emergency is important.[6]

De la Campa also emphasized the availability of the FEMA phone application as a tool to facilitate the creation of a family plan:

> We have an app that all citizens can access through any smartphone. It is an app that will help you create your family plan,

will alert you whenever there is any type of emergency, flooding, or any other type of emergency. And at the same time, it will help your family to be better prepared. I recommend everyone to access it because it is something that [is] available to all citizens, including the family, where we emphasize so much family preparedness.[7]

Ironically, after the catastrophic outcomes of hurricanes Irma and Maria, the emphasis on family preparedness seemed like a self-fulfilling prophecy but with little or no government support for what lie ahead. Residents of Puerto Rico relied on their families and neighbors to fulfill their most basic needs for days, weeks, and, in many cases, months. The catastrophic situation that followed is a reminder of the historical reality in Puerto Rico, as in other places, where the immediate emergency response takes place within communities. Almost two years after the event, in many communities, the recovery is also stemming from the commitment of leaders, volunteers, and residents who are actively engaged in home repairs, public area restoration, fundraising, action-oriented planning, community organizing, and overall preparedness activities. While many processes are also taking place at the institutional level, only a small portion of the funding has been received and the delivery of repairs and services has been delayed.

The Economic Situation Prior to Hurricane Maria

For the last decades, Puerto Rico has been in a dire and ever-compounding economic situation. The establishment of the North American Free Trade Agreement (NAFTA) eliminated the exclusive tax haven that Puerto Rico offered to U.S. corporations.[8] Some research and development companies that were located in Puerto Rico are now in Mexico, which has developed industrial and technology hubs offering cheaper labor, production, and lower transportation costs. The elimination of the tax and tariff exemptions to U.S. investors in Puerto Rico accelerated deindustrialization, and the island was both unable to grow a service economy or to portray Puerto Rico as a good venue for investment in the global economy.

In 2015 Governor Alejandro García Padilla publicly announced that the government could not pay the debt accumulated as a result of this economic downtown and emphasized the need to develop a restructuration plan. The situation emphasized the paradoxical outcomes of Puerto Rico's development program. While it is not the scope of this chapter to discuss in detail the development trajectory of Puerto Rico's economy, it is crucial to understand the dynamic pressures and the unsafe conditions that left the island socially vulnerable to disasters.

Puerto Rico has been a territory of the United States since 1898 following the Spanish American War. One of the main development programs implemented in Puerto Rico in the 1950s was Operation Bootstrap, in Spanish *Operación Manos a la Obra*. The development program sought to reduce population growth, poverty, unemployment, and underemployment, mainly through family planning, industrialization, education, and migration to the U.S. mainland. Operation Bootstrap tapped into the main challenges to Puerto Rico's development: unemployment, underemployment, poverty, and high birth rates.

At the beginning of the 1970s, "Operation Bootstrap" was perceived as a resounding success. Nevertheless, the rapid transformation of the island from an agricultural to an industrial society had paradoxical results.[9] After the 1970s, economic growth stalled. The industrialization of the island was insufficient to produce the jobs expected, and federal controls imposed on Puerto Rico over international commercial activities did not allow full integration of the island into the global economy.[10]

Rivera-Batiz and Santiago document that unemployment rapidly increased in the 1970s, reaching 14.3 percent for men and 16.1 percent for women by the end of that decade.[11] The insufficient growth in employment required the public sector – government – to absorb a good portion of the unemployed labor force and forced thousands of residents to join the informal economy and rely on federal nutritional assistance programs.[12] The government of Puerto Rico also became the primary employer on the island.[13]

To compound matters, federal and local tax exemptions and other benefits granted to industries to attract or retain external investment resulted in a fragile tax-based economy. Efforts to finance the design, construction, and maintenance of public infrastructure, increased the government's debt significantly.[14] The arrangement led to a pattern of economic insolvency and increasing public sector employment as a response to the decline in the industrial sector. The pattern of economic insolvency generated a critical and fallible economic reality: Puerto Rico's spending practices and returns were out of balance and not sustainable. May 1, 2006 was the first time in the history of Puerto Rico that the government had to shut down because they were not able to cover the payroll for the rest of the fiscal year. The shutdown was mainly due to the inability of the two main political parties, the Popular Democratic Party (PPD) and the New Progressive Party (PNP), to agree on the establishment of a sales tax to reduce the island's debt. Many perceived the situation as a struggle among political parties, and for the next decade, the commonwealth employed different economic steering strategies. Looking back, the shutdown had little to do with the annual budget and instead called for attention to the burden of decades of governmental maneuvering to promote an unsustainable economic growth that undermined the accumulation of public debt.

The economic instability of Puerto Rico increased as the local government was unable to pay creditors. To tame the spiraling economic crisis, President Obama signed the Puerto Rico Oversight, Management, and Economy Stability Act, known as PROMESA, on October 30, 2016. This controversial law, declared unconstitutional in February 2019 by the U.S. Court of Appeals for the First Circuit of Boston, imposed an unelected Fiscal Control Board in charge of developing an austerity plan to repay and restructure over $72 billion in public debt. The reverberations of this economic crisis in the lives of residents of Puerto Rico were many and diverse. Reductions in and elimination of numerous services ensued. The costs of services increased significantly, and those services offered at a higher cost have become precarious because of the limited availability of operational resources.

Similarly, the postponed maintenance of government-owned infrastructure continues, and its deterioration is evident. The result of the precarious situation in the island has been the most massive migratory wave of residents to the mainland in history, leaving elders behind or responsible for raising grandchildren. The Center for Puerto Rican Studies at CUNY-Hunter estimates that over 135,000 Puerto Ricans relocated to the United States after Hurricane Maria.[15]

Over two years after hurricanes Irma and Maria, and for the years to come, their impact continues to be present in the lives of thousands of Puerto Ricans. The hurricanes, in many ways, represent the ultimate blow to an agonizing economy. In the weeks before the hurricanes, local conversations revolved around the reduction of work hours for public employees and pensions for retirees to balance the fiscal plan that was to be approved by the U.S.–imposed Fiscal Control Board. Thus, the context that drove how Hurricane Maria affected the island was one of precariousness, austerity, and rapid changes to maintain government operations and to avoid legal conflicts with creditors.

Unsurprisingly, the reverberations of the economic situation of Puerto Rico are observable at all levels. At the institutional level, government agencies and decision makers are implementing budget cuts that leave administrative units with almost no operational resources to safeguard jobs and avoid massive layoffs. Thousands have lost their sources of income due to the elimination of temporary positions throughout government agencies or due to closures in the private sector. At the community level, neighborhoods, particularly those recently built, have many vacant units, and community relations are disrupted because members have relocated. Increasingly more geographically dispersed families appear throughout the island, because job opportunities are concentrated in the metropolitan area of San Juan. Ultimately, hurricanes Irma and Maria affected a place that was in a socially, economically, and politically produced crisis, and in the midst of devising reactive mechanisms to steer its stagnant economy as well as other forms of social and cultural capital forward.

Preparedness and Warning Process

The first NOAA product generated for the system that became Hurricane Irma was a tropical storm advisory released on August 30, 2017. The next day, Governor Rosselló issued an executive order directing the Puerto Rico Office of Management and Budget to pay insurance policies to the National Flood Insurance Program. Since Hurricane Georges in

1998, the government of Puerto Rico has absorbed the costs of the flood insurance policies of families with limited economic resources who have received FEMA assistance for property losses.

On August 30, 2017, public advisories issued through different media outlets urged continued monitoring of the event and associated bulletins. The first hurricane watches for Irma on September 3, 2017, were for Antigua, Barbuda, Anguilla, Montserrat, St. Kitts, Saba, St. Eustatius, Saint Maarten, Saint Barthelemy, and Nevis. On September 4, 2017 hurricane watches were issued at 11:00 a.m. AST for Guadeloupe, the U.S. Virgin Islands, Puerto Rico, Vieques, and Culebra, and a tropical storm watch issued for Dominica. At that time, Governor Rosselló declared a state of emergency, canceled classes in public schools, activated the National Guard, and authorized agencies to use necessary funds to carry out emergency activities. As the hurricane continued intensifying, government officials and news reporters expressed their concern about the imminent direct impact of hurricane Irma. Expecting tropical storm winds in the island of Culebra on Wednesday morning, advisories urged residents to complete preparations by Tuesday evening.

At 11:00 p.m. AST on September 5, 2017 Hurricane Irma, now a Category 5 hurricane, was approximately 35 miles from Barbuda. The first wind and rain bands of Irma reached Puerto Rico the next day. At 2:00 p.m. AST on September 6, 2017, the eye of hurricane Irma was located over St. Thomas with sustained winds of over 160 miles per hour. Although the eye of the hurricane stayed north of Puerto Rico, the island of Culebra experienced sustained winds of over 115 miles per hour and wind gusts of over 150 miles per hour. The Municipality of Culebra and the northeastern coast of Puerto Rico sustained the greatest damage from hurricane Irma.[16]

In Puerto Rico, aid drives organized by emergent groups sent food, clothing, medicines, construction supplies, tools, and house products to the British and U.S. Virgin Islands. One of those groups named themselves the Puerto Rican Navy. In coordination with local and federal authorities, the group organized, from a meeting room at a yacht store in San Juan, aid drives at different marinas and locally owned businesses throughout the island. The Puerto Rican Navy organized and carried out dozens of trips to deliver donated goods and to transport passengers to Puerto Rico.

On September 16, 2017 as state and federal agencies in Puerto Rico were increasingly assisting neighboring islands, a tropical disturbance was detected. The warning and preparedness processes were very similar to those undertaken for Hurricane Irma. In different press conferences, the authorities recounted that Hurricane Irma mostly affected the Municipality of Culebra and northeastern Puerto Rico and emphasized that this new event would cross the island diagonally. Residents in coastal and low-lying areas were asked to evacuate. In what many considered a polemical way of communicating the risk faced, Hector Pesquera, Secretary of the Department of Public Safety, on September 18, 2017 mandated that those who lived in flood-prone areas evacuate to one of the 450 designated shelters or expect to die. Shelters habilitated by the local government had enough room to receive 240,000 evacuees.[17]

Impacts and Response to Hurricane Maria

The first day after the event, residents evaluated their losses and most businesses were closed. Some gas stations began opening on Friday, and there were long lines of customers, although many were out of gas because of the demand before the event. There was little information available; only one local radio station was operational. The media covered reports of situations experienced during the event in different parts of the island in the weeks after. Some of those reports were of accidents, unfolding emergencies, rescues, deaths, medical needs, or of those who lost their lives as they were serving or helping others. One of those cases is the situation at the Corozal Police Station as the hurricane was crossing the island. A flash flood completely submerged the station and officers held onto to each other as they were laying down on the roof to withstand the winds. Residents from a nearby housing project and the Fire Department came to their rescue as waters receded. Another case was that of the two police officers in the Northwest part of the island, who went home after a 24-hour shift the morning after the hurricane and were dragged by the Culebrinas River and drowned in the Coloso Valley.

At the federal level, President Donald J. Trump approved a major disaster declaration that only included the eastern half of the island of Puerto Rico.[18] Emergency funds covered individual assistance, assistance for temporary housing and home repairs, low-cost loans to cover uninsured property losses, and other programs to help individuals and business owners recover from the effects of the disaster. Other municipalities were eligible for federal funding for emergency work on a cost-sharing basis. On October 2, 2017, an amended disaster declaration included all municipalities in Puerto Rico. Nevertheless, many residents of Puerto Rico were not familiar with FEMA's DisasterAssistance.gov website, and only those in certain areas of San Juan had internet service in the immediate aftermath.

In the days immediately after the event, residents scrambled for fuel, food, medicine, water, cash, and other essential resources. Long lines gathered at hospitals, gas stations, supermarkets, banks, and stores. Most gas stations limited their sales to $10 per customer. Customers could spend five or six hours waiting in line for fuel and leave without any if the expected delivery truck did not show up.

Damages to Infrastructure and Disruption of Basic Services

The extensive damage to critical infrastructure such as energy, water supply, transportation, and telecommunications increased the impact of Hurricane Maria on the island's residents. This was in addition to losses to houses and for many, access to vital health care services.

Energy

Before the strongest winds of Hurricane Maria, most of the electric grid had failed and as the event crossed through the island, it destroyed the deteriorated energy distribution system. The whole island of Puerto Rico was without electricity the morning after Maria. Some areas had been without electricity since Hurricane Irma. Families relied mostly on generators fueled with gasoline or natural gas. Figure 8.2 shows the percentage of gas stations that opened in the weeks after the event. The Army

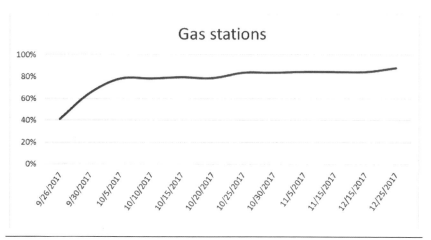

Figure 8.2 Percentage of Gas Stations Opened After Hurricane Maria

Source: StatusPR, www.status.pr. Figure drawn by authors

Corps of Engineers was tasked with the reconstruction of the power grid, and repairs required over 50,000 wood and cement poles and thousands of kilometers of wire. While the energy grid has been restored, the task is incomplete as many poles still need to be replaced and damaged wires must be removed. Several initiatives supporting a transition to alternative energy sources have emerged.

Telecommunications

While there were many cascading impacts associated with the destruction of the energy grid, telecommunication and water services also failed. The first updates on the status of cell phone towers became available on September 28. At that point, 92 percent of the cell phone towers were not working. There was also no Internet or landline phone service. The lack of telecommunications and electricity made it very difficult for emergency responders at the municipal level to communicate with regional or with the State Emergency Management Bureau. Volunteer ham radio operators were vital in facilitating communications throughout the island for the Red Cross, hospital facilities, and emergency management agencies. Only a very small portion of San Juan had limited telecommunication. As days passed, mayors and municipal personnel slowly started visiting the Emergency Operations Center relocated from the agency's headquarters to the San Juan Convention Center in Miramar.

Water

There was limited access to potable water in the aftermath of the event. Water storage, distribution, sewage, and treatment services declined, mainly because of the lack of electricity. According to data provided by the government of Puerto Rico, over half of the customers (52 percent) were without potable water on October 4, 2017.[19] In some areas, residents collected water from streams and rivers for domestic use. The use of contaminated water resulted in over 120 cases of leptospirosis with four associated deaths by the end of October 2017.[20] In many cases, people would go to sites identified by word of mouth and collect water from streams without knowing whether dead animals and other pollutants could have contaminated the water.

Damage to the Guajataca dam, located in the municipality of Isabela, caused another major disruption to water services in the northwest part of the island. Part of the dam collapsed after Hurricane Maria and the dam is still under reconstruction. To repair the dam, reservoir water levels were lowered and a 24-hour water-rationing program initiated. Different areas of the region only received water every other day, instead of having daily water service.

Ports, Airports, and Ground Transportation

The United States is the leading trading partner of Puerto Rico. Section 27 of the U.S. Merchant Marine Act of 1920, known as the Jones Act, regulates maritime commerce and requires that goods transported between U.S. ports must use U.S. vessels. In Puerto Rico, over 80 percent of food is imported, and there is a state tax on stored inventory or goods. Therefore, continuity in the supply chain is essential to ensure the availability of products. The ports of San Juan reported no significant damages, which allowed them to reopen on September 23, 2017. However, there were delays in the release of containers for ground transportation because several main roads were inaccessible, drivers did not have access to fuel, or consignees were not able to receive the goods.

The main airport in San Juan partially reopened for emergency flights in the afternoon of September 21, 2017. Airport congestion was immediate with relief supplies and personnel flying in, leaving only a limited number of authorized flights to Florida for emergency evacuations. As weeks passed and as the public complained about the increasing costs of airfares between Puerto Rico and the U.S. mainland, airlines denied the claims and published the capped prices offered.

Health Services

Health services were another of the functions that showed great difficulties in the storm's aftermath. Before Hurricane Maria, the privatized health care system of Puerto Rico already faced great challenges. Close to half of Puerto Ricans rely on Medicaid, and unlike states, the territory of Puerto Rico has an annual spending cap for services.

Because Hurricane Maria had severely affected transportation systems, many residents could not reach a health care facility. Those who were able to reach a regional hospital often found only limited services were available and that only some patients could be admitted in the absence of electricity. In remote areas, it was virtually impossible to visit a health care facility. Regularly, the closest health care facility in remote areas, such as the municipalities of Maricao and Orocovis, is over an hour away. Health care services providers outside of the Metropolitan area, including pharmacies, dialysis centers, and doctors, offered services for weeks, and in more remote areas for months, without electricity, water, telecommunications, or access to computers.[21] Even in urban areas, residents often lacked information on services available. An example of that situation is the limited use and understanding of the services provided by the U.S.N.S. Comfort. Doctors and patients alike were often unclear of the services available at the hospital ship.

Access to a healthy diet was also difficult in the immediate aftermath of the event. Many individuals with chronic health conditions spent weeks on a diet high in salt and sugars. Community kitchens emerged to facilitate access to hot meals and as a point of convergence for local and visiting volunteers to provide their services. Food delivery was another

area of concern during the immediate response because some of the contractors hired by emergency response agencies to prepare and distribute
meals could not complete the task.

Housing Losses and Damages

According to FEMA, owners built 45% of the housing units in Puerto
Rico, developers built the rest of the units, and professional engineers or
architects certified the latter.[22] According to FEMA reports there were
772,682 valid home owner assistance registrations and 339,380 valid
renter registrations. FEMA only approved 40% of the owners and 42%
of the renters who applied.[23] Following FEMA inspections, there are
over 307,000 homes classified as having moderate, major, or total damage. Many of the homes affected had roof damage, and in the interior
part of the island, many homes had their structure compromised because
of landslides. One of the challenges, in terms of housing and population
distribution, is that many elders in remote areas experienced damage to
their homes. That was the case of the home in Figure 8.3. To compound

Figure 8.3 Damaged Home in Puerto Rico

Source: Photo by author

matters, in many rural areas affected by landslides, younger generations moved away from their communities and were not present during the event. Many elders took upon themselves the difficult task of cleaning up the dirt that was around or inside their homes, or of repairing their homes with little support from others. Solidarity was observed, and many relied on a neighbor for help, in the absence of familial support.

Disruption of Economic Activities

As is the case in all disasters, those affected by extreme events, including businesses, actively try to return to their normal activities. Research has found that while structural damage is a poor predictor of economic disruption, damage to lifeline infrastructure is an important factor.[24] Between September 25 and October 6, 2017, visits to 154 businesses located along the main commercial avenues of San Juan allowed us to document the status of activities.[25] Of the businesses visited, only 45 (29%) had opened. Fifty-four businesses showed visible structural damage, while nineteen of those with visible damage were open at the time of the visit. Further research needs to show how the lack of basic services in the aftermath of Hurricane Maria affected businesses, particularly in areas where those services took months to restore.

Businesses rely on transportation to acquire the commodities they need to produce and to maintain their relationships with their clients. Paradoxically, those businesses based on local resources and clients probably do better than their counterparts do. During field observations, it was common to see a small business open their doors, or whatever was left of its structure, and improvise services they could offer given the circumstances. Barbers figured out a way to power their clippers with their vehicles. In some cases, barbers would plug their clippers to a car lighter power inverter. Other barbers were using their car batteries directly. Figure 8.4 captures a barber in San Juan who connected his clippers to his car and was serving customers outside of his shop.

In other cases, small business structures were destroyed, or owners temporarily relocated to the mainland. Figure 8.5 shows the Fish Market at Crash Boat Beach in the Municipality of Aguadilla, located in the northwest coast of the island. Fishers in Aguadilla are building a

Figure 8.4 Makeshift Barbershop

Source: Photo by author

Figure 8.5 Fish Market, Aguadilla

Source: Photo by author

new site to sell their product very close to the old structure. Concerns have been raised about the proximity to the shore of the new structure, however.

Four Scenarios in the Immediate Aftermath

The impact of hurricane Maria halted the daily routines of Puerto Ricans. Most of the island lost electricity as the first wind bands of the hurricane made landfall. Most residents of Puerto Rico had to adapt to a life without electricity for months. Articulating some of the challenges that residents of Puerto Rico experienced during the blackout after Hurricane Maria is a challenging task. The blackout, now recognized as the longest one in U.S. history, accounts for a substantial portion of the death toll. According to the Milken Institute of Public Health at The George Washington University, total excess mortality from September 2017 to January 2018, using the migration displacement scenario, is an estimated 2,975.[26]

For most, the weeks following hurricane Maria involved long lines to obtain gas, ice, cash, and generators. Even after service was restored, most areas experienced outages. A photograph of doctors working with flashlights in the surgery room of Centro Medico, the main hospital of Puerto Rico, circulated in social media for weeks. In many areas, the service took several months to be reestablished. Although daily updates on the progress made to restore the generation of electricity were available, there was no information on the number of residents that were receiving the service. The lack of information on customer demand and accidents in the reconstruction of the grid also caused disruptions to the service.

While the whole island experienced a major catastrophe resulting from Hurricane Maria, there were many contrasts in the experiences of residents. Those with more resources were able to adapt slowly, as much as possible, to their new reality. Some left the island and stayed with relatives for weeks or months. Those who stayed returned to their jobs without having power service at home and many used the moratorium on the payment of mortgages to be able to cover the costs of fuel to energize their homes for part of the day. Most families had a schedule to accommodate their domestic activities to the availability of electricity.

Activities such as brewing coffee, cooking, washing cloth, or taking a hot shower became a privilege. A balanced meal and access to health services also became a privilege for those with more resources. Older males (65+) living in municipalities with low socioeconomic development had a 45 percent higher risk of death.[27] The following sections present field observations made in the first three weeks after the event. The island is divided into four areas or regions to highlight the differentiated patterns observed. The four areas described include field observations conducted in the San Juan Metropolitan area, coastal municipalities, the interior/mountainous region, and the southeast.

San Juan Metropolitan Area

The metropolitan area of San Juan generally had more resources than other areas of Puerto Rico after Hurricane Maria. As the capital of Puerto Rico, San Juan is the center of social, economic, political, and cultural activities on the island. However, it is essential to highlight that the experience of those living in San Juan was not uniform. The San Juan Metropolitan area houses a very diverse population, although often only portrayed as a touristic destination. Outside of the hotels in El Condado, Isla Verde, and Old San Juan, residents of those same areas had to organize *in situ* to respond to the immediate needs of their neighbors. Every social class was affected, but residents living in marginalized and disadvantaged communities, occupants without title deeds, households with very limited financial resources, patients with chronic ailments, elders living alone, and employees that were laid off and without a stable source of income seemed to be affected the most. In many of the marginal areas, it took several days, weeks, or even months for aid to arrive. While there are marginalized communities, such as La Perla in Old San Juan, who received media coverage and assistance from celebrities and politicians, there are others like Cantera and Buena Vista, where leaders had limited access to emergency supplies for affected residents. Today there are areas where residents claim that aid never arrived. In many of these communities, local and emergent leaders took on the response themselves and visited distribution sites daily to pick up and distribute food, water, and other essential products to fellow residents.

The Southeast

Because of the trajectory of hurricanes Irma and Maria, the eastern part of Puerto Rico experienced the strongest impact. The municipalities of Yabucoa and Humacao experienced storm surge flooding of over 5 feet. Beyond the force of the hurricane as an extreme weather event, with sustained Category 4 winds, researchers documented that there were also technical problems that exacerbated the exposure of specific areas. For instance, Mercado documented that the levee system built in the community of Punta Santiago in Humacao acted as a barrier that increased the level of the flood and increased the amount of time that it took to drain, keeping homes flooded with seawater for several days.[28]

Interior/Mountain Region

Residents of the interior part of the island experienced the greatest difficulty in accessing available resources. The U.S. Geological Survey estimated that the area experienced over 40,000 landslides.[29] Damage to bridges either eliminated faster routes or made remote areas inaccessible. Brigades of self-organized local volunteer groups, often accompanied by groups arriving from other states and countries, visited many remote and disconnected areas where residents improvised ways to receive the aid.

Coastal Municipalities

Not all coastal municipalities were affected in the same way even when the storms impacted all coastal areas. Low-lying areas were generally the most damaged by storm surge and riverine floods. Barreto and colleagues observed that most beaches had a loss in elevation. In the west-northwest, north-central, and southeast regions of the island, their team observed significant losses in beach width.[30] The storm exacerbated coastal erosion, particularly in constructed or built-up areas. Areas with coastal barriers in the northeast and southwest parts of the island experienced fewer changes. In the constructed areas where drastic beach loss is observed, structures were also likely damaged. The management and cleanup of damaged structures along the coast remain a challenge. Some of the units are second homes, now in foreclosure, or second homes to owners who live outside of the island.

Population Loss

Preliminary estimates released by the U.S. Census indicate that, between July 1, 2017, and July 1, 2018, close to 130,000 residents left Puerto Rico for the mainland.[31] As stated earlier, the current exodus of Puerto Ricans to the U.S. mainland is the largest in history and expected to continue. By 2050, the projected population of Puerto Rico will be 2.9 million, down from an estimate 3.7 million in 2015.[32]

One of the social arrangements observed through fieldwork, and mentioned by key informants such as teachers, is that of grandparents responsible for children as parents work outside of the island. Figure 8.6 presents a map generated by the research team, using data from the American Community Survey 5-year estimates to illustrate the distribution in the percentage of children living with grandparents. Further research and attention need to address the impacts of children living with their grandparents in Puerto Rico on the children themselves, but also their elderly caregivers.

Opportunities and Challenges for Emergency Management and Long-term Recovery in Puerto Rico

In line with the features of catastrophes described by Quarantelli, the catastrophe that has unfolded after hurricanes Irma and Maria in Puerto Rico is politically rooted and loaded.[33] Response and recovery post-Maria have become extremely politicized. Although Puerto Rico was included in all supplemental appropriations bills passed by Congress, receiving the funding has progressed very slowly. Different grants from a variety of sources potentially serve as investments to promote local capacity and alleviate the fragility of different sectors – community development block grants for disaster recovery, hazard mitigation grants, rural community development grants, and coastal resilience grants, among others. However, funds allocated through supplemental bills can be redistributed so it is not clear how much access Puerto Rico will have to the available funds.

Figure 8.6 Grandparents Responsible for Children Under 18, 2017

Source. U.S. Census Bureau, American Community Survey. Map reproduced by Erika Pham, University of South Carolina

Moreover, concerns have been raised over the management and administration of the funds previously allocated. According to the Center for the New Economy, of the $5 billion in federal recovery funds awarded through August 2018, companies and organizations from the U.S. mainland received $4.3 billion.[34]

Puerto Rico was a society in a socially produced condition of vulnerability when hurricanes Irma and Maria made landfall in 2017. The island had been struggling for over a decade to promote economic growth, after the economic downturn stemming from NAFTA. The tax-savings arrangement allowed corporations, particularly pharmaceutical companies, to realize great profits as they avoided federal taxes and had access to a skilled and educated workforce.

The extractive arrangement for investment in Puerto Rico has led to decades of accumulated disadvantage. The challenge of long-term recovery in Puerto Rico is not just about emergency management capacity but also – mainly – about development and inequality. Puerto Rico prioritized immediate needs over risk-reduction options according to researchers.[35] With declining incomes, Puerto Rican households will be increasingly less likely to have money for mitigation and preparedness.

Environmental planners have argued that Puerto Rico development was at the cost of the environment through extractivist policy arrangements.[36] The environment was, in some cases, even perceived as an obstacle to economic activity. Historical records show how disruptions to construction projects by natural hazards was often undermined and more considerable attention was placed on the number of jobs and in the financial investment that they represented. As a society, there is an opportunity to reflect upon the legacies of the American development model to promote political, economic, cultural, social, and policy changes that assure recovery, allowing an adaptive, secure, equitable, and resilient future for Puerto Rico. Community development and capacity-building initiatives must address the root causes of vulnerability and nurture community preparedness as a process for long-term recovery.

An important takeaway from the experience of Hurricane Maria is that immediate emergency response takes place within communities connected to different subsystems that allow customary daily routines to continue. Communities and all the actors present in them should be motivated to engage in collective planning and preparedness processes. Moreover, developing a culture of preparedness in which residents and community emergency response teams regularly think through the emergent needs and cascading effects of emergencies and disasters is vital to promote adaptive resilience. Ultimately, tightly knit and cohesive communities may have more capacity to absorb the shocks of extreme events or disasters.

The 2017 season served as a reminder of the threat posed by a changing climate. The case of Puerto Rico, in many ways, is not unique and illustrates the dynamics of the globalized planet. Therefore, there is an urgent need to rethink not only development models but also the relations among different actors and levels of that globalized planet to address their ever-compounding environmental reality.

Over ten years ago, William Easterly discussed the "other tragedy" of the world's poor, one in which billions of dollars are spent in aid but services are not delivered.[37] He highlighted how economies are successful in the delivery of entertainment goods to the privileged, while lifesaving aid does not make it to those in need. In Puerto Rico, as it is the case in post-disaster sites, planning activities have become part of everyday life. As time goes by, and "big plans" are discussed, focusing more attention and expanding inclusion helps to understand the needs, goals, and desires of those served.

Notes

1. "Puerto Rico Hurricane Irma Disaster Declaration DR-4336," FEMA, last updated September 18, 2017, www.fema.gov/disaster/4336; "Puerto Rico Hurricane Maria Disaster Declaration DR-4339," FEMA, last updated December 6, 2017, www.fema.gov/disaster/4339.
2. Richard J. Pasch, Andrew B. Penny, and Robbie Berg, *Tropical Cyclone Report AL 152017: Hurricane Maria* (Miami: National Hurricane Center Report, National Oceanic and Atmospheric Administration, February 14, 2019), www.nhc.noaa.gov/data/tcr/AL152017_Maria.pdf.
3. Gobierno de Puerto Rico, *Orden Ejecutiva del Gobernador de Puerto Rico, Hon. Ricardo Rosselló Nevares, para viabilizar y acelerar la recuperación de Puerto Rico luego del paso del Huracán María* (San Juan: La Fortaleza, Executive Order 2017-53, September 28, 2017), www.estado.pr.gov/en/executive-orders/.
4. Enrico L. Quarantelli, "Catastrophes Are Different from Disasters: Some Implications for Crisis Planning and Managing Drawn from Katrina," *Understanding Katrina: Perspectives from the Social Sciences* (New York: Social Science Research Council, 2016), http://understandingkatrina.ssrc.org/Quarantelli/.
5. Negociado de Manejo de Emergencias y Administración de Desastres, "Conferencia de Prensa: Puerto Rico se Prepara," Live Conference Broadcasted on May, 1, 2017, www.youtube.com/watch?v=RpmGuywV-jY.

6. Ibid.
7. Ibid.
8. Section 936 from the Internal Revenue Code gave a tax credit for U.S. corporations investing in export manufacturing in Puerto Rico that was equal to their tax liabilities. In other words, corporations paid no federal income taxes on income generated from Puerto Rican sources, thus providing an economic competitive advantage to the island.
9. Francisco L. Rivera-Batiz and Carlos E. Santiago, *Island Paradox: Puerto Rico in the 1990s* (New York: Russel Sage Foundation, 1996).
10. J. Alameda, "Puerto Rico: Tratados de Integración Sub-regional (Puerto Rico: Sub-Regional Integration Treaties, 2003)," Paper presented at the Puerto Rican Planning Society Conference, San Juan, PR. [Online], https://archivo.ictal.org/.
11. Rivera-Batiz and Santiago, *Island Paradox*.
12. Richard Weiskoff, *Factories and Food Stamps: The Puerto Rico Model of Development* (Baltimore, MD: The John Hopkins University Press, 1985).
13. James Dietz, *Economic History of Puerto Rico: Institutional Change and Capitalist Development* (Princeton, NJ: Princeton University Press, 1986).
14. Business International Corporation, *Puerto Rico: Critical Choices for the 1980s* (New York: Business International Corporation, 1980).
15. Center for Puerto Rican Studies (CENTRO), *Puerto Rico Post María* (New York: City University of New York-Hunter College, 2018), https://centropr.hunter.cuny.edu/sites/default/files/PDF/puerto_rico_post_maria-2018-final.pdf.
16. John P. Cangialosi, Andrew S. Latto, and Robbie Berg, *Tropical Cyclone Report (AL 112017): Hurricane Irma* (Miami, FL: National Hurricane Center, National Oceanic and Atmospheric Administration, June 30, 2018), www.nhc.noaa.gov/data/tcr/AL112017_Irma.pdf; John P. Cangialosi, *2017 Hurricane Season Forecast Verification Report* (Miami, FL: National Hurricane Center, National Oceanic and Atmospheric Administration, June 19, 2018), www.nhc.noaa.gov/verification/pdfs/Verification_2017.pdf.
17. Puerto Rico Emergency Management Bureau, "Hurricane María Press Conference," September 18, 2017, www.youtube.com/watch?v=Tex9dxtDDN4.
18. Federal Emergency Management Agency, "President Donald J. Trump Approves Major Disaster Declaration for Puerto Rico," News Release Number HQ-17-129, September 21, 2017, www.fema.gov/news-release/2017/09/21/president-donald-j-trump-approves-major-disaster-declaration-puerto-rico.
19. StatusPR, "Government of Puerto Rico Hurricane Maria Data Portal," Data retrieved daily September 27, 2017–September 29, 2018, www.status.pr/.
20. Josh Michaud and Jennifer Kates, "Public Health in Puerto Rico after Hurricane Maria," The Henry Kaiser Family Foundation, Issue Brief, November 17, 2017, www.kff.org/other/issue-brief/public-health-in-puerto-rico-after-hurricane-maria/view/footnotes/.
21. Kyle Melin, Wanda T. Maldonado, W., Angel López-Candales, "Lessons Learned from Hurricane Maria: Pharmacists' Perspective," *Annals of Pharmacotherapy*, 52, no. 5 (2018): 493–494.
22. Federal Emergency Management Agency, *Hurricanes Irma and Maria in Puerto Rico: Building Performance Observations, Recommendations, and Technical Guidance* (Washington, DC: FEMA P-2020. Mitigation Assessment Team Report, 2018), www.fema.gov/media-library/assets/documents/173789.
23. Jennifer Hinojosa and Edwin Meléndez, *The Housing Crisis in Puerto Rico and the Impact of Hurricane Maria* (New York: CUNY-Hunter, Center for Puerto Rican Studies Report RB2018-04, 2018), https://centropr.hunter.cuny.edu/sites/default/files/data_briefs/HousingPuertoRico.pdf.

24. Kathleen Tierney, "Business Impacts of the Northridge Earthquake," *Journal of Contingencies and Crisis Management* 5, no. 2 (1997): 87–97.

25. Coauthors were deployed as a research team after Hurricane Irma. The team visited municipalities along the Northern coast and the island of Culebra after Hurricane Irma. We reconvened as a team on September 25, 2017. A cursory field survey of business closures and damage was done by the coauthors in the commercial arteries of Calle Andalucía in Puerto Nuevo, Calle Loíza in Santurce, and Ave. 65 de Infantería in San Juan, Puerto Rico.

26. The number of fatalities ranges from 2,658 to 3,290 at the 95% confidence interval. Milken Institute School of Public Health and University of Puerto Rico Graduate School of Public Health, *Project Report: Ascertainment of the Estimated Excess Mortality from Hurricane María in Puerto Rico* (Washington, DC: The George Washington University and University of Puerto Rico, 2018), https://publichealth.gwu.edu/sites/default/files/downloads/projects/PRstudy/Acertainment%20of%20the%20Estimated%20Excess%20Mortality%20from%20Hurricane%20Maria%20in%20Puerto%20Rico.pdf.

27. Carlos Santos-Burgoa et al., "Differential and Persistent Risk of Excess Mortality from Hurricane Maria in Puerto Rico: A Time-Series Analysis," *Lancet Planet Health* 2, no. 11 (2018): e478–e488.

28. Aurelio Mercado "María y su marejada ciclónica (María and its storm surge)," *El Nuevo Día* 20, no. 11 (November 2017), www.elnuevodia.com/opinion/columnas/mariaysumareaciclonica-columna-2375420/.

29. Erin K. Bessette-Kirton et al., "Landslides Triggered by Hurricane Maria: Assessment of an Extreme Event in Puerto Rico," *GSA Today* 29, no. 6 (June 2019), https://doi.org/10.1130/GSATG383A.1; Erin K. Bessette-Kirton et al., *Preliminary Locations of Landslide Impacts from Hurricane Maria, Puerto Rico October 25, 2017: Map Data Showing the Concentration of Landslides Caused by Hurricane Maria in Puerto Rico* (Reston, VA: U.S. Geological Survey, 2017), https://landslides.usgs.gov/research/featured/2017/maria-pr/.

30. Maritza Barreto-Orta et al., "State of the Beaches in Puerto Rico after Hurricane Maria (2017)," *Shore and Beach* 87, no. 1 (Winter 2019): 16–23.

31. U.S. Census Bureau, "Newsroom: Nevada and Idaho are the Nation's Fastest-Growing States," Release Number CB18-193, December 19, 2018, www.census.gov/newsroom/press-releases/2018/estimates-national-state.html.

32. Toshiko Kaneda, Charlotte Greenbaum, and Kaitlyn Patierno, *2018 World Population Data Sheet with Focus on Changing Age Structures* (Washington, DC: Population Reference Bureau, 2018), www.prb.org/2018-world-population-data-sheet-with-focus-on-changing-age-structures/.

33. Quarantelli, "Catastrophes Are Different."

34. Deepak Lamba-Nieves and Raúl Santiago-Bartolomei, *Transforming the Recovery into Locally-led Growth: Federal Contracting in the Post-Disaster Period* (San Juan, PR: Center for the New Economy, September 26, 2018), http://grupocne.org/wp-content/uploads/2018/09/Federal_Contracts_FINAL_withcover-1.pdf.

35. Tania López-Marreo and Brent Yarnal, "Putting Adaptive Capacity into the Context of People's Lives: A Case Study of Two Flood Prone Communities in Puerto Rico," *Natural Hazards* 52, no. 2 (2010): 277–297.

36. Carmen M. Concepción, *Environmental Policy and Industrialization: The Politics of Regulation in Puerto Rico* (Graduate Division, University of California-Berkeley, Ph.D. Dissertation, 1990).

37. William Easterly, *The White Man's Burden: Why the West's Efforts to Aid the Rest Have Done So Much Ill and So Little Good* (New York: The Penguin Press, 2006).

9

LOSS REDUCTION AND SUSTAINABILITY

Melanie Gall

Living with risk requires making choices: Migrate and avoid risks from natural hazards, stay and accept one's fate, or adapt by reducing exposure to natural hazards and/or minimizing consequences from them. In the United States, reducing the exposure and/or consequences from natural hazards is called hazard mitigation – also referred to as disaster loss reduction in non–U.S. contexts, or adaptation in the climate change realm. Hazard mitigation is squarely situated within the emergency management field. Until 2011, the Federal Emergency Management Agency (FEMA) explicitly included the reduction of loss of life and property in its mission statement.[1]

The elimination of loss reduction from FEMA's mission did not occur because the United States had successfully built a resilient society. Quite the opposite is the case: The socioeconomic impacts from weather- and climate-related disasters continued to escalate after 2011 (Figure 9.1). The year 2017 set a new record for losses in excess of $300 billion in direct and indirect damage and more than 3,250 fatalities, largely driven by the catastrophic impacts of hurricanes Harvey, Irma, and Maria and the California wildfires. The damage tally in 2017 banished the hurricane season of 2005 to the second costliest year (at least $220 billion, and 2000 fatalities) and 2012 to the third costliest year (at least $125 billion

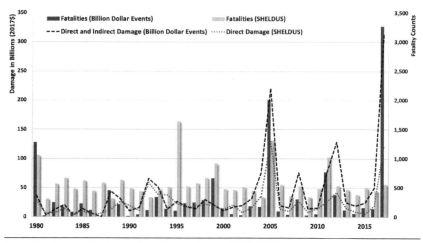

Figure 9.1 Comparative Losses From Disaster Events, 1980–2015

Comparisons of disaster loss statistics from two different sources tell a different story about the socioeconomic burden from natural hazards. In most years, the death toll across minor to catastrophic events as documented by the Spatial Hazard Events and Losses Database for the United States (SHELDUS) exceeds the annual death toll from catastrophic events as reported by the National Centers for Environmental Information's (NCEI) Billion-Dollar estimates. However, the annual combined direct and indirect economic damage of catastrophic events as represented by NCEI's estimates often far exceeds the direct damage as reported by SHELDUS, especially for events with widespread, regional impact such as hurricanes Katrina (2005), Sandy (2012), and Maria (2017). Note that the cumulative, annual impacts are adjusted for inflation and that SHELDUS includes geological hazards whereas the National Centers for Environmental Information's Billion-Dollar estimates cover only hydrological, meteorological, and climatological events.

Source: The author

and 375 fatalities).[2] The combined damage from hurricanes Michael and Florence along with California wildfires in 2018 produced another top-ranking year – fourth – with more than $90 billion in direct and indirect damage and 247 fatalities.[2]

The U.S. National Preparedness Goal considers hazard mitigation, i.e. all efforts to reduce loss of life and property from future events, as the "critical linchpin to reduce or eliminate the long-term risks to life, property, and well-being" when it comes to stabilizing or reversing "the trend of increasing impacts from extreme events and catastrophic incidents."[3] Research shows that hazard mitigation fosters a more resilient society by reducing damage and speeding up recovery, among others.[4] Actions taken during the mitigation and/or the recovery phase allow communities to integrate principles of community resilience and sustainability by build-ing back better.[5] *Building back better* means converting hazard-prone areas into greenspace, instituting stronger building codes, elevating homes, opting for fortified home construction, enhancing capacity for natural flood retention environments, prohibiting development in hazard-prone areas, and are smart choices of, by, and for more resilient communities. Forensic engineering surveys post–Hurricane Irma in Florida and the U.S. Virgin Islands, for example, underscored dividends from mitigation and, generally speaking, validated that newer construction built in com-pliance with stronger/newer building codes "sustained much less damage than older construction."[6]

At present, hazard mitigation and loss reduction remain confined to government-led initiatives. Through hazard mitigation plans, jurisdic-tions assess their risks, devise mitigation strategies, and apply for federal mitigation dollars to implement some of these actions. Most mitigation dollars spending is on elevating homes post-disaster, flood control struc-tures, and the purchase of generators.[7] Thus far, these actions have proven to be insufficient, ineffective, or both in curbing the nation's damage and recovery burden associated with natural hazards.

Much of the damage from natural hazards occurs in the existing resi-dential building stock. Unfortunately, hazard mitigation is not a priority for most homeowners.[8] For those affected by a disaster, recovery equates to rebuilding bigger, not necessarily better. Lazarus et al. found with regard to post-hurricane development that "despite decades of regulatory efforts in the United States to decrease vulnerability in developed coastal zones, exposure of residential assets to hurricane damage is increasing – even in places where hurricanes have struck before."[9]

Engaging the whole community, informing residents and business owners, and changing rebuild behavior of those living in at-risk zones, particularly homeowners, is critical to moving the needle toward resil-ience and sustainability. However, critical elements of a better-informed society are missing: 1) complete and accurate data on the socioeconomic burden of natural hazards; 2) availability of and access to data; and 3) con-version of these data into meaningful and useful products that inform decision-making processes across the whole community. This chapter spotlights these knowledge gaps by delving deeper into disaster loss statistics, comparing and contrasting different data sources, and by taking a closer look at how loss data are sourced and leveraged.

The Evidence Base for Loss Reduction: Historic Accounts of Impacts

Since the Disaster Mitigation Act of 2000 (DMA), local, state, and tribal jurisdictions are bound by law to develop and update hazard mitigation plans to maintain eligibility for various federal mitigation dollars (largely post-disaster) administered by FEMA. At the core of a hazard mitigation plan are the documentation of impacts from past, present, and future hazard risks (risk assessment) and the identification of mitigation strategies to reduce the exposure and impacts outlined in the plan's risk assessment. The risk assessment with its evidence of past impacts and identification of vulnerability hot spots, as well as modeling outputs of future scenarios establishes the baseline and risk profile of a jurisdiction. Data to compile this evidence base may originate from a combination of state and local (e.g., insurance claims filed for public properties, public health records, and disaster after-action or expenditure reports). Federal sources contribute data as well (e.g., the National Centers for Environmental Information's Storm Data, U.S. Geological Survey, post-disaster federal assistance, payouts through federal insurance program such as the National Flood Insurance Program or disaster crop insurance), as do private sources (e.g., property or life insurance claims). Private sources, though, are proprietary and thus mostly inaccessible for hazard mitigation planning. Given the multitude, disparity, and complexity in these data sources, many jurisdictions outsource data collection and analysis to consultants or data consolidation services such as the Spatial Hazard Events and Losses Database for the United States (sheldus.org) or the forthcoming National Risk Index by FEMA.

The data provided by the various sources listed above fall into two categories: quantification of 1) direct damage related to the immediate effects of a natural hazard on human and animal life as well as the damage to property and crops; and 2) insurance payouts related to any of these effects (e.g., life insurance) or reimbursement of disaster-related costs (e.g., business interruption, temporary housing costs). Although direct damage figures are available, they are for the most part unverified estimates generated by local weather forecasting offices from sources such as emergency managers, law enforcement, fire departments, broadcast media, trained spotters, or the public.[10] Few economic damage estimates are the result of official observations or surveys by National Weather Service (NWS) employees. Thus, the completeness and accuracy of weather-related, direct damage information depends heavily on the vigilance and value judgements by local NWS forecasters and the quality and quantity of estimates shared with them. The local NWS officers then transmit data to the National Centers for Environmental Information (NCEI), which compiles it into *Storm Data* reports and *Storm Events Database* (www.ncdc.noaa.gov/stormevents/) and through which data become accessible to third-party loss repositories such as the Spatial Hazard Events and Losses Database (SHELDUS).

The same process applies to fatality and injury counts. Local forecast offices do not receive information from state or local health departments due to privacy restrictions related to the Health Insurance Portability and Accountability Act (HIPAA) of 1996. As a result, there are discrepancies between hazard-related fatalities and injuries as reported by NCEI, the National Vital Statistics Systems, and others.[11] One example is 2017's Hurricane Maria, for which NCEI reports 20 fatalities (and only $18.3 billion in direct property damage) although studies using excess mortality calculations – a standard methodology common in estimating heat-related fatalities – assert much higher fatality counts of around 2,975[12] up to 4,645 fatalities.[13] The example of Hurricane Maria highlights not only nationwide reporting challenges, i.e. sourcing complete and accurate data regarding direct damage, but also the challenges associated with capturing this information during and after an event (see Box 9.1).

Box 9.1 Three Avenues for Sourcing Hazard-Related Fatality Counts

There are three avenues for sourcing hazard-related fatality counts. The first are fatality reports obtained from public sources such as news/social media outlets, highway patrol, and emergency managers, which are incorporated and compiled into official publications such Storm Data reports by the National Centers for Environmental Information (NCEI). The second source is the utilization of statistical methods, so-called 'excess death' calculations, which reconstruct fatality counts during a specific time period by comparing the event-specific fatality counts to historic fatality counts incurred during the same time period in years prior. The third source is a state's vital records system as compiled from death certificate information. With regard to the latter, the initial information listed on a death certificate – the demographic data, and the immediate disease or condition resulting in death as well as the underlying diseases or injuries that triggered the disease/condition resulting in death – is often provided by a funeral home, and subsequently reviewed and certified by a coroner, physician, or medical examiner based on their best medical opinion.

Mass fatality events such as Hurricane Maria in 2017 tend to be characterized by a confluence of adverse conditions such as the shortage in medical certifiers and limited/no communication between exchange between certifier and family members. This results in incomplete death certificates regarding the causal chain of events and subsequently an under-allocation of hazard-caused fatalities. The official death count for Hurricane Maria stood at 64 until the Government of Puerto Rico increased the official tally to 1,427 fatalities based on the findings from an excess death study by George Washington University's Milken Institute School of Public Health in 2018.

Due to differences in methodologies, even scientific excess death studies arrive at divergent fatality counts – albeit all generate estimate significantly higher than the initial figure of 64 fatalities. The Milken study estimates that 2,975 people died from the effects of Hurricane Maria whereas a Harvard-led study purports a fatality count as high as 4,645. This is not new. Fatality counts related to Hurricane Katrina rose from an initial estimate of 1,100 to 1,833 deaths at present although the latter is a combination of both direct and indirect fatalities with the exact number of direct fatalities still unknown. In sum, the more catastrophic the disaster, the more uncertain and underreported fatality and injury counts become.

Source: Milken Institute School of Public Health (MISPH), *Ascertainment of the Estimated Excess Mortality from Hurricane Maria in Puerto Rico,* (George Washington University, 2018); Nishant Kishore et al., "Mortality in Puerto Rico after Hurricane Maria," *The New England Journal of Medicine* 379, no. 2 (2018): 162–170; John L. Beven et al., "Annual Summary: Atlantic Hurricane Season of 2005," *Monthly Weather Review* March (2008): 1109–1173. DOI: 10.1175/2007MWR2074.1

Thus, compiling the evidentiary basis on the historic impacts of natural hazards is largely limited to very conservative – underestimates or guestimates – of direct injuries, fatalities, and property damage that, at best, date back to the 1960s. The estimates exhibit various levels of completeness by state and hazard type with chronic events like heat and drought, often lacking estimates entirely.[14]

A similar pattern emerges with the impacts on economic sectors such as agriculture. For example, direct crop estimates as provided by NCEI are fraught with many uncertainties as the comparison with federal crop insurance payout shows. Figure 9.2 demonstrates not only discrepancies in the severity of impacts (as expressed in the NCEI annual direct crop damage versus the annual U.S. Department of Agriculture – USDA – crop insurance payouts) but also in when those impacts occurred over time. It is safe to assume that direct crop damage should always be higher than crop insurance payouts, a trend observable until 2000. With the exception of 2005 and 2006, crop insurance payouts have consistently exceeded the direct crop estimates provided by NCEI.

Other types of losses such as indirect or uninsured damage, while equally or perhaps even more important with regard to a community's ability to recover and long-term effects on community resilience, do not

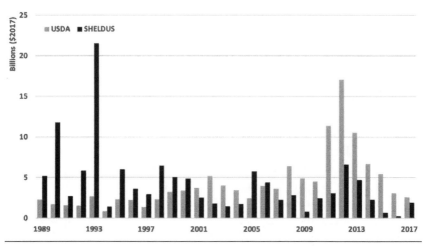

Figure 9.2 Crop Damage and Payouts

The divergent timelines of direct crop damage and federal disaster crop insurance payouts highlight gaps in documenting the direct damage from natural hazards. In theory, direct damage should exceed insurance payouts since not all crops are insurable and not all farmers take out insurance for insurable crops.

Source: Data compiled by the author using data from SHELDUS Version 17

factor into local hazard mitigation plans and risk assessments due to lack of documentation and/or quantification. While the documentation of direct damage is itself incomplete and underestimates the actual impacts on local communities for a variety of reasons, indirect, and uninsured damages go entirely unaccounted for with the exception of NCEI's estimates for large-scale billion-dollar events.[15] This is despite the fact that simplistic economic modeling approaches exist to calculate estimates for indirect damage.[16]

For some places, like tribal nations or U.S. territories, documentation is often completely missing (willingly or unwillingly) across all loss types, i.e. direct, indirect, insured, and uninsured damage. This makes it extremely challenging for communities to comply with federal mandates for hazard mitigation plans and/or successfully justify and receive federal funding for mitigation projects.

Trends in Natural Hazard Losses

According to SHELDUS – a loss database maintained by Arizona State University that consolidates weather-related loss estimates from the

National Weather Services along with geological loss estimates from the U.S. Geological Survey and other sources – the cumulative U.S. burden from natural hazards stands at more than $1 trillion (in 2017$) in direct property and crop damage, 245,250 injuries, and 33,350 fatalities since 1960.[17] This baseline is likely to be much higher given the systemic issues surrounding loss estimation as discussed earlier. Hurricanes and thunderstorms are responsible for most of damage with a third of the losses followed by flooding (25 percent) and severe weather including tornadoes (21 percent) (Figure 9.3). The impacts stemming from the 2004 and 2005 hurricane seasons make up the largest share based on a single hazard type during the past decades. However, with nearly annual urban flood disasters characterizing the 2010s thus far, flooding may be on track to outpace the hurricane damage from the prior decade.

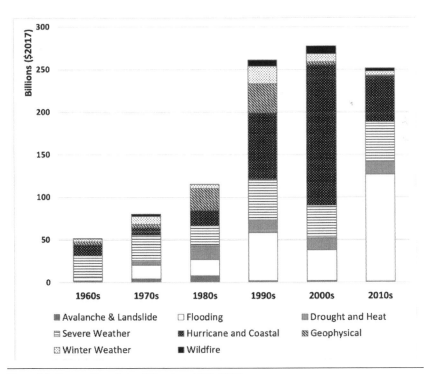

Figure 9.3 Damage From Natural Disasters, 1960–2017

Source: Author created

Geophysical hazards – earthquakes, volcanic eruptions and tsunamis – stand at a share of seven percent. Drought damage ($64 billion in 2017 dollars) tends to be vastly underestimated by NCEI and is highly likely to contribute a much bigger portion than the 6 percent currently reported. Wildfires account for 2 percent in damage (nearly $24 billion in 2017 dollars) with the vast majority of them occurring in a single state (California, $15.5 billion).

California ranks third in overall property and crop damage ($108 billion in 2017 dollars) after Texas ($170 billion) and Florida ($120 billion) (Figure 9.4). More than half of California's damage occurred in one county – Los Angeles County, which holds the top rank of the most severely property damaged county nationwide with a tally of $46 billion. This is followed by Harris County and Galveston County, Texas, as the top three counties in damage since 1960 with $22 and $21 billion (in 2017 dollars) respectively. These facts may not be surprising given that urban places tend to dominate damage tallies based on the prevalence of assets and people at risk.

Iowa stands out as the most severely affected state with regard to crop damage ($27 billion in 2017$) followed by Texas ($24.6 billion) and California ($20.1 billion). Similarly, Iowa received more than $8.5 billion (in 2017$) in crop insurance indemnities payments by USDA since 1989

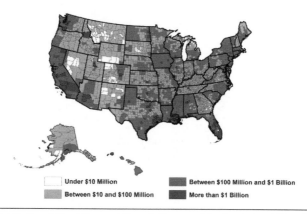

Figure 9.4 Distribution of Direct Crop and Property Damage at the County Level Since 1960

Source: Author created

ranking fourth after Texas ($17.5 billion), North Dakota ($11.7 billion), and Kansas ($9.5) according to SHELDUS.

When translating absolute damage figures into relative impact metrics such as per capita values, Skamania County, Washington tops the list with more than $1.2 million (in 2017 dollars) in property damage per county resident since 1960. This is attributable to a singular event: the 1980 eruption of Mount St. Helens and a massive earthquake-triggered debris avalanche. In Louisiana, residents in Plaquemines Parish suffered nearly $289,000 (in 2017 dollars) in property damage due to Hurricane Katrina. The residents of Alpine County, California saw about $260,000 (in 2017 dollars) of property damage per person, mostly due to wildfires, between 1960 and 2017.

In summary, Figure 9.1 shows that over the past 38 years, 18 years exceeded a value of $15.7 billion in direct damage – the annual average in direct disaster damage according to SHELDUS. The very active hurricane seasons of the 1990s produced excess direct damage in 9 out of 10 years. In the two subsequent decades, excess loss years were not as frequent (3 out of 10 years in the 2000s and 4 out of 8 years in the 2010s thus far). The two most recent decades have accumulated higher loss totals than any prior decade. This means that in recent years, 1) the annual swings in direct damage between years have increased (i.e. below average year(s) followed by well-above average year(s)); and 2) milestone events of catastrophic proportion (magnitude and/or impacts) have set new damage records in short succession.

These findings track with global trends along with the predicted effects of climate change.[18] Munich Re reports that between 1980 and 2017, the economic losses and frequency of significant loss events have increased, especially those caused by hydrological and meteorological hazards. In 2017 alone, natural hazards were responsible for about 10,000 fatalities and $340 billion in damage, with less than half insured.[19] For the United States and Europe, Munich Re found that economic damage increased even when adjusting for inflation and wealth with similar findings reported elsewhere,[20] countering the argument of rising losses due to more assets at risk[21] and explicitly identifying "the plausibility of climate change already influencing some types of event in a number of regions."[22]

The Evidence Base for Loss Reduction: Historic
Accounts of Recovery Costs

Relying solely on direct damage data or NCEI's more comprehensive estimates of singular, catastrophic events to quantify a community's exposure to natural hazards (or lack thereof) says little about the costs of recovery. The investments and expenditures needed at all levels – from private to federal – to "get back to normal" or "bounce back better" generally far exceed the immediate damage of a disaster. The total costs of a disaster go beyond (market or replacement) value of damaged property and infrastructure (direct damage) or lost revenue (indirect damage). It also encompasses the spending needed to recover from the disaster consequences such as clean up or remediation costs, temporary housing costs, congressional appropriations for community development, and more. For a more nuanced discussion of disaster costs, consult the sources listed here.[23]

Until 2013, the now-defunct PERI Presidential Disaster Declarations database was the only entity collating county-level data on federal, post-disaster funds. The database documented the allocation of federal dollars to local jurisdictions for rehabilitation public infrastructure, disaster cleanup costs, and more, along with direct financial assistance to individuals such as temporary housing costs whenever counties received a presidential disaster declaration.[24] Forced by a 2013 Executive Order 13642 "Making Open and Machine Readable the New Default for Government Information," FEMA now offers select datasets through its OpenFEMA portal (www.fema.gov/openfema). Based on a compilation of multiple data sources including these FEMA data sets (Table 9.1), we now know that disaster recovery has cost the nation at least $446 billion (in current dollars) since the 1980s. By contrast, less than $3.5 billion have been invested into *ex ante* hazard mitigation, i.e. less than one percent of disaster-related expenditures are invested prior to or independent of any disaster.

While the Hazard Mitigation Grant Program (HMGP) allocated nearly $20 billion in mitigation dollars over the past decades, this funding stream blurs the separation between disaster recovery and hazard mitigation. A precondition for HMGP funds is a disaster declaration

Table 9.1 Federally Obligated Funds for Disaster Mitigation, Response, and Recovery

Agency	Program	Data Availability	Obligated (in billion, current$)	Source
Dept. of Agriculture	Disaster Crop Insurance	1989–2017	$102.3	CEMHS 2018
Federal Emergency Management Agency	Public Assistance	1993–2017	$83.8	OpenFEMA
Federal Emergency Management Agency	National Flood Insurance Program	1978–2018	$68.0	NFIP Loss Statistics
Dept. of Housing and Urban Development	Community Development Block Grants-Disaster Recovery	2006–2018	$55.6	HUD 2018
Dept. of Homeland Security**	Disaster-specific Obligations	2005–2014	$39.0	GAO 2016
Federal Emergency Management Agency	Individual Assistance	2005–2014	$25.4	GAO 2016
Federal Emergency Management Agency	Hazard Mitigation Grant Program	1990–2018	$19.9	OpenFEMA
Dept. of Transportation	Disaster-specific Obligations	2004–2015	$15.5	GAO 2016
Dept. of Defense	Disaster-specific Obligations	2004–2015	$10.8	GAO 2016
All Federal Agencies	Disaster Relief Fund Mission Assignment Reimbursements	2004–2015	$7.3	GAO 2016
Small Business Administration	Disaster-specific Obligations	2004–2015	$4.9	GAO 2016
Dept. of Health and Human Services	Disaster-specific Obligations	2004–2015	$3.9	GAO 2016
Environmental Protection Agency	Disaster-specific Obligations	2004–2015	$3.6	GAO 2016
Dept. of the Interior	Disaster-specific Obligations	2004–2015	$1.9	GAO 2016
Federal Emergency Management Agency	Pre-Disaster Mitigation*	2001–2017	$1.4	OpenFEMA
Federal Emergency Management Agency	Emergency Management* Preparedness Grants	2014–2018	$1.0	OpenFEMA
Federal Emergency Management Agency	Flood Mitigation Assistance*	1997–2017	$0.9	OpenFEMA
Dept. of Commerce	Disaster-specific Obligations	2004–2015	$0.8	GAO 2016
Federal Emergency Management Agency	Severe Repetitive Loss	2008–2011	$0.3	OpenFEMA
Dept. of Education	Disaster-specific Obligations	2004–2015	$0.2	GAO 2016
Federal Emergency Management Agency	Repetitive Flood Claims	2008–2012	$0.04	OpenFEMA
Total			**$446.54**	

Note:
(*) denotes a mitigation program independent of the presence of a disaster. Note that this excludes state and local shares of project costs.
(**) denotes disaster-specific obligations for FEMA and Coast Guard outside of the Disaster Relief Fund.

Source: Author from various sources listed in the table

with the funding calculated as a share (sliding scale between 7.5 up to 15 percent) of federal *ex post* disaster assistance.[25] Thus, there is a concern regarding the (mis-)use of HMGP funds for recovery purposes and the disincentive for pre-disaster (*ex ante*) mitigation – a phenomenon many call "welfare economics of post-disaster government aid."[26]

FEMA is one among several federal agencies dispersing response and recovery funds. According to the Government Accountability Office (GAO), 17 federal agencies and departments obligated at least $277 billion for disaster response and recovery between 2005 and 2014 alone.[27] In GAO's assessment, FEMA's disaster relief fund (i.e. public and individual assistance, hazard mitigation, fire management assistance, mission assignment, and administration) accounted for nearly 38 percent of federal obligations ($104.5 billion). About 48 percent ($132.2 billion) were authorized for the explicit purpose of disaster response and recovery and involved agencies such as USDA, the Department of Housing and Urban Development (HUD), Department of Defense, Department of Education, and Department of Labor. Among the non-FEMA agencies, HUD emerged as a key agency responsible for long-term community disaster recovery. Since Hurricane Katrina in 2005, HUD now awards disaster recovery funds via community development block grants (CDBG-DR). Since 2006, HUD has awarded 106 CDBG-DR worth nearly $55 billion (in current dollars).[28]

Not surprisingly, the list of federal obligations related to disaster mitigation, response, and recovery is incomplete leading to an underestimation of overall federal disaster expenditures. The GAO found

> more than half of the 17 departments and agencies in the scope of this review reported that obligations for certain disaster assistance programs or activities during this time frame are not separately tracked or are not available. For example, some disaster assistance programs or activities are not separately tracked because spending related to these activities is generally subsumed by a department's general operating budget or mission-related costs.[29]

In other words, despite the nation's susceptibility to natural hazards and recurring disasters, the overall fiscal burden disasters exercise on federal budgets is unknown.

How much is the federal government spending on disaster recovery and risk reduction? As shown in Table 9.1, expanding many of GAO's numbers in the original estimate by extending the timeframe under consideration and fiscally by including additional expenditure data through OpenFEMA provides a better assessment of spending. Based on these publicly available sources and without adjusting for inflation, federal disaster-related expenditure accounted for at least $446 billion in tax dollars (e.g., public assistance, HMGP, CDBG-DR), nearly double the estimate by the GAO – albeit calculated over a longer time period when data were available.

The hidden fiscal burden of disasters extends to state and local governmental budgets. While some states maintain disaster funds, many state and local agencies subsume disaster-related expenses under their operating or contingency budgets and/or make supplemental appropriations.[30] For presidentially declared disasters, the federal government generally covers 75 percent of project costs with state and local governments shouldering the remaining share. Occasionally, the federal government may cover a higher percentage and/or local jurisdictions may be able to use federal CDBG-DR funds as a local match. Nevertheless, as federal disaster-related expenditures increase, so do state and local expenditures. Add to this the recovery costs carried by the private sector, nonprofit organizations, and disaster survivors, it becomes clear that recovery expenditures are substantial but largely unbudgeted liabilities for most stakeholders.

Poor Data Leads to Poor Decisions

Not knowing how much federal, state, local, and tribal governments spent on disasters is not just a question of budgeting and tracking. It is also a question of being able to make evidence-based decisions. This includes having access to data in a way that is informative, useful, and usable.

First, many reports including those by GAO utilize federal disaster spending figures expressed as cumulative, absolute numbers at current cost. This means that spending figures are unadjusted for inflation or wealth. Even less common is the contextualization of disaster impacts using population counts, population density, or local productivity, which would provide some indication of the relative impacts on a local community.[31] The result is a distortion of the impacts of past disasters and the long-term adverse impact of past events skewed toward population centers like Los Angeles or Harris County. Agencies accustomed to economic research such as GAO or the Federal Reserve would be well suited to generate and incorporate relative or per capita impact disaster metrics into future reports.

Access to digital data over the lifetime of an entire program, not just a few select years, is imperative to evaluate program effectiveness and efficiency. For example, OpenFEMA provides information on Public Assistance projects dating back to 1993 only. In the case of the National Flood Insurance Program (NFIP), privacy concerns are the given reason for suppressing specific address level data. As a result, public NFIP data are aggregated at the state or jurisdictional level – not the ZIP code or census boundaries. While consumers are able to retrieve reports for cars to educate themselves on historic flood damage among other things, homebuyers must rely on local disclosure laws – if they exist – to uncover if a prospect residence may be at risk of flooding.

Furthermore, many disaster-related datasets require extensive post-processing by the end user due to 1) the infancy of the open data initiative and 2) technological deficiencies. A case in point is FEMA's Integrated Financial Management Information Management System. According to reports by the Department of Homeland Security (DHS) Office of Inspector General, FEMA's internal system suffers from:

> a) inability to integrate FEMA's internal systems to perform end-to-end mission functions; b) inability to track and manage disaster-related funds effectively; c) inability to share information with external emergency management partners; and d) limited real-time awareness or coordination across disaster response efforts.[32]

These deficiencies require not only many manual workarounds by FEMA personnel but also by the data end user. Compatibility and data integration issues are common due to frequent changes in output formats, data quality/typos, etc.

State-level data regarding disaster spending and mitigation is even more sporadic than federal spending data even though some states offer state-local cost shares similar to federal public assistance projects. Others, such as North Dakota, invest in their own hazard mitigation programs and/or offer cost-sharing incentives.[33] Such a poor and incomplete baseline misrepresents the impact and burden from natural hazards and stymies the development of effective counter measures. For example, any hazard mitigation project application must show (based on existing data) that the proposed project costs (including construction, maintenance, etc.) will be lower than its socioeconomic benefits (avoided losses). An incomplete documentation of past losses and investments makes it extremely difficult, especially for less populated and resource poor communities, for the math to come out in favor of mitigation investments.

In addition, the siloed domains of hazard mitigation planning and community development hamstring any sustainability-related coordination and capacity building. Hazard mitigation is central to sustainable and resilient community development. Sustainable community development practices are difficult to operationalize by a single department or public official, and neither can hazard mitigation. For example, the development in hazardous areas without disclosing risks to potential homebuyers or nearby/downstream neighborhoods places not only the inhabitants at risk but adversely affects community resilience. The whole community approach has not yet fully embraced citizens, nonprofit organizations, and the private sector.[34]

The call for a culture of preparedness[35] rings hollow when investments are neither properly tracked nor monitored, and program evaluations left to occasional GAO reports or Multi-Mitigation Council reports. While important, these assessments lack a comprehensive investigation beyond singular mitigation projects or agencies that include long-term effects on community resilience.

What the Future Holds: Loss and Damage From Climate Change

So why is the United States continuing to ignore the socioeconomic impacts of natural hazards? Without comprehensively documenting and tracking the indirect, indirect, insured, and uninsured damage from natural hazards along with federal, state, local, tribal, private, nonprofit, and personal expenditures related to disaster mitigation and recovery, there is no comprehensive baseline from which to initiate strategic planning and monitor progress. Failure to measure the burden of disasters means failing to manage them through more effective (i.e., resilience-inducing) policies and actions. Without informative data, policies will fail to address root causes, communities will not be able to fiscally justify long-term resilience investments or quantify return on resilience investments, and the general public will continue to buy at-risk homes suckered in by amenities and the latest design promoted by do-it-yourself television programs and other mass media.

The international community through the Sendai Framework for Disaster Risk Reduction[36] as well as the Sustainable Development Goals set a target date of 2030 to

> significantly reduce the number of deaths and the number of people affected and substantially decrease the direct economic losses relative to global gross domestic product caused by disasters, including water-related disasters, with a focus on protecting the poor and people in vulnerable situations.[37]

This target, measured as a) the number of deaths, missing persons, and persons affected by disaster per 100,000 people; and b) the direct disaster economic loss in relation to global GDP, including disaster damage to critical infrastructure and disruption of basic services, is part of the Sustainable Development Goal 'Sustainable Cities and Communities' (SDG #11). The United States is struggling to track progress along those metrics.[38] Significant improvements in data collection on the overall costs of disasters are needed to facilitate evidence-based policies and decision making to effectively reduce disaster risk and impacts.

Living in the Anthropocene[39] and adjusting to a new normal means coming to terms with the fact that the United States has yet to decisively act and implement effective policies and measures to curb the impact from natural hazards, let alone face the new realities associated with climate change. In a review of disaster-related governmental budgeting mechanisms in ten states (including California, Florida, and New York), the GAO found that some utilized disaster funds for ongoing or recovering from past disasters though only for the current fiscal year. None budgeted or developed reserves for future disasters.[40]

Our new normal will not only require adaptation and hazard mitigation by those currently at risk from natural hazards. According to the Union of Concerned Scientists (UCS), business as usual will lead to nearly doubling the number of U.S. coastal communities facing chronic inundation from moderate sea level rise within the next 20 years.[41] UCS estimates this number to increase to 270 coastal communities within the next 45 years and to nearly 490 communities (40 percent of all East/Gulf Coast coastal communities) by the end of the century. This includes a substantial number of communities that either have never flooded or only seldom flooded from tidal waters.

Humans' ability to think short-term, forget the past, hope for the best, stick with business as usual, and ignore complexities and feedback loops[42] calls for a shift toward valuing hazard mitigation beyond emergency management. The portfolio of a sustainability or resilience officer as well as an emergency manager, for example, overlaps closely when it comes to reducing the socioeconomic impacts from hazards and disasters. Fusing the responsibilities of hazard mitigation and sustainability planning and necessitating co-production of knowledge seems a prerequisite to be successful in the Anthropocene. This demands that communities "defy simple arrangements [and initiate] institutional arrangements that are able to meaningfully engage the institutional and ecological complexity and dynamism" of communities.[43] At the city and county of Honolulu, Hawaii, for example, hazard mitigation and long-term recovery planning now reside at the newly established (in 2016) Office of Climate Change, Sustainability, and Resilience. Similar organizational restructuring, i.e. shifting hazard mitigation planning – and even emergency management as a whole – away from public safety domains and integrating it with resilience and sustainability efforts are on the rise.

Conclusion

New approaches along with an evaluation of existing investments and smarter strategies need to harness the transformative potential of hazard mitigation.[44] Resilience is the connective tissue between emergency management, hazard mitigation, and sustainability.[45] To move forward, we need better and more comprehensive data on disaster impacts and expenditures to assess and audit progression toward a more resilient and sustainable future.

This is especially critical for local communities, which are at the forefront of climate change adaptation and are more actively preparing for climate change than is widely known.[46] Loss reduction from natural hazards is one of the areas that allows for leveraging tangible co-benefits cross-sector.[47] Without piggybacking loss reduction onto climate adaptation, "unforeseen" disaster liabilities will create socioeconomic, financial, environmental, cultural, and intergenerational burdens that will infringe on our ability to prepare for the future.

Even in the absence of comprehensive data on disaster losses and recovery expenditures, the trends are clear both nationally and internationally: First, the economic damage from disasters is on the rise. Second, catastrophic damage records occur in increasingly shorter succession. Finally, current efforts to curb these trends are insufficient. States like California and Louisiana face a seemingly perpetual state of disaster response and recovery with one disaster chasing another with cascading and compounding impacts. Disasters are becoming the new normal and the accounting of their impacts – their economic, social, cultural, and environmental burden – must improve to trigger effective counter measures and reduce disaster risk long-term.

Notes

1. FEMA, *FEMA Strategic Plan, Fiscal Years 2008–2013* (Washington, DC, 2008), www.fema.gov/pdf/about/fy08_fema_sp_bookmarked.pdf; FEMA, *FEMA Strategic Plan, Fiscal Years 2011–2014* (Washington, DC, 2011).
2. "Billion-Dollar Weather and Climate Disasters," National Centers for Environmental Information (NCEI), 2018, www.ncdc.noaa.gov/billions/summary-stats.
3. Department of Homeland Security (DHS), *National Preparedness Goal*, 2nd edition (Washington, DC, 2015), www.fema.gov/media-library-data/1443799615171-2aae 90be55041740f97e8532fc680d40/National_Preparedness_Goal_2nd_Edition.pdf, quote from p. 10.

4. Multi-Mitigation Council, *Natural Hazard Mitigation Saves: 2017 Interim Report* (Washington, DC, 2017), www.fema.gov/media-library-data/1516812817859-9f86 6330bd6a1a93f54cdc61088f310a/MS2_2017InterimReport.pdf; National Research Council (NRC), *Disaster Resilience: A National Imperative* (Washington, DC: National Academies Press, 2012).

5. Katja Brundiers and Hallie C. Eakin, "Leveraging Post-Disaster Windows of Opportunities for Change towards Sustainability: A Framework," *Sustainability* 10, no. 5 (2018): 1390, https://doi.org/10.3390/su10051390.

6. FEMA, *Mitigation Assessment Team Report: Hurricane Irma in Florida* (Washington, DC, 2018); FEMA, *Mitigation Assessment Team Report Hurricanes Irma and Maria in the U.S. Virgin Islands* (Washington, DC, 2018), quote from p. 5–2.

7. Melanie Gall and Carol J. Friedland, "If Mitigation Saves $6 Per Every $1 Spent, Then Why Are We Not Investing More? A Louisiana Perspective on a National Issue," *Natural Hazards Review* (forthcoming 2019).

8. Debra Javeline and Tracy Kijewski-Correa, "Coastal Homeowners in a Changing Climate," *Climatic Change* 152, no. 2 (2019): 259–274, https://doi.org/10.1007/s10584-018-2257-4.

9. Eli D. Lazarus, Patrick W. Limber, Evan B. Goldstein, Rosie Dodd, and Scott B. Armstrong, "Building Back Bigger in Hurricane Strike Zones," *Nature Sustainability* 1, no. 12 (2018): 759–762, quote from p. 759.

10. National Weather Service (NWS), *Storm Data Preparation* (Silver Spring, MD: Department of Commerce, National Oceanic & Atmospheric Administration, National Weather Service, 2007), www.nws.noaa.gov/directives/.

11. Kevin A. Borden and Susan L Cutter, "Spatial Patterns of Natural Hazards Mortality in the United States," *International Journal of Health Geographics* 7, no. 1 (2008): 64, https://doi.org/10.1186/1476-072X-7-64.

12. Milken Institute School of Public Health (MISPH), *Ascertainment of the Estimated Excess Mortality from Hurricane Maria in Puerto Rico* (George Washington University, 2018), https://publichealth.gwu.edu/sites/default/files/downloads/projects/PRstudy/Acertainment%20of%20the%20Estimated%20Excess%20Mortality%20from%20Hurricane%20Maria%20in%20Puerto%20Rico.pdf.

13. Nishant Kishore et al., "Mortality in Puerto Rico after Hurricane Maria," *The New England Journal of Medicine* 379, no. 2 (2018): 162–170, https://doi.org/10.1056/NEJMsa1803972.

14. Melanie Gall, Kevin A Borden, and Susan L Cutter, "When Do Losses Count? Six Fallacies of Natural Hazards Loss Data," *Bulletin of the American Meteorological Society* 90, no. 6 (2009): 799–809, https://doi.org/10.1175/2008BAMS2721.1; Adam B. Smith and Richard W. Katz, "US Billion-Dollar Weather and Climate Disasters: Data Sources, Trends, Accuracy and Biases," *Natural Hazards* 67, no. 2 (2013): 387–410, https://doi.org/10.1007/s11069-013-0566-5.

15. Ibid.

16. Stéphane Hallegatte, "The Indirect Cost of Natural Disasters and an Economic Definition of Macroeconomic Resilience," *Policy Research Paper Working Paper 7357* (Washington, DC, 2015), http://documents.worldbank.org/curated/en/1866314679 98501319/The-indirect-cost-of-natural-disasters-and-an-economic-definition-of-macroeconomic-resilience; Nathaniel Heatwole and Adam Rose, "A Reduced-Form Rapid Economic Consequence Estimating Model: Application to Property Damage from U.S. Earthquakes," *International Journal of Disaster Risk Science* 4, no. 1 (2013): 20–32, https://doi.org/10.1007/s13753-013-0004-z.

17. Center for Emergency Management and Homeland Security (CEMHS), *The Spatial Hazard Events and Losses Database for the United States, Version 17 [Online Database]*

(Phoenix, AZ: CEMHS at Arizona State University, 2018), www.sheldus.org. All damage estimates are in 2017 dollars.

18. Intergovernmental Panel on Climate Change (IPCC), *Managing the Risks of Extreme Events and Disasters to Advance Climate Change Adaptation, A Special Report of Working Groups I and II of the Intergovernmental Panel on Climate Change* (Cambridge: Cambridge University Press, 2012), http://doi.org/10.1017/CBO9781139177245.

19. "Topics Geo Natural Catastrophes 2017," Munich RE, 2018, www.munichre.com/touch/naturalhazards/en/publications/topics-geo/2017/index.html.

20. Fabian Barthel and Eric Neumayer, "A Trend Analysis of Normalized Insured Damage from Natural Disasters," *Climatic Change* 113, no. 2 (2012): 215–237, https://doi.org/10.1007/s10584-011-0331-2; Melanie Gall, Kevin A. Borden, Christopher T. Emrich, and Susan L. Cutter, "The Unsustainable Trend of Natural Hazards Losses in the United States," *Sustainability* 3, no. 11 (2011): 2157–2181, https://doi.org/10.3390/su3112157.

21. Roger A. Pielke and Daniel Sarewitz, "Bringing Society Back in to the Climate Debate." *Population and Environment* 26, no. 3 (2005): 255–268.

22. "Topics Geo Natural Catastrophes 2017." Quote from p. 23.

23. Adam Rose. 2004. "Economic Principles, Issues, and Research Priorities in Hazard Loss Estimation," in *Modeling Spatial and Economic Impacts of Disasters*, edited by Yasuhide Okuyama and Stephanie E. Chang (New York: Springer Verlag), 13–36; Stéphane Hallegatte, and Valentin Przyluski, *The Economics of Natural Disasters: Concepts and Methods* (The World Bank Group, 2010), https://openknowledge.worldbank.org/handle/10986/3991.

24. Richard T. Sylves, "Federal Emergency Management Comes of Age: 1979–2001," in *Emergency Management: The American Experience 1900–2010*, edited by Claire B. Rubin (Boca Raton, FL: CRC Press, 2012), 112–166.

25. FEMA, *Hazard Mitigation Assistance Guidance Hazard Mitigation Grant Program, Pre-Disaster Mitigation Program, and Flood Mitigation Assistance Program* (Washington, DC, 2015), www.fema.gov/media-library-data/1424983165449-38f5dfc69c0b-d4ea8a161e8bb7b79553/HMA_Guidance_022715_508.pdf.

26. Philip R. Berke, Ward Lyles, and Gavin P. Smith, "Impacts of Federal and State Hazard Mitigation Policies on Local Land Use Policy," *Journal of Planning Education and Research* 34, no. 1 (2014): 60–76, https://doi.org/10.1177/0739456X13517004; Dwight Jaffee and Thomas Russell, "The Welfare Economics of Catastrophe Losses and Insurance." *Geneva Papers on Risk and Insurance-Issues and Practice* 38, no. 3 (2013): 469–494, https://doi.org/10.1057/gpp.2013.17.

27. GAO, *Federal Disaster Assistance* (Washington, DC, 2016), www.gao.gov/assets/680/679977.pdf.

28. HUD, *Monthly CDBG-DR Grant Financial Report, December 30, 2018* (Washington, DC, 2018), www.hudexchange.info/resources/documents/CDBG-DR-Financial-Report-2019-01-01.pdf.

29. GAO, *Federal Disaster Assistance*, 12.

30. GAO, *Budgeting for Disasters: Approaches to Budgeting for Disasters in Selected States* (Washington, DC, 2015), www.gao.gov/assets/670/669277.pdf.

31. Kevin D. Ash, Susan L. Cutter, and Christopher T. Emrich, "Acceptable Losses? The Relative Impacts of Natural Hazards in the United States, 1980–2009," *International Journal of Disaster Risk Reduction* 5, no. 9 (2013): 61–72, https://doi.org/10.1016/j.ijdrr.2013.08.001.

32. John V. Kelly, *Using Innovative Technology and Practices to Enhance the Culture of Preparedness* (Washington, DC, 2018), www.oig.dhs.gov1, quote from p. 2.

33. Pew Charitable Trusts, *What We Don't Know About State Spending on Natural Disasters Could Cost Us* (Washington, DC, 2018), www.pewtrusts.org/-/media/assets/2018/06/statespendingnaturaldisasters_v4.pdf.
34. NRC, *Disaster Resilience*.
35. FEMA, *2018–2022 Strategic Plan* (Washington, DC, 2018), www.fema.gov/media-library/assets/documents/160940.
36. UNISDR, *Sendai Framework for Disaster Risk Reduction 2015–2030* (Geneva, Switzerland, 2015), www.preventionweb.net/files/43291_sendaiframeworkfordrren.pdf.
37. UN, *Transforming Our World: The 2030 Agenda for Sustainable Development* (Geneva, Switzerland, 2015), https://sustainabledevelopment.un.org/content/documents/2125 2030 Agenda for Sustainable Development web.pdf.
38. Susan L. Cutter and Melanie Gall, "Sendai Targets at Risk," *Nature Climate Change* 5, no. 8 (2015): 707–709, https://doi.org/10.1038/nclimate2718.
39. Simon L. Lewis and Mark A. Maslin, "Defining the Anthropocene," *Nature* 519, no. 7542 (2015): 171–180, https://doi.org/10.1038/nature14258.
40. GAO, *Budgeting for Disasters*.
41. Erika Spanger-Siegfried, Kristina Dahl, Astrid Caldas, Shana Udvardy, Rachel Cleetus, Pamela Worth, and Nicole Hernandez Hammer, *When Rising Seas Hit Home* (Union of Concerned Scientists (UCS), 2017), www.ucsusa.org/global-warming/global-warming-impacts/when-rising-seas-hit-home-chronic-inundation-from-sea-level-rise.
42. Robert J. Meyer and Howard Kunreuther, *The Ostrich Paradox: Why We Underprepare for Disasters* (Philadelphia, PA: Wharton Digital Press, 2017).
43. Tischa A. Muñoz-Erickson, Clark A. Miller, and Thaddeus R. Miller, "How Cities Think: Knowledge Co-Production for Urban Sustainability and Resilience," *Forests* 8, no. 6 (2017): 1–17, quote from p. 14.
44. Hallie C. Eakin, Tischa A. Muñoz-Erickson, and Maria Carmen Lemos, "Critical Lines of Action for Vulnerability and Resilience Research and Practice: Lessons from the 2017 Hurricane Season," *Journal of Extreme Events* 5, no. 02n03 (2018): 1850015, https://doi.org/10.1142/S234573761850015X.
45. Susan L. Cutter, "Building Disaster Resilience: Steps toward Sustainability," *Challenges in Sustainability* 1, no. 2 (2014): 72, https://doi.org/10.12924/cis2013.01020072.
46. Jerry M. Melillo, Terese C.T.C. Richmond, and Gary W. Yohe, eds., *Climate Change Impacts in the United States: The Third National Climate Assessment* (Washington, DC: U.S. Global Change Research Program, 2014).
47. Jason Vogel, Karen M. Carney, Joel B. Smith, Megan O. Grady, Alexis St Juliana, and Missy Stults, *The State of Practice in Us Communities* (Kresge Foundation, 2016), https://kresge.org/sites/default/files/library/climate-adaptation-the-state-of-practice-in-us-communities-full-report.pdf.

10

GLANCING BACKWARD WHILE MOVING FORWARD

Susan L. Cutter and Claire B. Rubin

As the authors and editors were at work on this book in the fall of 2018 and spring of 2019, the disaster events kept coming. Knowing where to stop in selecting events to document was difficult. In 2018, costly and deadly events continued to affect the United States, some of the impacts foreshadowed by previous events and the preexisting conditions in those communities.

For example, the beginning of 2018 saw the arrival of the rainy season in California, producing deadly debris flows from the November 2017 Thomas fire in the Santa Barbara region, aptly illustrating another example of a cascading event.[1] Mudslides in wildfire-scarred areas near Montecito, a wealthy enclave outside of Santa Barbara, killed 23 people, crushed homes, and filled major transportation corridors with mud and debris. Anticipating heavy rainfall, local officials ordered evacuations, but only for neighborhoods closest to the mountains, underestimating both the extent of the flooding due to the denuded slopes and the reduction in catchment basin capacities caused by a poorly maintained and aging flood control system.[2] The year ended with the deadliest, costliest, and largest wildfires in California's recorded history.

Two additional events in 2018 illustrated the continuing pattern of cascading events and the production of new extremes. Hurricane

Florence in September 2018 produced rainfall records in two states (36 inches in North Carolina; 24 inches in South Carolina) creating massive flooding in the coastal rivers reminiscent of Hurricane Matthew's impact in 2016 and the floods of 2015.[3] Less than a month later, Hurricane Michael made landfall in the Florida panhandle, devastating the Mexico Beach community and Tyndall Air Force Base with Category 5 winds and storm surge inundation of 14 feet.[4] The storm made its way north through Georgia and the Carolinas, with many residents still in shelters and schools closed from the Hurricane Florence flooding in the Carolinas the previous month.[5] Given the widespread damage and death toll – 51 from Florence; 45 from Michael – these two storm names were retired from future use.[6]

The chapters in the book have provided dramatic examples of signature events that not only received a Presidential Disaster Declaration (PDD) but also provided valuable insights into recovery and resilience issues. The documentation provided soon after the events are a lens for viewing past practices, but it will take many more years to document the full recovery of the communities highlighted here. The recency of hurricanes Florence and Michael, unfortunately, precludes their inclusion in our case studies, despite their significance.

We did not attempt any cross comparison of these signature events as the nature of disaster agents and the focus of each chapter is different. Rather, we sought chapter authors who worked or lived in the affected communities. They not only describe what went well or badly, but also called attention to the many opportunities to learn from these case studies and improve recovery and resilience for future disaster events.

It is also important to note that during our period of study, 2010–2019, there were two dissimilar political administrations at the national level. Each demonstrated profoundly different attitudes and actions to address disasters and their impacts on communities and the people who lived there. As we reflected on each chapter, we found one unanswered question arising repeatedly: Are the deficiencies and distortions of the U.S. emergency management system short-term aberrations or significant lasting changes? That question provides the focus of this concluding chapter.

Knowledge, Experience, and Research Gains

Each year more research products are completed and shared, providing a growing knowledge base regarding disasters – preparing for and dealing with them. For example, between 2000 and 2019 there were 28,940 journal articles on some aspect of U.S. hazards or disasters, with 73 percent appearing between 2010 and 2018.[7] More notable, however, was the increase in publications on U.S. hazards and disasters after 2005, setting Hurricane Katrina and its aftermath as a tipping point in scholarly interest and output in the hazards and disasters field. A similar post-Katrina increase in research is also evident in hazard and disaster-related grants from the National Science Foundation.[8]

Globally, one of the leading publishers of scientific research, Elsevier, found that despite the societal significance of disasters, less than one percent of the global scientific research output from 2012–2016 focused on disaster science and management topics.[9] Their report noted that while the needs are large, the research output (and by inference the research community) is rather small, but often very timely. For the United States, the research output is similar to the global average in preparedness and prevention but it leads the world in disaster response and recovery research, particularly on meteorological and biological disasters.[10]

In virtually all of the disaster case studies described in the book, emergency management practitioners worked with local universities. University personnel often documented the events and actions taken and, in some cases, advised local practitioners about options and alternatives; one notable example was in Houston, Texas. The added experiential knowledge benefits practitioners, academics, and students of emergency management and contributes to the rich narratives in the book.

What Went Right

The Federal Emergency Management Agency is roughly 40 years old. Over the years, there have been peaks and troughs in its effectiveness and public confidence with the agency.[11] Mechanisms are in place and the laws, regulations, and policies exist for the federal government to aid state and local governments with disaster response and recovery. Nevertheless, there are variations in political will, competence, and knowledge at the federal level by the executive and legislative branches of government that directly affect the lives and livelihoods of the American public in times of crises and disasters. Nowhere is this better illustrated than in the contrasts between the Obama and Trump administrations.

Advancements in federal processes and capabilities under FEMA's National Planning Frameworks (see Chapter 2) became a crucial step forward in implementing the national preparedness goal. Another positive sign was the development of FEMA's Strategic Foresight Initiative in 2011, which set out to identify future challenges affecting the emergency management operating environment based on the drivers of future change and strategic needs for improving capabilities in response to these challenges. As the report concludes:

> [W]e have learned that blistering rapid change and complexity will define the emergency management environment over the next few decades. Even demographics, here in the U.S. traditionally one of the more slow-moving and predictable trends, could be subject to sudden and unpredictable lurches, in the face of climate change, pandemic outbreaks, refugee surges or some other factor not even considered today. Meanwhile, new service challenges are arising as government agencies – from Washington down to the smallest towns – wrestle with new responsibilities and extremely challenging fiscal conditions. All of this is playing out in a data-rich but often knowledge-poor environment, where nearly everyone is an information consumer, contributor, and critic. Not surprisingly, these dynamics will drive demand for new, augmented, or otherwise different emergency management capabilities.[12]

Another positive sign was the consistency of the leadership team at FEMA (2008–2016) and its emphasis on enhancing the capabilities of the whole community. Other positive conditions were 1) a FEMA administrator who lasted 8 years; 2) efforts to foster and use research findings; and 3) efforts to improve the reservist cadre. As the outgoing FEMA administrator in the Obama administration testified to Congress:

> [I]t's important that the incoming Administrator not get bogged down in bureaucracy. My parting advice for the FEMA team was to continue going big, going early, going fast, and being smart about it. The Agency currently has the authorities and resources needed for success, but they are both in jeopardy. It is vitally important for the next Administrator to continue building upon the strides the Agency has made since Katrina and working with Congress to ensure authority and funding are not diminished. . . . Challenges in emergency management are a constant. Also, failure is not an option and is not well-received by the American public; we've seen time and again how failures related to federal emergency management contribute to or even establish a narrative of ineffective leadership of a president.[13]

What Went Wrong: The Federal Government No Longer Is a Reliable Partner

There has been a loss of public will to provide effective aid to victims of major disasters and an intentional reduction of capabilities at the national level of government in the past few years. The federal government is no longer a reliable partner for disaster planning or response and recovery implementation. Since 2017, it has become clear that emergency management in the United States is at a low point in terms of acknowledging and dealing with major disasters, particularly those large and costly enough to be eligible for a presidential disaster declaration. There are a number of systemic reasons and unique individual actions by Congress and the executive branch supporting our conclusion.

Executive Agency Senior Staffing and Management Failures

Whether by design or lack of familiarity with executive duties of the Office of the President, the Trump administration has chosen since the beginning to understaff many of the political appointments to federal agencies, including agency and division heads at some Cabinet-level agencies. In many agencies, there is no permanent administrator; instead, temporary acting appointees staff these key positions. As a result, leadership in key areas related to natural hazards or hazardous materials is lacking or very limited, especially in FEMA, EPA, and HUD. This is especially detrimental at FEMA, which has seen two directors in less than two years, with many of the high-level positions still vacant or filled by acting appointments including the FEMA administrator and deputy administrator.[14] Several GAO and Inspector General Reports exposed major management failures in the past two years regarding contracting problems, data leaks, and faulty implementation of the "blue tarp" temporary roofing effort by FEMA, much of this attributable to inexperienced – or worse, incompetent – leadership.[15]

At EPA, the Office of Homeland Security (OHS) has responsibilities for prevention, preparedness, mitigation, response, and recovery efforts for homeland security incidents, including biological, chemical, or radiological contamination, natural hazards, and disasters functioning as a lead agency or support agency as identified in the National Response Plan. As of 2019, the OHS has an acting associate administrator and an acting deputy associate administrator.[16] At HUD, the disaster recovery program (CDBG-DR) is under the General Deputy Assistant Secretary for Community Planning and Development, with an incumbent operating in an acting capacity.[17] Major flaws in the slow distribution of CDBG-DR funds from the 2017 hurricanes identified a number of structural problems including lack of staffing to monitor block grants, guidance for staff to use in assessing grantees, developing monitoring plans, and workforce development to oversee it.[18] More significantly, the GAO report suggested that CDBG-DR appropriations should have permanent statutory authority and regulations for disaster recovery funding to bring it more in line with other disaster assistance programs, rather than leaving it up to ad hoc rule customization for each disaster published in *Federal Register* notices.

Presidential Vision and Petulance

Since the start of Trump Administration in 2017, serious deficiencies in emergency management understanding, thinking, and capability have become apparent and are having seriously negative effects on federal agencies involved with the emergency management community – FEMA, EPA, HUD, Department of Defense (DoD) – who often receive conflicting directions from the White House. This lack of vision and support at the top filters down to reduced funding and assistance for state and local emergency management agencies. Federal responses to disasters, a core governmental function seemingly only recognized by the public when their lives and property are threatened, has political consequences if an administration bungles a response or fails to fully consider the needs of those affected as was seen in the George W. Bush administration after Hurricane Katrina.[19] As noted in *The New York Times* during the 2018 hurricane season, "Since Hurricane Katrina in 2005, the federal response to deadly storms has taken on overt political implications, often standing in for an administration's competence and empathy."[20] Governors and mayors have lost re-elections due to failed responses from federal and state agencies to natural hazards in their states, as have many senior administrators in federal agencies.

There is a noticeable lack of presidential sympathy and support for disaster-stricken communities in California, but most especially in Puerto Rico. Treating Puerto Rico as a foreign country and engaging in name-calling and shaming of local and commonwealth officials by the President are unprecedented actions. As noted in Chapter 8, President Trump began feuding with the Governor of Puerto Rico and the Mayor of San Juan immediately after Hurricane Maria passed over the island, and has not stopped since. He has used public forums to berate the disaster survivors and public officials. He has also threatened the loss of approved recovery funds for Puerto Rico and the California wildfires for his border wall construction, when Congress failed to appropriate funds for it.

Heightened Partisanship on Disaster Relief Funding

The appropriation of disaster relief has always been political, but since Hurricane Sandy, disaster relief has become an extremely partisan issue. Disaster relief bills pit regional representatives against one another (Texas Republican representatives voting against disaster relief aid for New York and New Jersey). Partisanship also occurs in trading off votes for disaster relief for votes on non-related issues (2016 disaster aid for the Zika virus crisis in Florida and Puerto Rico in exchange for defunding Planned Parenthood clinics in Puerto Rico), or not even recognizing the event as worthy of relief funding (Flint water crisis).[21]

Congress is also deadlocked in its willingness to pass disaster relief legislation. Almost two years after hurricanes Irma and Maria affected Florida and Puerto Rico respectively, Congress has not authorized funds for those two places, among others. Politics has interfered with the humanitarian aid for the recent catastrophic hurricanes and fires. President Trump personally interfered in the congressional grant process for disaster relief through verbal shaming, threats of legislative vetoes, and shutting down the government. With increasing need for disaster relief not only for flooding in the Midwest, storms in the Southeast, and more food and infrastructure aid for Puerto Rico, Congress remains stalled as Democrats push for additional money for Puerto Rico and Republicans stand behind Trump and refuse to give in. As the summer of 2019 began and the floodwaters continued to rise, affecting farm states throughout the Midwest, the disaster relief bill finally passed, despite months of unnecessary delay due to partisan infighting. Providing disaster relief to communities in times of need is a core function of the federal government that now appears somewhat derelict in the timeliness of its actions.

Scientific Literacy: Facts Versus Fiction

As we head toward the end of the second decade of the century, we see a trend toward events larger in size, amount of destruction, and costs from those occurring the decade before. At the same time, we note the rapid succession of events, the increased duration of both response and recovery, and increasing income inequality that limits response and recovery efforts for many Americans; trends clearly documented by statistical evidence.

The most important trend influencing disaster events is climate change and the associated sea level rise. Yet, the Trump administration refuses to acknowledge climate change or its impacts, let alone the United States' contribution to greenhouse gas emissions, unlike the previous administration. Development of mitigation plans and adaptive strategies for climate impacts by response agencies such as FEMA, EPA, NOAA, and DoD that began under the Obama administration stopped. Climate change has been and continues to be a national security issue. In response to a congressional mandate, the Department of Defense published a report in 2019 on the effects of a changing climate to the DoD.[22] The report clearly acknowledges climate change threats to missions, installations, and operational plans and the increasing exposure of military installations to recurrent flooding, drought, and wildfire. Yet, there is no mention of the devastation of two military bases from the 2018 hurricanes – Tyndall Air Force Base near Panama City, FL and Camp Lejeune, NC – both facing multimillion-dollar price tags for recovery.[23]

Climate change denial is just one manifestation of the Trump administration's anti-science bias. Starting from his first day in office, the administration has undermined the role of science in public policy, waging a *de facto* war by ignoring it, misrepresenting it, distorting the facts, defunding it, harassing federal scientists, and reducing access to scientific information by the public. This is pervasive throughout the federal government, and most seriously affects public health and safety. A Union of Concerned Scientists report of actions in the first six months of the Trump administration provides a scary primer of the assault on science in support of public policy that continues.[24] In an interesting move to improve public awareness of government attempts to restrict climate science and scale back federal climate mitigation and adaptation measures, the Sabin Center for Climate Change Law at Columbia University maintains a web-based Silencing Science Tracker and a Climate Deregulation Tracker.[25]

Since the Trump administration will not deal with real science and its input into public policy and governance, it is unlikely that any major improvements in emergency management including disaster response will occur until administrations change. As pointed out by *The New York Times* editorial board:

> From Day 1, the White House and its lackeys in certain federal agencies have been waging what amounts to a war on science, appointing people with few scientific credentials to key positions, defunding programs that could lead to a cleaner and safer environment and a healthier population, and, most ominously,

censoring scientific inquiry that could inform the public and government policy.[26]

Deconstructing the Whole Community Approach

Given the uncertainties of federal agency responsibilities and federal funding in recent years, it will be essential to work smarter and to rely more on other sectors of society for all phases of emergency management. The hierarchical structure of command and control employed in the federal incident management system (ICS) and to a lesser extent in the National Response and National Recovery Frameworks led to a reexamination of the prior government-centric emergency management approach, especially in light of potentially catastrophic events. Rolled out in 2011, the whole community approach combined with local partnerships created a shared-partnership business model for emergency management with three key principles: 1) understand and meet the actual needs of the community; 2) engage and empower all parts of the community; and 3) strengthen what works well in communities on a daily basis.[27]

With the dismantling of federal agencies and other governance structures, the federal government may no longer be a reliable partner in emergency management. The transformation of whole community to "you're on your own" community could fundamentally alter how to conduct emergency management in the future. A shift from a federal-centric vertical hierarchy structure to a more locally based horizontal but vertically integrated structure is underway. Increasingly, communities are developing stronger relationships with a broad array of groups in state and local governments, the private sector, nonprofit organizations, faith-based organizations, and others.

These relationships guide preparedness, response, and resilience efforts but are more significant in recovery efforts, where the philanthropic sector also has stepped up efforts to provide financial support to nonprofits assisting in recovery. For example, the Center for Disaster Philanthropy provides consulting services – technical assistance, strategic planning, research, and analysis – to other philanthropy organizations wanting to engage in disaster recovery.[28] It also provides recovery funding for vulnerable populations filling the gaps when public resources are unavailable, scarce, or insufficient to satisfy unmet needs. Presently they have multiple national campaigns underway including 2019 Midwest floods recovery fund, 2018 Atlantic hurricane season recovery fund, and California wildfire recovery fund. Examples include grants to nonprofits in Northern California to support the rapid rehousing of 40 families displaced by the 2018 wildfires, emergency financial assistance and comprehensive case management for six months for fire-affected families, and support for low-income individuals including immigrants and seniors living and working in one of the wildfire-affected counties.[29] In Puerto Rico, with more than $100 billion in damages, philanthropic giving from individuals and organizations totaled more than $375 million primarily for relief, recovery, and rebuilding, much of it from the Puerto Rican diaspora.[30]

Planning for post-disaster recovery by a community is another mechanism for building local capacity for response and recovery with an eye toward more resilient reconstruction.[31] The development of recovery plans before a disaster occurs helps to identify vulnerable groups and structures, helping networks, and the range of institutional arrangements present in communities that can either thwart or enhance recovery. One example is the mayor's office in Houston, which is working on several aspects of recovery and provides not only a listing of recovery resources, but also a pre-disaster recovery plan template.[32] The collaborative planning effort engaged local government, community organizations, the private sector, and recovery partners in a coordinated and networked process designed to reduce future disaster impacts. A much longer comprehensive pre-disaster recovery plan written by Fairfax County to guide recovery actions in the event of a large or catastrophic incident addresses long-term housing restoration and reconstruction, economic recovery, infrastructure and lifeline restoration/recovery, provision of public safety, security, and community services, and protection of natural and cultural resources.[33] However, many communities may lack the expertise and resources for such comprehensive planning efforts such as Fairfax County, making Houston's pre-disaster recovery plan template a more viable option for many communities.

Facing the Flood Challenge

Almost 75 year ago, Gilbert F. White wrote in his dissertation "Floods are acts of God, but flood losses are largely acts of man [sic]."[34] As one of many advisors to President Lyndon Johnson regarding the establishment of the National Flood Insurance Program (NFIP), White argued for an integrated approach for managing flood risk, including insurance. As we round out the second decade of the 21st century, flood problems are escalating in frequency, intensity, and duration resulting in more lives lost and skyrocketing costs to homes, businesses, infrastructure, and crops. The passage of the National Flood Insurance Act of 1968 creating the NFIP has gone through many iterations over the years to strengthen its provisions, improve its risk mapping and insurance rate setting, and ensuring its overall fiscal soundness in an attempt to control development in flood-hazard areas and reduce federal expenditures for post-flood disaster assistance.

Significant changes occurred in 2012 with the Biggert-Waters Flood Insurance Reform Act (implementation of more risk-based premiums for policyholders). To appease interest group campaigns suggesting widespread premium increases of tens of thousands of dollars for many policyholders,[35] Congress reversed itself in 2014 by actually repealing some provisions of Biggert-Waters regarding affordability with the passage of the Homeowner Flood Insurance Affordability Act, thereby illustrating one of the many inherent conflicts in the fragmented federal approach to flood hazards. Since September 2017, the NFIP has had 11 short-term reauthorizations without any substantive changes to the program. The latest short-term reauthorization runs through September 30, 2019, after which time:

1. Authority to provide new flood insurance contracts ceases but contracts entered into before the expiration date would continue until the end of their one-year policy term;
2. Authority for FEMA to borrow funds from the Treasury reduces to $1 billion, and if funds to pay claims were depleted from premiums or the reserve fund, then claimants would have to wait

for payments until Congress appropriated supplemental funds or increased the borrowing limit.[36]

The inability of Congress to pass bipartisan comprehensive reforms to the NFIP program continues the fragmented and short-term approach to flooding, in contrast to the integrated, comprehensive approach envisioned in 1968. The principal issues with NFIP reform and reauthorization vary among different stakeholders but generally fall into six broad areas.[37]

- **Financial solvency**: Need to address the $20.5 billion debt to Treasury (at the end of 2018 after Congress canceled a $16B debt in 2017);
- **Premiums and affordability**: Make insurance rates risk-based and eliminate subsidies; provide some measure of affordability to those who need it;
- **Flood mapping**: Complete flood mapping for the nation, improve the accuracy of existing flood maps;
- **Mitigation and repetitive loss**: Enhance and reward pre-flood mitigation through premium reductions and restrict policies for repetitive loss properties;
- **Private insurance**: Remove federal ambiguities that limit growth of private flood insurance;
- **Reauthorization timing**: Extend the reauthorization periods beyond five years, for example, to enable more time for reforms to take place to reduce partisan bickering and unwillingness to commit to needed reforms.

Despite the longevity of the NFIP and the periodic renewal of its statutory authority (i.e. reauthorization), there have been relatively few audits or evaluations of the entire program. It is unclear whether the NFIP is increasing or decreasing flood losses in the nation. There has been no comprehensive assessment of the entire program since 2006, despite periodic reviews of individual elements such as flood hazard mapping or insurance rates. The 2006 review did target its evaluation on progress toward meeting the NFIP's four goals: "decrease the risk of future flood losses; reduce the costs and adverse consequences of flooding; reduce the demands and expectations for disaster assistance after floods; and preserve and restore the natural and beneficial uses of floodplains."[38] The conclusions are telling and help explain why, 13 years later, Congress has still not made significant reforms to the NFIP including whether the program increases or decreases flood losses.

> Although the overall goals of the NFIP are clear, consensus has not been reached on specific, interim national floodplain management goals and objectives. Further, the data available to measure progress towards such objectives are limited. Progress towards goals cannot be evaluated if information is not available. . . . The NFIP operates in coordination with state governments, but the states' potential for furthering the goals of the program has not been fully utilized.[39]

Meanwhile the flood problem is increasing – in our coastal communities due to sea level rise, in our streams and rivers due to extreme precipitation events, and in our urban areas as a consequence of poor storm water management and the increasing frequency of heavy rainfall events. Urban flooding and sunny day flooding (also called high tide or nuisance flooding) in coastal areas are distinct types of flooding that will increase in the next decade due to climate change and increasing urbanization along the coast. They will necessitate a different approach for risk estimation and management.[40] According to a NOAA report,

> the risk of coastal flooding is rapidly increasing; in fact, annual high tide flood frequencies are already linearly increasing or accelerating at most locations examined. . . . Such a flood frequency "tipping point" is becoming more apparent as several coastal cities with infrastructure increasingly vulnerable to high tide flooding undertake large scale and costly upgrades to combat effects.[41]

As the late Margaret Davidson was fond of saying, "Today's flood will become tomorrow's high tide."

Governance Structures for Recovery and Resilience

There is no formal legislative or legal structure for disaster resilience or disaster recovery such as the Stafford Act. While the National Recovery Framework and the National Mitigation Framework focus on recovery and resilience respectively, there are no regular funding streams nor consistent guidelines for distributing funds, and programmatic incentives/disincentives for communities. The bifurcation of recovery between FEMA (generally short-term, e.g. 180 days) and HUD (long-term) presents challenges to communities in the post-disaster period in knowing the responsibilities, rules, and documentary evidence required as they navigate the federal bureaucracy. For instance, with the CDBG-DR program at HUD, grantee requirements change from disaster to disaster as there is no permanent statutory authority for CDBG-DR appropriations for "unmet disaster recovery needs," nor a consistent set of rules, regulations, or guidance for states to follow to obtaining funds. A GAO report suggested, "legislation establishing permanent statutory authority for a disaster assistance program administered by HUD or another agency that responds to unmet needs in a timely manner and directing the applicable agency to issue implementing regulations."[42] Thus far, there has been no congressional movement in this direction.

Within the FAA Reauthorization Act of 2018 is Division D, otherwise known as the Disaster Recovery Reform Act of 2018 (DRRA). The Act specifically applies to each major disaster and emergency declared on or after August 1, 2017 under the Stafford Act. It has over 50 provisions that require policy or regulatory changes designed to amend the Stafford Act and reduce the complexity of FEMA.[43] Unfortunately, the Disaster Recovery Reform Act does not address long-term recovery because of its sole focus on FEMA, saying nothing about the HUD's CDBG-DR program or unmet disaster recovery needs.

A more positive element in the Disaster Recovery Reform Act is the increased emphasis on community resilience by providing a consistent and reliable funding stream for pre-disaster grant funding for public infrastructure projects in its new Building Resilient Infrastructure and Communities (BRIC) program. Building on the 2012 National Academies landmark report, *Disaster Resilience: A National Imperative*, FEMA's new strategic plan focuses on pre-disaster mitigation. The plan highlights three goals to reduce losses from natural hazards:

1. Build a culture of preparedness for state and local governments including capacity and investment in pre-disaster mitigation;
2. Ready the nation for catastrophic disasters whereby FEMA focuses its efforts and resources on the largest of events with the assumption that state and local are better prepared under the first goal; and
3. Reduce the complexity of FEMA.[44]

The plan suggests a new model of disaster recovery programs that are "federally supported, state managed, and locally executed," echoing what the federal government has long argued, namely that FEMA cannot lead recovery efforts for every disaster, thus necessitating state and local management and execution.[45] While lofty in aspiration, the utility and effectiveness of the new federal Disaster Recovery Reform Act remains unknown at this time.

A Concluding Note of Optimism

Unless there is a major change in mindset, and the political will to think strategically, improvements in enhancing the nation's disaster resilience and facilitating post-disaster recovery will have to wait until a new administration takes office. As evidenced by the case studies in the preceding chapters, there are many bright spots of local engagement and support before, during, and after a disaster. However, the known prospect of weather-related disasters increasing due to climate change and the denial of the science does not bode well for handling the surprise of multiple disasters occurring back-to-back in the same season or the same region of the country. Our federal institutions ignore the new realities in the fundamental shifts in natural and human systems – more people are moving into hazard zones which themselves are changing and expanding, ultimately putting more people and places at risk. Congress has been dysfunctional, the current executive branch is ignorant of the responsibilities and complexities of governance, and the American electorate are seemingly apathetic unless a hazard event hits close to home, which is happening more frequently than in the past.

There is hope and indeed a possibility or some say a necessity for change – in our electoral politics, in our understanding of science, and in the value we ascribed to community service and helping others. There are signs that the many efforts to champion the cause of disaster mitigation and resilience are coming to fruition. However, it is the next generation, many of whom have contributed chapters to this book and many more who will read it, that offers the best opportunity to right the ship and steer us into the messy future with all of its challenges, opportunities, and excitement. The pace of technological change is accelerating with new ways of producing and communicating risk information to inspire action, seemingly translating what once appeared as science fiction into forecasts, creative visualizations, and now reality.[46]

Notes

1. See Chapter 2 for the discussion on the temporal and spatial connection of discrete events and Chapter 7 for a description of the fires.
2. Joe Mozingo, "Santa Barbara County Knew Mudslides Were a Risk. It Did Little to Stop Them," *Los Angeles Times*, December 20, 2018, www.latimes.com/local/california/la-me-montecito-debris-basins-20181220-htmlstory.html.
3. Stacy R. Stewart and Robbie Berg, *National Hurricane Center Tropical Cyclone Report: Hurricane Florence (AL062018) 31 August–17 September 2018* (Washington, DC: NOAA, May 3, 2019), www.nhc.noaa.gov/data/tcr/AL062018_Florence.pdf.
4. John L. Beven II, Robbie Berg, and Andrew Hagen, *National Hurricane Center Tropical Cyclone Report: Hurricane Michael (AL 142018) 7–11 October 2018* (Washington, DC: NOAA, May 17, 2019), www.nhc.noaa.gov/data/tcr/AL142018_Michael.pdf.
5. Chris Dixon and Campbell Robertson, "They Were Still Recovering from Hurricane Florence. Then Michael Came," *The New York Times*, October 11, 2018, www.nytimes.com/2018/10/11/us/carolinas-hurricane-florence-michael.html.
6. National Oceanic and Atmospheric Administration (NOAA), "Florence and Michael Retired by the World Meteorological Organization," March 20, 2019, www.noaa.gov/media-release/florence-and-michael-retired-by-world-meteorological-organization.
7. This was based on a *Web of Science* search using keywords, U.S. hazards or disasters for the period 2000–2019, conducted by the author.
8. Adam Behrendt, Kathryn Lukasiewicz Daniel Seaberg, and Jun Zhuang, "Trends in Multidisciplinary Hazard and Disaster Research: A 1982–2017 Case Study," *Risk Analysis* (2019), https://doi.org/10.1111/risa.13308.

9. Elsevier, *A Global Outlook on Disaster Science* (Amsterdam, The Netherlands: Elsevier, 2017), www.elsevier.com/__data/assets/pdf_file/0008/538091/ElsevierDisaster ScienceReport-PDF.pdf.

10. Ibid., 35–36.

11. C.B. Rubin, *Emergency Management: The American Experience 1900–2005* (Fairfax, VA: Public Entity Risk Institute, 2007); George J. Haddow, Jane Bullock, and Damon Coppola, *Introduction to Emergency Management*, 6th edition (Cambridge, UK: Butterworth-Heinenmann, 2017).

12. Strategic Foresight Initiative, *Crisis Response and Disaster Resilience 2030: Forging Strategic Action in an Age of Uncertainty* (Washington, DC: FEMA, January 12, 2012), 13, www.fema.gov/media-library-data/20130726-1816-25045-5167/sfi_report_13. jan.2012_final.docx.pdf.

13. W. Craig Fugate, "The Future of FEMA: Recommendations of Former Administrators," Testimony before the Committee on Homeland Security, Subcommittee on Emergency Preparedness, Response, and Communications, U.S. House of Representatives, February 28, 2017, https://docs.house.gov/meetings/HM/HM12/ 20170228/105585/HHRG-115-HM12-Wstate-FugateW-20170228.pdf.

14. FEMA, "FEMA Leadership Organizational Structure," April 30, 2019, www.fema. gov/media-library-data/1556626489884-311cb457d271cf5c4b7aa04bc6a10df7/ orgchart.pdf.

15. Government Accountability Office (GAO), *Puerto Rico Hurricanes: Status of FEMA Funding, Oversight, and Recovery Challenges* (Washington, DC: GAO Report GAO-19-256, March 14, 2019); GAO, *2017 Hurricanes and Wildfires: Initial Observations on the Federal Response and Key Recovery Challenges* (Washington, DC: GAO Report GAO-18-472, September 4, 2018).

16. EPA, "About the Office of Homeland Security (OHS)," accessed May 22, 2019, www.epa.gov/aboutepa/about-office-homeland-security-ohs.

17. HUD, "Principal Directory," accessed May 22, 2019, www.hud.gov/contact/ principal_directory.

18. Government Accountability Office, *Disaster Recovery: Better Monitoring of Block Grant Funds is Needed* (Washington, DC: GAO Report GAO-19-232, March 25, 2019). www.gao.gov/assets/700/697827.pdf.

19. Richard T. Sylves, "President Bush and Hurricane Katrina: A Presidential Leadership Study," *Annals of the American Academy of Political and Social Science* 604 (March 2006): 26–56.

20. Ron Nixon, Julie Hirschfeld Davis, and James Glanz, "Hurricane Florence Is a Formidable Test for FEMA and Trump," *The New York Times*, September 12, 2018, www. nytimes.com/2018/09/12/us/politics/trump-hurricane-florence-fema.html.

21. Susan Milligan, "Playing Games with a Disaster," *U.S. News and World Report*, September 30, 2016, www.usnews.com/news/articles/2016-09-30/the-partisan-politics-of-disaster-relief.

22. Office of the Under Secretary of Defense for Acquisition and Sustainment, *Report on Effects of a Changing Climate to the Department of Defense* (Washington, DC: Department of Defense, January 2019), https://media.defense.gov/2019/ Jan/29/2002084200/-1/-1/1/CLIMATE-CHANGE-REPORT-2019.PDF.

23. John Conger, "New Pentagon Report: 'The Effects of a Changing Climate are a National Security Issue'," January 18, 2019, https://climateandsecurity.org/2019/01/18/new-pentagon-report-the-effects-of-a-changing-climate-are-a-national-security-issue/.

24. Jacob Carter, Gretchen Goldman, Genna Reed, Peter Hansel, Michael Halpern, and Andrew Rosenberg, *Sidelining Science Since Day One: How the Trump*

Administration Has Harmed Public Health and Safety in Its First Six Months (Boston, MA: Center for Science and Democracy at the Union of Concerned Scientists, July 2017), www.ucsusa.org/sites/default/files/attach/2017/07/sidelining-science-report-ucs-7-20-2017.pdf.

25. See the Silencing Science Tracker at http://columbiaclimatelaw.com/resources/silencing-science-tracker/ and the Climate Deregulation Tracker at http://columbia climatelaw.com/resources/climate-deregulation-tracker/ for both daily and weekly updates.

26. Editorial Board, "President Trump's War on Science," *The New York Times*, September 9, 2017, www.nytimes.com/2017/09/09/opinion/sunday/trump-epa-pruitt-science. html?searchResultPosition=1.

27. FEMA, *A Whole Community Approach to Emergency Management: Principles, Themes, and Pathways for Action* (Washington, DC: FEMA FDOC 104-008-1, December 2011). www.fema.gov/media-library-data/20130726-1813-25045-3330/whole_community_dec2011__2_.pdf.

28. See the Center for Disaster Philanthropy website https://disasterphilanthropy.org/who-we-are/, accessed May 23, 2019.

29. Regine A. Webster, "Northern California Wildfire Grants Support Most Vulnerable," Center for Disaster Philanthropy, February 22, 2018, https://disasterphilan thropy.org/blog/wildfires/northern-california-wildfire-grants-support-vulnerable/.

30. Janice Petrovich, *Philanthropy and Puerto Rico after Hurricane Maria: How a Natural Disaster Put Puerto Rico on the Philanthropic Map and Implications for the Future* (Red de Fundaciones de Puerto Rico, December 2018), accessed May 23, 2019, http://redfundacionespr.org/wp-content/themes/virtue-child-theme/pdf/Philantropy_PR_v5.pdf.

31. Gavin Smith, *Planning for Post-Disaster Recovery: A Review of the United States Disaster Assistance Framework*, 2nd edition (Washington, DC: Island Press, 2012).

32. Houston Urban Area Security Initiative (UASI) Regional Recovery Workgroup, *Pre-Disaster Recovery Plan*, accessed May 23, 2019, http://onestarfoundation.org/wp-content/uploads/2019/01/Pre-Disaster-Recovery-Plan-Template.pdf.

33. Fairfax County Office of Emergency Management, *Fairfax County Pre-Disaster Recovery Plan*, January 5, 2012, www.fairfaxcounty.gov/emergencymanagement/sites/emergencymanagement/files/assets/documents/ffx%20pdrp%20complete%20 document%20(bos%20endorsed%20indexed)%20032112.pdf.

34. Gilbert F. White, *Human Adjustment to Floods*. Research Paper No. 29 (Chicago: University of Chicago Press, 1945, republished 1953), quote from p. 2.

35. Two National Academy of Sciences reports addressed the affordability issue with suggestions for protocols for evaluating policy options. These are National Academies of Sciences, Engineering, and Medicine, *Affordability of National Flood Insurance Program Premiums: Report 1* (Washington, DC: National Academies Press, 2015); and National Academies of Sciences, Engineering, and Medicine, *Affordability of National Flood Insurance Program Premiums: Report 2* (Washington, DC: National Academies Press, 2016).

36. Diane P. Horn, "What Happens if the National Flood Insurance Program (NFIP) Lapses?," *CRS Insight*, January 14, 2019, https://fas.org/sgp/crs/homesec/IN10835. pdf.

37. Government Accountability Office, *Flood Insurance: Comprehensive Reform Could Improve Solvency and Enhance Resilience* (Washington, DC: GAO Report GAO-17-415, April 2017), www.gao.gov/assets/690/684354.pdf; EveryCRSReport.com, "Selected Issues for National Flood Insurance Program (NFIP) Reauthorization and

Reform: Homeland Security Issues in the 116th Congress," *CRS Insight*, February 19, 2019, www.everycrsreport.com/reports/IN11050.html.

Maria Cox Lamm, Chair, Association of State Floodplain Managers "Testimony: National Flood Insurance Program Reauthorization and Reform," Before the House Financial Services Committee, Washington, DC, March 13, 2019, https://financial services.house.gov/uploadedfiles/hhrg-116-ba00-wstate-coxlammm-20190313.pdf; Association of State Floodplain Managers, "ASFPM Detailed Priorities for 2019 NFIP Reauthorization and Reform," last updated April 1, 2019, www.floods.org/ ace-images/ASFPMPriorities4NFIP2019ReauthorizationApr1_2019.pdf.

38. American Institutes for Research, *The Evaluation of the National Flood Insurance Program, Final Report* (Washington, DC: American Institutes for Research, October 2006), www.fema.gov/media-library-data/20130726-1602-20490-1463/nfip_eval_final_report.pdf, quote from p. 4.

39. Ibid., p. 42.

40. National Academies of Sciences, Engineering, and Medicine, *Framing the Challenge of Urban Flooding in the United States* (Washington, DC: National Academies Press, 2019), https://doi.org/10.17226/25381; Elizabeth Rush, *Rising: Dispatches from the New American Shore* (Milkweek Editions, June 2018); Jason Samenow, "Federal Report: High Tide Flooding Could Happen 'Every Other Day' by Late this Century," *The Washington Post*, March 28, 2018, www.washingtonpost.com/news/ capital-weather-gang/wp/2018/03/28/federal-report-high-tide-flooding-could-happen-every-other-day-by-late-this-century/?utm_term=.5bdcc0a8fd68.

41. William V. Sweet, Greg Dusek, Jayantha Obeysekera, and John J. Marra, *Patterns and Projections of High Tide Flooding Along the U.S. Coastline Using a Common Impact Threshold* (Silver Spring, MD; NOAA, Technical Report NOS CO-OPS 086, February 2018), https://tidesandcurrents.noaa.gov/publications/techrpt86_PaP_of_HTFlooding.pdf, 31.

42. GAO, *Disaster Recovery*, 54.

43. See www.fema.gov/disaster-recovery-reform-act-2018 for the provisions in the bill and updates on FEMA's status in their implementation.

44. FEMA, *2018–2022 Strategic Plan* (Washington, DC: FEMA, 2018), www.fema.gov/ media-library-data/1533052524696-b5137201a4614ade5e0129ef01cbf661/strat_plan.pdf.

45. Jieyi Lu, "Congress and FEMA Indicate Shift toward Resilience in National Disaster Policy," Environmental and Energy Study Institute, June 27, 2018, www.eesi.org/articles/ view/congress-and-fema-indicate-shift-in-national-disaster-policy-toward-resilie.

46. Namwali Serpell, "When Science Fiction Comes True," *New York Times Book Review Essay*, March 12, 2019, www.nytimes.com/2019/03/12/books/review/namwali-serpell.html.

ABOUT THE AUTHORS

Sergio Alvarez (Chapter 6) is an assistant professor of natural resource economics researching how natural resources and the environment contribute to human well-being through the provision of ecosystem services such as food, recreation, and protection from natural and man-made hazards. He holds a BA in Environmental Sciences and MS and Ph.D. degrees in Food and Resource Economics, all from the University of Florida. Alvarez has published articles on a range of topics including the economics of marine resources, the costs and management of biological invasions, and the value of ecosystem services such as clean water and outdoor recreation. Between 2013 and 2018, he served as the Chief Economist at the Florida Department of Agriculture and Consumer Services. As part of this role, Dr. Alvarez worked in the Florida State Emergency Operations Center during Hurricane Irma. He joined the faculty at the University of Central Florida in 2018.

Génesis Álvarez-Rosario (Chapter 8) is a student in the Graduate School of Social Work at the University of Puerto Rico – Río Piedras and a research assistant for Dr. Jenniffer Santos-Hernández at Centro de Investigaciones Sociales (CIS). She is a graduate fellow of the NSF Urban Resilience to Extremes Sustainability Research Network (UREx

SRN). Álvarez holds a bachelor's and master's degree in social work. Her research focuses on the experiences of grandparents raising children during disasters. She has also researched the knowledge, values, and skills of social workers managing cases of same-sex couples interested in adoption.

Lucy A. Arendt (Chapter 3) is a professor of management in the Donald J. Schneider School of Business and Economics at St. Norbert College. She received her Ph.D. in Management Science from the University of Wisconsin-Milwaukee, and teaches strategy, leadership, and organizational behavior to both undergraduate and graduate students. Her scholarly work focuses on organizational and community decision making in the aftermath of disasters. Arendt studies how organizational and community leaders perceive and address risks associated with disasters and how organizations and communities engage in long-term recovery and resilience-building. The overarching goal of her interdisciplinary research is to discover and communicate lessons that may be used to enhance public policy and practice.

Jane Cage (Chapter 3) is Principal at InsightFive22, a consulting firm in Joplin, Missouri specializing in strategic planning and long-term community recovery and resilience. She served as the Chair of the Joplin Citizens Advisory Recovery Team (CART) after the Joplin tornado. The CART developed a long-term recovery plan for the city based on a citizen visioning process. Since that time, she has become a national resource and public speaker to disaster-affected communities as well as federal agencies. Cage published an essay collection, *Joplin Pays It Forward*, in 2013 with the practical lessons learned of 50 people involved in all sectors of the Joplin Recovery. She is an instructor with the FEMA EMI specializing in the role of the community post-disaster. Cage graduated from Wake Forest University with a degree in economics and is a graduate of the Harvard National Preparedness Initiative.

David Calkin (Chapter 7) is a supervisory research forester at the Human Dimensions Program of the U.S. Forest Service Rocky

Mountain Research Station in Missoula, Montana. He leads the Wildfire Risk Management Science team (www.fs.fed.us/rmrs/groups/wildfire-risk-management-team) working to improve risk-based fire management decision making through improved science development, application, and delivery. His research incorporates economics with risk and decision sciences to explore ways to evaluate and improve the efficiency and effectiveness of wildfire management programs. Calkin has an MS degree in natural resource conservation from the University of Montana and a Ph.D in economics from Oregon State University.

Susan L. Cutter (Coeditor, Chapter 2) is Carolina Distinguished Professor of Geography at the University of South Carolina and director of the Hazards & Vulnerability Research Institute. She is a nationally and internationally recognized scholar publishing more than 14 books and 175 refereed articles and book chapters. Her primary research interests are in the area of vulnerability and resilience science, with a particular focus on its measurement, monitoring, assessment, and usage in policy and practice. Cutter is an elected fellow of the American Association for the Advancement of Science (AAAS) and a former president of the American Association of Geographers (AAG) and the Consortium of Social Science Associations (COSSA). She served on many national advisory boards and committees, including those of the National Academies of Science, Engineering, and Medicine, National Institute of Standards and Technology, and the National Science Foundation, and was a juror for the Rebuild by Design competition for Hurricane Sandy Recovery Projects. She also is an elected foreign member of the Royal Norwegian Society of Science and Letters. She received her master's and doctorate in geography from the University of Chicago.

Christopher T. Emrich (Chapter 6) is Endowed Associate Professor of Environmental Science and Public Administration within the School of Public Administration and a founding member of the newly formed National Center for Integrated Coastal Research at University of Central Florida (UCF Coastal). His research/practical service includes applying geospatial technologies to emergency management planning and practice, long-term disaster recovery, and the intersection of social vulnerability and community resilience in the face of catastrophe. He provided geospatial support for response and long-term recovery to Florida from 2004–2007 and has assisted other states and U.S. territories with their recovery plans. He earned his master's in geography from the University of South Florida and his Ph.D from the University of South Carolina.

Donovan Finn (Chapter 4) is Assistant Professor in the Sustainability Studies Program and School of Marine and Atmospheric Sciences at Stony Brook University where he also directs Stony Brook's undergraduate degree in Environmental Design, Policy and Planning. His research interests include urban sustainability, coastal resilience, environmental justice, and participatory planning. A longtime resident of New York City, Finn has been involved in research on the recovery process across the region since Hurricane Sandy, especially in the neighborhoods of Red Hook, Midland Beach, and the Rockaways. He holds a master's degree in urban planning and a Ph.D in regional planning, both from the University of Illinois at Urbana-Champaign.

Melanie Gall (Chapter 9) is a research professor in the College of Public Service and Community Solutions at Arizona State University and teaches in the online master's program in Emergency Management and Homeland Security. She co-directs the Center for Emergency Management and Homeland Security and manages the Spatial Hazard Events and Losses Database for the United States (SHELDUS). As a hazards geographer, her expertise lies in geospatial technologies, risk assessments, and hazard mitigation planning. She received a bachelor of science from the University of Heidelberg in 1998, a master's from the University of Salzburg in 2002, and a doctorate from the University of South Carolina in 2007.

Claire Connolly Knox (Chapter 6) is an associate professor and the Master of Emergency and Crisis Management Program Director in the School of Public Administration at the University of Central Florida. Her primary research interests include environmental vulnerability and disaster response, coastal resiliency, Habermas' critical theory, and the scholarship of teaching and learning. Dr. Knox is Chair of ASPA's Section for Emergency and Crisis Management and FEMA's Scholarship of Teaching and Learning Group. In 2015, she received the Florida Emergency Preparedness Association's Gary Arnold award for her dedication to improving Florida's emergency management community through higher education. She has an MPA and Ph.D in public administration from Florida State University.

Ashley J. Méndez-Heavilin (Chapter 8) is a student in the Graduate School of Planning at the University of Puerto Rico – Río Piedras and a research assistant for Dr. Jenniffer Santos-Hernández at Centro de Investigaciones Sociales (CIS). She is a graduate fellow of the NSF Urban Resilience to Extremes Sustainability Research Network (UREx-SRN). Méndez holds a BA magna cum laude in sociology and a minor in human resources from the UPR-RP. Her interests include environmental justice, gender studies, climate change adaptation, and special needs populations in disasters.

Ashley D. Ross (Chapter 5) is an assistant professor in the Marine Sciences Department at Texas A&M University at Galveston where she teaches coastal policy and environmental management courses in the Marine Resources Management master's program. Her research examines disaster resilience with a specific focus on local governance. Her book *Local Disaster Resilience: Administrative and Political Perspectives* analyzes the resilience of coastal communities along the U.S. Gulf Coast. She is a faculty fellow with the Texas A&M University Center for Texas Beaches and Shores. She has a master's degree in political science from Louisiana State University and a Ph.D also in political science from Texas A&M University.

Claire B. Rubin (Coeditor, Chapter 1) is president of Claire B. Rubin & Associates, LLC (clairerubin.com), a small business specializing in disaster research and consulting located in Arlington, Virginia. She is a social scientist with forty years of experience in emergency management and homeland security. Her experience includes independent researcher, consultant, practitioner, and educator. She was an affiliate of The George Washington University's Institute for Crisis, Disaster, and Risk Management from 1998 through 2014. In recent years, her firm has produced a variety of educational products and services, most notably the Disaster Time Line series and the Disaster Bookstore. For eight years she has maintained the blog on disaster recovery called Recovery Diva. She also is the cofounder and moderator for three Facebook groups regarding emergency management. Ms. Rubin is the author or editor of three books to date. She has almost 100 additional publications and has presented numerous talks and lectures on emergency management and homeland security topics. She was the cofounder and, for six years, managing editor of *The Journal of Homeland Security and Emergency Management.*

Abdul-Akeem Sadiq (Chapter 6) is an associate professor in the School of Public Administration at the University of Central Florida. He received his joint Ph.D in Public Policy from Georgia State University and Georgia Institute of Technology in 2009. Dr. Sadiq's research focuses on organizational disaster preparedness and mitigation, hazard risk perceptions, community resilience to floods, and collaborative governance. He has received research funding from the National Science Foundation including a fellowship for the NSF Enabling the Next Generation of Hazards and Disasters Researchers. Sadiq has published 31 peer-reviewed articles and several book chapters. His teaching interests include emergency management, homeland security, and public administration. Sadiq serves on the *Journal of Emergency Management* advisory board, as a board member of ASPA Section on Emergency and Crisis Management, and as President of the Central Florida Chapter of the American Society for Public Administration (ASPA).

Jenniffer M. Santos-Hernández (Chapter 8) is a sociologist and research professor for Centro de Investigaciones Sociales at the University of Puerto Rico – Río Piedras. She is the co-city lead for the city of San Juan in the NSF Urban Resilience to Extremes Sustainability Research Network (UREx SRN) and the external evaluator of the NSF Scholars from Under-Represented Groups in Engineering and the Social Sciences Capacity in Disasters (SURGE). Dr. Santos-Hernández holds a BA magna cum laude in sociology from the University of Puerto Rico, an MA and Ph.D in sociology from the University of Delaware, and several certifications. As a graduate student, she held research positions at the Disaster Research Center (DRC) and Oak Ridge National Laboratory (ORNL). Santos-Hernández' research focuses on issues of development and policy transfers, social vulnerability to disasters, climate change adaptation and education, and the increasing "rationalization" of emergency management.

Karen Short (Chapter 7) is a research ecologist with the USDA Forest Service, Rocky Mountain Research Station, Human Dimensions program. She received her BSc in Wildlife and Fisheries Science from the University of Arizona and her Ph.D in Organismal Biology and Ecology from the University of Montana. Her work has included fire-effects research in southwestern ponderosa pine forests; development and maintenance of spatial datasets on vegetation, fuels, and fire-occurrence for several national applications; and mapping of wildfire hazard for risk assessment and other applications. One product of this work is a spatial database of wildfires in the U.S., now spanning 1992–2015: www.fs.usda. gov/rds/archive/Product/RDS-2013-0009.4/.

Meg Traci (Chapter 7) is a senior scientist at the University of Montana Rural Institute for Inclusive Communities. Her work focuses on strengthening public systems through the inclusion of persons with disabilities. For the past 15 years, her work has included a focus on strengthening emergency management to better serve the whole community by integrating supports and solutions designed to support the health and participation of people with disabilities.

Renee White (Chapter 3) was the Chairperson of the Joplin Area Long-Term Recovery Committee after the May 2011 tornado, a volunteer position, for over 2.5 years. It was her first opportunity to be involved in disaster recovery. She continues to work with disaster-effected communities via the Disaster Leadership Team, a national group of experienced community organizers post-disaster. She received a bachelor's in social work in 1983; a master's in social work in 1994, and an educational doctorate in 2010. Since 2015 she has been the Department Chair and Associate Professor of Social Work at Missouri Southern State University in Joplin, Missouri.

Yao Zhou (Chapter 6) is Boardman Preeminent Postdoctoral Scholar of Environmental Science and Public Administration at the University of Central Florida. She holds a BS in geographic information systems from Wuhan University, an MS in physical geography from Beijing Normal University, and a Ph.D in geography from the University of Florida. Her research uses GIS techniques and spatial statistics to examine tropical cyclone precipitation, natural hazards, and social vulnerability.

INDEX

Note: Page numbers in *italic* indicate a figure and page numbers in **bold** indicate a table on the corresponding page.

NAFTA *see* North American Free Trade
Agreement (NAFTA)
National Centers for Environmental
Information (NCEI) 213, 215–216
National Cohesive Wildfire Management
Strategy (NCWMS) 172, 176
National Disaster Recovery Framework
(NDRF) 19, *20*
National Disaster Recovery Reform Act 4
National Fire Protection Association
(NFPA) 53, 170
National Flood Insurance Program
(NFIP) 5, 32, 67, 174, 224, 244–247;
see also flood insurance
National Incident Management System
(NIMS) 15
national recovery policies 80–83; *see also*
Obama, Barack; Trump, Donald
National Research Council (NRC) 27
National Response Framework (NRF) *20*
National Security Council (NSC) 27
National Weather Service (NWS) 94,
213, 217
New Jersey 5
New York City 5, *63*, *70*, *71*, *78*;
and business recovery 72–74; and
community recovery 74–75; and housing
recovery 66–72; and recovery 61–66
New York City Housing Authority
(NYCHA) 72, 79
NIMS *see* National Incident
Management System (NIMS)
North American Free Trade Agreement
(NAFTA) 183
nuclear weapons 11
nursing homes 138–139; *see also* seniors
NYS 2100 Commission 28

Obama, Barack 15, 22, 24–25; and
disaster recovery 83; and Hurricane
Sandy Rebuilding Task Force 29, 80;
and Puerto Rico 189; and Tuscaloosa-
Birmingham, Alabama Tornado 45

Office of Homeland Security (OHS)
see Department of Homeland
Security
Operation Bootstrap 188

policies 4–5; and action 22–25; and
climate change 12–15; and disaster
resilience 25–31; and recovery
18–22; and situational awareness
15–17; and social cascades 17–18; and
Trump administration 31–32; *see also*
Biggert-Waters Flood Insurance
Reform Act; Disaster Recovery
Reform Act; Homeowners Flood
Insurance Affordability Act; National
Flood Insurance Program; Sandy
Improvement Reform Act; Sandy
Recovery Improvement Act (SRIA);
Weather Research and Forecasting
Innovation Act
policy action 22–25
population 13–14
ports 195–196
poverty *186*
preparedness 190–192, 205–206
property taxes 114–115
public assistance 133–135, *136*, **221**
Puerto Rico 6, 17–18, *197*, *199*, *204*;
and disaster preparedness 190–192;
economic vulnerability of 187–190;
evacuees from 139; and long-term
recovery 203–206; social vulnerability
of 185–187; and Trump, Donald 239;
see also Hurricane Maria

race: and digital divide 15; and Hurricane
Harvey 101–103; and income
inequality 14
Rapid Repairs 68–69; *see also* housing
recovery
Rebuild by Design (RBD) 29–30, 81;
see also Department of Housing and
Urban Development (HUD)

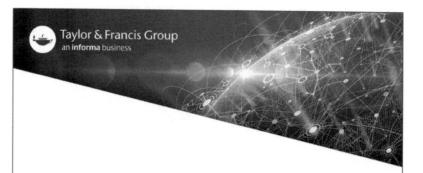